A TV GUIDE TO LIFE

This book provides an important contribution to the economic history of modern China. It examines the history of the coal mining industry – one of China's largest and most important – from the beginnings of modernization around 1895 to the start of the Sino-Japanese War in 1937. It addresses questions of both economic and socio-political history and contributes to our knowledge of many aspects of early twentieth-century Chinese history. It examines the slow growth of the modern sector of the Chinese economy and considers the effects of foreign investment and ownership, the supply of capital, the technology of production, the availability of local entrepreneurship, and compares the evolution of the Chinese coal industry with development elsewhere.

Part I analyses the determinants of the rate and pattern of the growth of coal output. It concludes that by the 1930s at least demand rather than supply was the crucial constraint on the growth of total output. Both the geographical and the temporal patterns of growth were affected by short-term political as well as by longer-term economic factors.

Part II looks at the industry in the context of China's social and political history. An examination of the role of foreign companies shows a more complex interaction between those enterprises and Chinese officials and firms than is usually assumed. A discussion of Chinese-owned companies again questions the accepted picture of 'bureaucratic capitalism' in the Chinese economy. Two chapters on labour and the labour movement give a detailed picture of the life and activities of the mine workers.

This book will be of interest to those concerned with the problems of industrial growth in general as well as to specialists on modern China.

Cambridge Studies in Chinese History, Literature and Institutions
General Editors
Patrick Hanan and Denis Twitchett

COAL MINING IN CHINA'S ECONOMY AND SOCIETY 1895–1937

Coal mining in China's economy and society 1895–1937

TIM WRIGHT
Murdoch University

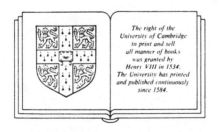

The right of the
University of Cambridge
to print and sell
all manner of books
was granted by
Henry VIII in 1534.
The University has printed
and published continuously
since 1584.

CAMBRIDGE UNIVERSITY PRESS

CAMBRIDGE

LONDON   NEW YORK   NEW ROCHELLE

MELBOURNE   SYDNEY

CAMBRIDGE UNIVERSITY PRESS
Cambridge, New York, Melbourne, Madrid, Cape Town, Singapore, São Paulo, Delhi

Cambridge University Press
The Edinburgh Building, Cambridge CB2 8RU, UK

Published in the United States of America by Cambridge University Press, New York

www.cambridge.org
Information on this title: www.cambridge.org/9780521258784

First published 1984
This digitally printed version 2008

A catalogue record for this publication is available from the British Library

Library of Congress Catalogue Card Number: 84–7099

ISBN 978-0-521-25878-4 hardback
ISBN 978-0-521-10188-2 paperback

CONTENTS

TABLES AND FIGURES

Tables

Figures

ACKNOWLEDGEMENTS

There are many people whom I want to thank for help in the compilation of this work, which has taken all too many years. Two, however, stand out. Denis Twitchett, now of Princeton University, was my supervisor at Cambridge; to him I owe the suggestion of a fruitful and interesting topic, perhaps the most important single contribution a supervisor can make. He has also been a source of helpful and probing suggestions as well as of friendship and encouragement throughout the long life of this project, as a PhD thesis and since. I met Shannon Brown, now of Stanford University, almost on the day I handed in my thesis; ever since then I have relied very heavily on his penetrating criticisms and suggestions. Now in a teaching job myself, I am even more appreciative that he found the time to read carefully and thoroughly the drafts of my articles and book. Without his advice this work would have been much poorer.

Many other people have read this work at various stages of its gestation. Christopher Howe of the School of Oriental and African Studies, and W. J. Macpherson and Suzy Paine of Cambridge were of great help in the early stages, in the course of my (still incomplete) metamorphosis from Sinologist to social scientist. Joe Moore, David Pong, Wang Gung-wu and Beverley Hooper have all read the manuscript at its almost final stage, saving me from error and making useful suggestions. Needless to say I have not been able to accept all the suggestions made and none of the people mentioned above are responsible for any mistakes in the content or argument of the book as it now stands.

A project like this is also very dependent on people outside the narrow academic sphere. Librarians in Cambridge, Oxford, London and Canberra have all been most helpful in obtaining materials for me and in offering bibliographical advice. Salli Demets and Ivy Witmer and the other typists in the School of Human Communication, Murdoch University, have ably and cheerfully coped with the thankless task of typing the manuscript, and the secretarial staff especially at the Australian National University were a major source of support in the course of my project. The staff of the graphics departments at the Australian National and Murdoch Universities kindly drew up the map and graphs for me.

A final mention also of Raymond Shaw-Smith, whose energy and enthusiasm as a teacher at Bradford Grammar School instilled in my mind the first vital spark of interest in China, and whose influence remains with me in this and many other respects.

ABBREVIATIONS

¢	Chinese cents
CEB	*Chinese Economic Bulletin*
CEJ	*Chinese Economic Journal*
CER	Chinese Eastern Railway
ILO	International Labour Office
IMC	Imperial Maritime Customs (later Inspectorate General of Customs)
IUP	Irish University Press
J¥	Japanese yen
KMA	Kailuan [Kailan] Mining Administration (also referred to in the text as Kailuan)
KYZB	*Kuangye zhoubao* (Mining weekly)
MCG	*Mantetsu chōsa geppō*
MMT or SMR	Minami Manshū tetsudō kabushiki kaisha (South Manchurian Railway Company)
NCH	*North China Herald*
NKGB	*Nongkuang gongbao*
NP	Nathan Papers, Bodleian Library, Oxford
NSGB	*Nongshang gongbao*
SKJ	*Shina kōgyō jihō*
¥	Chinese silver dollar
ZGJJNJ 1936	China, shiyebu, Zhongguo jingji nianjian bianzuan weiyuanhui, *Zhongguo jingji nianjian disanbian* (Shanghai, 1936)

Chinese Railways

An–Feng	Sujiatun–Andong
Bei–Ning	Beijing–Shenyang
CER	Manzhouli–Suifenhe
Dao–Qing	Daokou–Qinghua

Ji–Dun	Jilin–Dunhua
Jiao–Ji	Qingdao–Jinan
Jin–Pu	Tianjin–Pukou
Jing–Han	Beijing–Hankou
Jing–Sui	Beijing–Baotou
Long–Hai	Lianyungang–Tianshui
Shen–Hai	Shenyang–Hailong
SMR	Changchun–Dalian
Yue–Han	Guangzhou–Hankou
Zheng–Tai	Zhengding–Taiyuan
Zhu–Ping	Zhuzhou–Pingxiang

For a reference list of the major Chinese coal mining companies, see Appendix B, pp. 200–1.

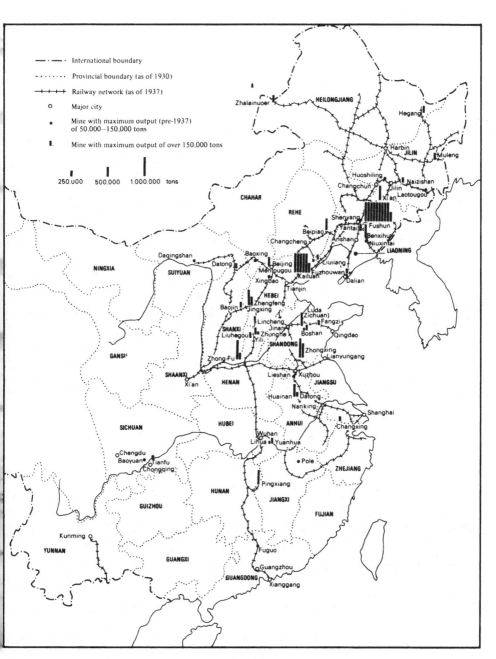

Map of major Chinese coal mines and railways

1
INTRODUCTION

The issues

China's prewar economic performance receives attention from historians of modern China for several reasons. Many see the economy's inability to provide the Chinese people with a decent standard of living as a major cause of the revolution, and there can be little doubt that a low per capita income left little leeway for the people to escape distress or even starvation if distribution was unequal or social upheavals disturbed the process of production. The greater equality and efficiency of distribution since 1949 and the Communist government's greater success in dealing with the effects of natural disasters have accounted for much of the contrast in the popular perceptions of pre-revolutionary and post-revolutionary China.

What is more questionable, however, is the extension of this gloomy view of the prewar economy to encompass not only a low per capita income in a static sense but also a lack of growth or dynamism within the economy, with again an implicit or explicit comparison being drawn with the post-1949 situation. Did underdevelopment necessarily imply stagnation, or did, in fact, growth occur in certain areas and sectors which formed the basis, in part, of the achievements of the Communist regime?

As a result of such doubts, the past emphasis in studies of Chinese industry on its failures and stagnation has more recently changed to one that acknowledges the substantial growth that did take place and tries to understand the reason for that growth. The evidence, which has long been available for those who wished to see it, has recently been systematically examined by John Key Chang and summarized in an index of industrial production which, despite the inevitable shortcomings resulting from an inadequate data base, supersedes previous efforts. Chang finds that China's net industrial output grew by a respectable 9.4% per annum between 1912 and 1936.[1] Although this figure needs to be qualified in several ways, it does suggest that 'stagnant' is not an appropriate description of pre-1937 Chinese industry.

There has recently been a gradual increase in the number and quality of studies of Chinese industrial history. Early studies published outside China after the war mostly concentrated either on broad generalizations about the factors promoting or impeding industrialization, such as (in the case of one of the best) the impact of foreign investment,[2] or on detailed studies of outstanding individuals or enterprises; in this latter category the work of Feuerwerker in English and Quan Hansheng in Chinese stands out.[3] These studies, excellent in themselves, had certain limitations. The generalizations made in the former were often too broad, being based mostly on summary statistics rather than on a firmer foundation of detailed monographic studies of individual industries. The latter, just because they dealt with outstanding cases, sacrificed typicality; moreover, their interest was often as much or more with inter-enterprise competition as with the growth of the sector as a whole.

Studies at the industry level of aggregation can fill some of these gaps, and a good start was made in the mid-1930s by Chinese scholars such as Fang Xianding, Ding Ji and He Lian.[4] Yan Zhongping's work on the cotton industry, published first in the 1940s, stands as one of the landmarks in modern Chinese economic historiography.[5] In the last few years several new works (most notably those by Chao and by Kraus) have appeared on the cotton industry, while Cochran's work on the tobacco industry, although still focussing mainly on inter-enterprise competition, has raised to a new level of sophistication studies on the history of modern Chinese industrial management.[6] Nevertheless these studies remain as isolated landmarks in the field, despite the fact that, as Fogel and Engerman point out, the explanation of industrial expansion is one of the most important desiderata for economic historians.[7]

This work seeks to add to those few pioneering efforts by undertaking an analysis of the Chinese coal industry between 1895 and 1937. Coal mining was one of China's largest industries, with a net value added of about ¥100 million in 1933, ranking behind only cotton yarn at ¥134 million and tobacco at ¥126 million. In terms of employment there were about 270,000 workers in modern coal mines, more even than the 199,000 working in cotton-spinning mills.[8] Its study is lent further interest and importance by the fact that coal was an intermediate product and thus vital also as an input into many other industries. Moreover, the industry was not concentrated in the treaty ports, as were other industries, but in the plains of north and north-east China, areas where the warlords held sway.

The shift of emphasis from the supposed stagnation of the industrial sector to its growth has also necessitated the use of a somewhat different framework of analysis. The concentration on stagnation involved an interest in a group of problems which could be used to explain this failure of industrial development. The theories adduced in this regard included both the technical and the social. Some pointed to the small and falling surplus available on peasant farms as a constraint on investment both in that sector and *a fortiori* in the secondary and tertiary sectors.[9] Others, however, have believed that there was sufficient surplus, but that the nature of Chinese society, which Chinese scholars have characterized as 'feudal', precluded its use in productive industry.[10] A further group of scholars has located the difficulty not in China's society or economy, but in the impact of imperialism, whether through the effect of foreign trade and investment on the Chinese economy,[11] or through the political debilitation of the Chinese state by foreign intervention.[12]

Many problems remain in these fields, but the discarding of the basic premiss on which this framework rests – that of industrial stagnation – indicates the need for a new type of framework. That used in Chapters 2–4 of this book is based on the analysis of the major influences on the secular growth of the supply of and the demand for coal during our period;[13] it is thus a type of analysis which puts the main stress on economic factors, and indeed I will argue that the rate of growth in total output is most easily understood in terms of at least proximate economic causes.

The factors examined as influences on the growth of the industry follow the standard categories of economics. The supply of coal depended on the price and availability of the major inputs: capital (and entrepreneurship) from sources Chinese and foreign; land or resources; and labour. Technological conservatism or change could maintain or transform the relationship between those inputs and the level of output. Changing demand for coal was also a function of various influences, comprising as it did demand from industries and from households, in rural and urban areas, and also demand from areas outside China.

Needless to say the Chinese data will not allow the sort of sophisticated econometric study done on American or European industries. Indeed, rather than make continual apologies about the quality of the figures, it would perhaps be best merely to state here that throughout this study the figures are at best approximate, but that they do in my opinion represent correctly the general trends and tendencies involved, and that the figures used are as reliable as possible when working in Chinese economic history. In the absence of any systematic data on many topics we have rather to use what quantitative and qualitative evidence there is to reach conclusions consistent with what we know. To refuse to follow such a path on the grounds that the data is insufficient would be to condemn ourselves to ignorance of most of prewar Chinese economic history.

The early chapters will, therefore, concentrate on the determinants of secular growth, but the temporal and geographical pattern of that growth was also important, and non-economic factors played a much greater role there. The geographical distribution of mining was partly determined by the economics of transport, but also by the strength of the foreign presence in certain areas and the ability and desire to build up and protect industries in those areas. Manchuria is such an outstanding example of this that it warrants a section to itself. Likewise the temporal pattern of growth, the short-term fluctuations not only in output but in the other indicators of the health of the industry, resulted partly from the, albeit incomplete, integration of China into the world economy, and its consequent suscepti-bility to world economic movements. But more important by far was the impact of the civil wars which wracked Chinese society, though that impact was felt very unevenly across the country.

Moreover, there were other aspects of the industry which sometimes assumed prime importance for contemporaries, aspects generally of the overlap between economic and political history. Central to this was the question of foreign investment in the industry. For today's economic historians it is a very difficult and complicated matter to draw up a balance sheet of the impact of foreign investment in the industry. But for Chinese nationalists in the early twentieth century the foreign impact posed urgent questions of national independence and left little time for considered statistical judgements. Indeed through this issue the coal industry came to play a central role in China's political history, particularly during the first decade of the century, and the issues continued to simmer throughout the prewar period.

Another major area where the history of the coal industry overlapped with China's broader political currents was in the types of entrepreneurs and investors involved. Mines formed one of the main targets for investment by the north-China warlords, so that they became involved inextricably in the continual wars and power struggles that marked China at that time. This was again an emotional issue for contemporaries, who left behind possibly exaggerated opinions of the damage that warlord involve-ment did to the industry. While modern economic historians may again doubt whether the impact was really so great, the subject cannot be ignored in any study of coal mining because of its importance in Chinese political history.

Last, but not least, we need to know about the men who worked in the mines; about their conditions of life and work, since they were by far the largest part of the proletariat outside the major cities. We also need to know about the organizations they formed to protect and further their interests, since the differences between their history and that of the urban workers throws much light on the evolving balance of the classes in prewar China.

To try to present a balanced and overall view of the development of the industry, this book adopts a pattern of organization that goes from the macro to the micro, from an industry-wide analysis to one of the factors affecting the fate of different enterprises; from the general to the particular, and from the economic to the political. Thus the first three chapters of Part I deal with the determinants of the secular growth of coal mining – the supply of the factors of production, technological change and the growth of demand – and the next two with those of the geographical and temporal pattern of that growth. Part II then considers the industry in the context of China's political history, and four chapters deal respectively with foreign investment, with Chinese investment and entrepreneurship, with the miners' conditions of work and living, and with the labour movement.

Coal in pre-modern China

Whereas in India before the arrival of the Europeans coal was only dug from outcrops,[14] in China output probably amounted to several million tons and pits were operated which were as large as those in seventeenth-century Europe. The growth of the industry was constrained both by the limitations of traditional technology and, more importantly, by the weakness of demand due to the steeply rising cost of coal as distance from the mine increased. Nevertheless coal mines supplied fuel to a wide variety of industrial and household users even before the mid nineteenth century.

The question of the development of the mining and use of coal in China is complicated by the confusing terminology used in the early texts. It appears that coal began to be used for both industrial and household purposes in the first few centuries AD.[15] The spread of its use was gradual until the late eleventh century, when a timber shortage in the north China plain brought about a rapid expansion in coal mining and consumption.[16] The industry never regained in later times the prominence it achieved in the twelfth century, but levels of output remained high in absolute terms and coal continued to be mined and used in many areas of the country.

Technologically, much the same problems were encountered as in Europe, although the solutions found for them generally involved more use of human power and less of animal or water power. The drainage of water from the mine was the main constraint on the depth of working and so, once the shallow outcrops had been worked out, both Chinese and European miners preferred to use drift mines sunk horizontally into the hillside. In such cases water could run straight out and no elaborate apparatus was

needed for raising coal and men from the mine. In the late eighteenth
century, British observers saw such mines in Guangdong, opening out
directly on to a river.[17] Only ventilation and roofing might limit the
expansion of such workings, and one drift mine in Sichuan had a haulage
way about 6.5 km long.[18] The second preference was for slope mines, which
allowed easy access and egress for men and coal, while drainage could often
be effected by sinking an adit (small tunnel) which came out lower down the
hill. The famous mines in Leiyang, Hunan, were mostly of this type; few of
them were deeper on the incline than 60 metres.[19]

Most outcrops had been worked out by the nineteenth century, and
especially in north China the shaft mine was the rule. Even in Boshan, where
mines lined the hillsides each side of the river, Richthofen emphasizes that
nearly all the mines were shaft mines, interpreting this as a result of the lack
of wood with which to hold up the roof in slope mines.[20] The lifting of water
out of such mines was the main constraint on the depth and size of working.
There are numerous references to mines abandoned because of flooding.[21]
When one mine was flooded the miners moved to another site and opened a
new mine, after which the process was repeated. The topography of a
particular area determined the actual possible depth of working, but in
general pre-modern Chinese technology permitted mines as deep as those in
Europe. Although, for instance, in Weixian in Shandong water limited the
workings to a depth of 30 metres, in areas such as Shanxi, where the plateau
afforded natural drainage, mines were as deep as 120 metres, and depths of
90 metres or more were reported from Henan and Manchuria.[22] This
compares with a maximum depth of 120 metres in Britain in 1700, although
by the end of the century the application of steam power to pumping had
increased this to 300 metres.[23]

Whereas in Europe various types of pump were developed to lift water
out of mines, in China miners mostly used leather buckets, raised with either
the same lifting gear as that used for winding the coal or else a similar kind of
apparatus.[24] At Kaiping in Hebei three buckets of water were taken from
the mine for every one of coal; these mines had, however, more or less
exhausted the possibilities of traditional technology, and in other coalfields
the proportion of water was lower.[25] One Westerner reported that the
buckets were equipped with an ingenious self-filling and emptying device.[26]
While the Chinese had a variety of pumps used for raising water, these were
rarely found in mines. The British Consul mentioned the use of pallet chain
pumps of the type used for agricultural irrigation in a mine in Taiwan,[27]
though a later reporter said that no pumps were in use.[28] Certainly
references to the use of buckets were much more common.

Coal could be carried or dragged out of drift or slope mines, and in

Sichuan one mine had an elementary system of wooden rails.[29] Some shaft mines were equipped with a system of ladders for carrying coal to the surface,[30] but most had some sort of winding mechanism. The most common was the Chinese windlass as described and illustrated by Hommel;[31] these could be quite large and complicated apparatuses, and many descriptions write of eight to ten men being required to operate them.[32] There are few reports of more elaborate types of engine to which animals could be harnessed, although one traditional mine in Henan in the early twentieth century used mule and bullock gins.[33]

The importance of ventilation varied very much in different coalfields, but little, if anything, is known about the methods used. The seventeenth-century Chinese writer, Song Yingxing, says that in many small mines a long bamboo pipe was let into the pit to draw off noxious fumes, but his illustration suggests that this method was primarily useful in small bell-type pits.[34] Nineteenth-century descriptions vary from saying that no provision at all was made for ventilation,[35] to a description of an elaborate airway providing good ventilation for a mine 6.5 km long.[36] The technique of furnace ventilation was known, but is seldom specifically mentioned.[37]

Consumption of coal in traditional China was substantial overall, but remained both highly localized and relatively small on a per capita basis. Demand from industry was probably the most important both quantitatively and as a dynamic factor in the industry's development. Some of the earliest references to coal are in the context of smelting methods, with the necessary technology spreading rapidly from the central plain to the outlying areas of China.[38] The great expansion of the industry during the northern Song was based mainly on iron smelting, and by the end of the eleventh century much of north China's iron production was smelted in coke-burning blast-furnaces.[39] The deforestation of much of north China had forced ironworks to turn to the use of coke made from bituminous coal (anthracite had long been used in primitive crucibles), which in turn led to the rise of a new group of ironworking centres along the Henan–Hebei border. Hartwell estimates that at least 140,000 tons of coal a year were used by the iron industry in this area.[40]

Hartwell's hypothesis of the later decline of the iron industry is less firmly based (as far as the whole of China is concerned) than his description of its earlier rise. It implies a very sharp fall in per capita consumption of iron in China, and the evidence for this is scanty.[41] Careful work with local histories and other sources may well show that the centre of the industry moved to other areas rather than that it underwent such a catastrophic and permanent decline. The industry certainly continued to use coal, with Song Yingxing suggesting that around 70% of iron was smelted with coal, only

30% using charcoal.[42] By late traditional times the industry was centred on Shanxi, which is richly endowed with coal, and Richthofen described the use of coal in iron-making in several areas of the province.[43] Many missionaries also reported its use in furnaces by all kinds of workmen.[44]

Other rural industries in which coal was used (and continued to be used in the twentieth century) included lime, glass, alcohol and ceramics. Potters used coal from the late Tang, according to a local tradition in Boshan, Shandong,[45] but the imperial kilns at Jingdezhen, Jiangxi, used firewood right up to 1949, despite rising costs as nearby timber supplies became exhausted.[46]

The use of coal for household purposes in China also goes back at least to the sixth century, when one writer remarked that food tasted different according to whether it was cooked over coal, charcoal, bamboo or grass. Although coal continued throughout the centuries to be burnt by households – even in Guangdong, where coal is scarce but in former times firewood was plentiful – it is difficult to gauge how widely it was actually used.[47] Its use in rural areas no doubt remained at most sporadic and scattered, at least while alternative fuels remained plentiful.

From the eleventh century, however, the shortage of alternatives led to a rapid expansion in the household use of coal in the capital at Kaifeng. In the first years of the twelfth century twenty new coal markets were established, and coal rapidly replaced charcoal as the fuel used by Kaifeng households.[48] This increase in demand stimulated the development of mining in many areas of Henan and Shandong.[49] Two centuries later Marco Polo claimed that coal was 'burnt throughout the province of Cathay', and stressed especially its use in bathhouses.[50]

Much more work on Ming and Qing China needs to be done before one can fully accept Hartwell's hypothesis that the twelfth century represented the peak of pre-modern Chinese use of coal.[51] It is, perhaps, unlikely that per capita consumption ever surpassed the levels attained in early twelfth-century Kaifeng, but coal was still widely used in households throughout later centuries. Certainly Beijing, situated almost astride a coalfield, mostly used coal for fuel, and the Qing government was as concerned as had been the Song to ensure a cheap and regular supply of fuel to warm the houses of the capital's inhabitants.[52] Outside Beijing Catholic missionaries reported the widespread use of coal for cooking and heating in private houses,[53] and Williamson in the 1860s observed its use for cooking in Shanxi.[54] The pressure put on fuel resources by the massive increase in population during the eighteenth century increased incentives to exploit coal resources, particularly with the expansion of settlement into the north China uplands which reduced the supply of timber in areas where coal was often available.[55]

Where mines were close to water transport, coal was carried over hundreds of kilometres to distant markets. The most important such long-distance trade was that in coal from Leiyang in southern Hunan, of which at least 150,000 tons a year were transported by boat up to Hankou and as far along the Yangzi as Shanghai.[56] Even in north China coal was carried for surprisingly long distances where water transport was available.[57] But in general both industrial and household use of coal remained highly localized. The price of coal rose steeply with distance from the mine and this, especially where land transport was used, soon prevented it from competing with other fuels. Richthofen reports that coal from a mine near Qinghua sold at the Yellow River, 50 km away, for five times its price at the mine.[58] In such areas proximity to a coalfield was a necessary condition for all but the most exiguous use of coal, and the concentration of water transport networks in central and south China but of coal resources in north China, where also the need for fuel was the most pressing, meant that these high transport costs were the single most important constraint on the growth of coal consumption.

So, although coal was available in widely scattered areas and its production and consumption were of considerable magnitude in absolute terms, China's use of coal remained very small on a per capita basis: the 5 million people in seventeenth-century England used almost 3 million tons of coal,[59] but a Chinese population eighty times that size by the mid nineteenth century used only a possibly similar amount of coal. Except perhaps in the twelfth century, the coal industry made little overall impact on the pre-modern Chinese economy.

The growth of output from modern coal mines

Details of Chinese coal output between 1896 and 1936 are shown in Table 1, which includes output in Manchuria even after its political separation from China in 1931; output in Taiwan is, however, excluded. The reliability of the figures compiled by the Geological Survey of China and the criteria used in compiling my own series are discussed in Appendix A. The brief conclusion is that it is possible to compile a series of reasonable reliability for large mines, but that the figures for small-mine output (and so, because of their inclusion in it, for total output) are of very little value.

Growth rates of large-mine output over the whole period and over several sub-periods are summarized in Table 2. The pattern that emerges is relatively clear. Growth was very rapid up to the early 1910s, but less than half as rapid in later years. The industry continued to grow, although more slowly, between 1914 and the mid-1920s, when it entered a period of stagnating output. From 1933 to 1936 there was a further spurt of rapid growth. Over the whole period the index indicates a 10.9% growth rate,

Table 1. *Chinese coal output, 1896–1936*
('000 tons)

Year	Large mines		Total output
	Wright	Survey	Survey
1896	489	—	—
1897	539	—	—
1898	783	—	—
1899	842	—	—
1900	n.a.	—	—
1901	521	—	—
1902	954	—	—
1903	1,026	—	—
1904	1,274	—	—
1905	1,345	—	—
1906	1,696	—	—
1907	2,189	—	—
1908	2,788	—	—
1909	3,868	—	—
1910	4,237	—	—
1911	5,266	—	—
1912	5,381	5,166	9,068
1913	7,432	7,678	12,880
1914	7,992	7,974	14,182
1915	8,371	8,493	13,497
1916	9,052	9,483	15,983
1917	9,963	10,479	16,982
1918	10,572	11,109	18,432
1919	12,222	12,805	20,147
1920	13,536	14,131	21,319
1921	12,675	13,350	20,507
1922	13,268	14,060	21,140
1923	16,354	16,973	24,552
1924	17,896	18,525	25,781
1925	16,732	17,538	24,255
1926	14,572	15,617	23,040
1927	17,132	17,694	24,172
1928	16,402	17,980	25,092
1929	17,527	18,854	25,437
1930	18,680	19,892	26,037
1931	19,948	21,093	27,245
1932	19,049	20,213	26,376
1933	20,904	22,075	28,379
1934	24,287	25,801	32,725
1935	25,699	30,093	36,092
1936	29,368	33,794	39,903

Note: n.a. – not available.
Sources: Appendix A; The Survey figures are taken
from Yan Zhongping, 1955, pp. 102–3.

Table 2. *Growth rates of the output of large Chinese mines, 1896–1936*

Period/sub-period	Average annual rate of growth (Percentage)
1896–1936	10.9
1896–1913	17.4
1914–36	5.2
1914–24	8.1
1925–33	3.6

Source: Calculated from my own series in Table 1, using least squares method.

over the 1914–36 period one of 5.2%. There is no doubt that these figures support the conclusions of earlier quantitative studies of industrial growth, such as that of Chang, which argue that the pre-1937 period saw substantial growth in the modern sector. While the details of the series on which the aggregate indices are based are certainly open to improvement, both in the case of coal mining and even more so for other industries, it is most unlikely that any such improvements would force a substantial revision in the overall picture of relatively rapid growth in modern industry. In the case of coal mining, moreover, it is also unlikely that this growth was offset by much of a decline in the output of unmodernized mines.

The growth rates in Table 2 are for large-mine output, which started from a very low base at the beginning of the period. If a (more or less) flat 6 million tons per annum is added to account for the output of small mines, as was done by the Survey, then total output grew at only about 4% per annum between 1913 and 1936. On the other hand small-mine output probably grew rather more than is suggested by this procedure, as we can see especially from the cases of those areas that benefited from railway transport, such as Boshan and the Western Hills outside Beijing. As some of the rest of the small-mine sector, which may have grown slowly or not at all, was in areas cut off from the national market, the figures for large mines do reflect fairly well the growth of a separate national (or at least regional) market for coal.

Table 3 compares the growth rate of Chinese coal output, 1896–1936, with those of coal industries in countries undergoing rapid industrialization. All the figures except the pre-1937 Chinese ones refer to total output, so the table flatters the Chinese performance. On the other hand none of the other countries had a market as fragmented as that of China, nor as large an output by small mines isolated from the main centres. So this qualification does not invalidate the conclusion that the growth rate of the Chinese coal industry before 1937 compares well with that of other countries.

Table 3. *Growth rates of various coal industries*

Country	Period	Rate of growth of coal output (Percentage)
Great Britain	1830–50	4.2
France	1830–60	5.1
Belgium	1830–60	5.2
China	1914–36	5.2
Japan	1900–20	6.9
China	1952–82	7.1
United States	1850–84	7.1
Russia	1890–1913	7.9
Germany	1850–73	8.4
China	1896–1936	10.9[a]
Japan	1874–1900	12.4[a]
USSR	1926–39	14.4

Note: [a] From a very low base.
Sources: Mitchell, 1975, pp. 360–70; Ohkawa, 1972, pp. 267–9; Howe, 1978, p. 106; Schurr and Netschert, 1960, pp. 491–2; Xue, 1982, 8:16.

Table 4. *Growth rates of various Chinese industries, 1912–36*

Industry	Average annual rate of growth (Percentage)
Modern coal mining	5.6
Modern iron- and steel-making	3.9 (1913–34[a])
Factory produced cotton yarn	8.3
Consumer goods (Chang's index)	10.1
Electricity	17.1

Note: [a] The figures for iron and steel are distorted by extreme figures for 1912 and 1935–6, which inflate the 1912–36 rate of growth to 8.2%.
Sources: Chang, 1969, pp. 78–9, 117–23; Wright, unpublished paper.

Table 4 compares the growth of coal output with that of other Chinese industries between 1912 and 1936. Because coal mining was relatively firmly established by 1912, as a result of the rapid growth during the preceding decade, output after 1912 grew rather less rapidly than that of other industries which were starting from a very low base. The more rapid growth of the other industries in Chang's index means that the contribution of coal output to that index fell from over 30% in the 1910s to just over 20% in the 1930s,[60] but coal mining remained throughout very important in the modern industrial sector.

The considerable growth even of modern industry as a whole made, however, little statistical impact on total domestic product; that of coal mining made even less of one. The whole modern industrial (and transport) sector contributed only 7.4% to gross domestic product in 1933: of this only about one-fifteenth came from coal mining – about 0.5% of domestic product. Although in earlier years coal mining was more important within the modern sector, that sector was a much smaller part of total product – only about 2.7% in the mid-1910s.[61]

Nevertheless, while it is necessary to remember this perspective, the modern sector was much more important than these bare figures suggest. It was the main source of dynamism in the economy, with a growth rate far higher than that of the agricultural sector. In it lay the hope of a strong and wealthy China, and there the foundations were being laid on which the Chinese government after 1949 was to base its much more purposeful drive for industrialization. Despite continuing and serious difficulties, China's post-1949 industrial growth has begun to transform the structure of China's national product and, more slowly, that of the employment of the population. Therefore, although superficially it held only a small place in the economy, the growth of the modern sector and the factors behind it deserve and demand attention and analysis.

2

THE FACTORS OF PRODUCTION

An adequate supply of the major inputs – land (resources), labour and capital – is a necessary condition for the growth of any industry.[1] If supply is inadequate, the price of the factor concerned will rise; the industry may then be able to substitute other factors, but even then the price of the final product will rise, reducing sales by an amount depending on the price elasticity of demand. The supply especially of capital and labour has been a controversial issue in development studies and in economic history: many scholars have talked of capital shortage in underdeveloped countries, and in India particularly but also elsewhere, contemporary observers stressed the difficulties of recruiting an industrial labour force even when the labour supplies seemed to be abundant.

Resources

China is one of the world's coal-rich countries. No accurate figures for total reserves are available, but K. P. Wang suggests that they may be as high as 1 million million tons, and some estimates made in the heady days of the Great Leap Forward were even higher.[2] In any case China's reserves are among the largest in the world, ranking behind only those of the Soviet Union at 6 million million tons, and those of the United States at 4 million million tons.[3] Known reserves before 1937 were substantially smaller than such estimates. While some areas had been properly surveyed by the Geological Survey of China, for others only rough estimates with no strict criteria were available. Most estimates at the time, however, put total reserves at around 250,000 million tons.[4]

The quality of those reserves was variable. Nearly 80% of known reserves before the war was bituminous coal (a proportion probably even higher now), about 20% was anthracite, and lignite made up the small remainder. The main quality problem since 1949 has proved to be the shortage of coking coal: although 35% of total reserves are now in the form of coking coal, this has been insufficient to prevent serious shortages of coke hampering the growth of the steel industry.[5] Nevertheless the level of development of the metallurgical industries before 1937 meant that supplies of coking coal were adequate to meet demand.

A further qualification that needs to be made to the apparent abundance of China's coal reserves is their often-inaccessible location. The Geological Survey estimates in the mid-1930s showed well over 80% of total reserves in the mountainous provinces of Shanxi and Shaanxi,[6] far away from the coastal industrial centres. Even in the case of those areas of Shanxi that were served by a railway, the long haul to the coast meant that Shanxi coal was very expensive there.

Despite these questions as to their quality and location, China's coal reserves were easily sufficient to support the prewar industry. Reserves of 250,000 million tons could have supported between 5000 and 10,000 years of production at current levels of output, so that, even if that figure has to be substantially reduced, the availability of resources was never likely to constrain the growth of output in China before 1937.

On a micro level the size of rent and royalty payments gives some indirect indication of the degree of pressure on resources. In Britain rents and royalties had been the focus of much concern especially in the eighteenth and nineteenth centuries – in the early nineteenth century royalty payments made up about 20% of cost, although a long process of attrition reduced this to around 3% by 1918.[7] In China, on the other hand, the fact that the sources are almost silent about the subject suggests that the issue was not seen as an important one. Where the level of payments is known, it was low. The modern mines at Jiaozuo, Henan, paid 0.04 taels per ton to landowners in 1915, around 10¢ in 1933. Since the pit-head price of the coal was around ¥5.0 in 1933, royalties amounted to only about 2% of selling price, below even the 1918 level in Britain.[8]

Capital

While contemporary sources showed little concern at the availability of natural resources, many studies of coal mines suggested that 'shortage of capital' was a central reason for their failure to develop. When discussing the problems of the Chinese coal industry, Tanaka Tadao, one of the leading Japanese observers of the economy, concentrated exclusively on the supply side, and included shortage of capital as one of the main reasons for the industry's difficulties.[9] The Chinese scholar Gong Jun, author of an early history of Chinese industry, produced a similar analysis.[10]

Shortage of capital was also cited as a reason for the failure of individual mines or areas. This was particularly true of the late nineteenth century and the first years of the twentieth. Niu Bingchen attributed the slow development of the mines at Lincheng in south Hebei to the failure to raise enough capital.[11] Later, many discussions of the Boshan mines in central Shandong cited capital shortage as a major determining factor of the development of that area.[12] Similarly the Ministry of Industry reported that the main complaint of mine owners in Hunan was shortage of capital.[13] Nevertheless in most cases other factors, the most important of which was the availability of cheap transport, were realistically given more prominence.

Other types of evidence can be cited to suggest a shortage of capital in the Chinese economy, or at least an inelastic supply of risk capital to industry. The payment of guaranteed dividends on share capital implies this: the practice was particularly prevalent in the late Qing[14] and was used in early coal-mining companies such as Luanzhou in north-east Hebei from 1908,[15] and Zhongxing in south Shandong up to the mid-1910s.[16] Even in the late 1920s this form of guaranteed dividend was still paid on the shares of the Baojin Company in Shanxi and on those of Jiawang in Jiangsu.[17] Nevertheless its incidence declined from the 1910s.

A corollary to the difficulty of attracting risk capital was heavy reliance on loans, often at high interest rates, and especially for working capital. The Hunan mine owners who bewailed their shortage of capital had to pay as much as 20% on short-term loans. As with many industrial firms,[18] mining companies also tended to be heavily reliant on loans: for instance over half the capital available to Zhongxing in 1915 was from loans rather than equity investment.[19] Such loans left any mine whose coal was less than highly profitable in a vulnerable position, and the poor financial situation of the Liuhegou Company in north Henan in the 1930s was attributed largely to the burden of interest payments on loans taken out in the previous decade. Attempts in the 1930s to raise large sums in equity capital to repay the loans failed, and the company was forced to fall further into debt with the banks, to a sum greater than its subscribed capital.[20]

As Chao Kang argues in the case of cotton mills,[21] such phenomena of undercapitalization are really a matter of the financial planning of the enterprises involved, and do not necessarily imply an overall shortage of capital in Chinese industry or in coal mining in particular at the levels of output which it had attained. Two theories do, however, postulate a shortage of capital in the economy or in the industrial sector.

One is the belief that there was too small a surplus above subsistence consumption in the economy, and thus insufficient savings and investment in both the agricultural and the industrial sector. Mark Elvin's 'high-level equilibrium trap' is probably the most sophisticated such theory, and certainly points to a potential constraint on Chinese growth, one that may have been important since 1949.[22] It is rather more doubtful if it was operative before 1937. In China, as in other underdeveloped countries especially in Asia, there did in fact exist a substantial surplus, not all of which was used for productive investment. Carl Riskin and Victor Lippit, using general concepts developed by Paul Baran, have attempted to calculate the extent of the surplus of production over subsistence and over actual consumption in China and, while their estimates include a wide margin of error and could in some respects be strengthened theoretically, they do show that: 'In a pre-World War II economy with a potential surplus above mass consumption of more than one-third of total product, there was bound to be much room for expanding the investment rate'; and that: 'The diversion of much of that surplus to investment and other growth-related activities would have involved very little opportunity cost, aside from the sacrifice of privileged consumption habits on the part of a relatively small portion of the population.' The real constraint implied by the 'high-level equilibrium trap' was, therefore, still only potential in pre-1937 China.[23]

Accepting this, implicitly or explicitly, the second theory postulates that institutional constraints discouraged the investment in industry of what capital was available. These constraints were of various kinds. The lack of an organized capital market for shares in Chinese companies meant that equity capital was recruited mainly through personal connections or, in some cases, telegraphed appeals.[24] The persistent strength of family and local ties and the slow emergence of a legal framework for economic activities meant that entrepreneurs preferred to rely on people they knew. This was, however, by no means peculiar to China, and capital was raised for coal mining in Britain in a very similar way up to the mid or late nineteenth century.[25]

These imperfections in the capital market were serious for industries with large and indivisible capital requirements, such as iron and steel.[26] So in south Wales patterns of entrepreneurship and capital formation differed considerably between ironworks, which needed to attract large amounts of capital from outside the locality, and coal mines, which did not.[27] Similarly in China, economies of scale in coal mining, at least in production, were smaller than in iron-making, and there was a large range of technologies available both to entrepreneurs opening up a new field and to existing companies wishing to increase output in the short term without heavy expenditure of capital. Large mining companies often used small pits operated with traditional technology to enable them to adjust rapidly to changing market conditions. The Zhongxing Company ran several dozen such pits up to the late 1920s, using them to expand output in boom times and cutting back production there first when economic conditions worsened.[28] Sometimes, as with the Zhongyuan Company in Jiaozuo, these pits were operated by contractors, with the company retaining the right to buy output.[29] This flexibility of production methods reduced the need for large lump sums of capital to be raised and reduced problems caused by imperfections in the capital market.

Finally, some scholars attribute the low level of industrial investment simply to the fact that investments in other parts of the economy were more secure and also promised greater returns, financial and other. Government bonds were a prime competitor to industrial investment in the modern sector, and their yields were generally higher than those from providing capital to industry.[30] Most of the funds raised by the government were of course consumed in unproductive military expenditure. These higher returns available elsewhere could lead to reluctance to invest even available capital in any but the most promising mining projects. When the Chinese were trying to raise their share of the capital for the establishment of the Sino-Japanese Luda Company in central Shandong in 1922, among the promoters was the warlord Wang Zhanyuan, whose reported ¥30 million fortune alone was far greater than the mere ¥1.25 million required. But low profit expectations for the company – later proved justified – meant that even the promoters were unwilling to commit their funds, and the Chinese failed to raise the full sum.[31]

Despite these difficulties, substantial investments were made in the Chinese coal industry up to 1937. Although far too little information exists to justify any attempt to reach an even approximate estimate of total investment either by the compilation of figures for individual companies or by using information on capital–output ratios, Yan Zhongping's estimate of a total of ¥430 million invested in coal mines in China (including Manchuria) in 1936 can be taken at least to indicate that several hundred million yuan had been invested by that time.[32] Such a conclusion is supported by any reasonable assumption regarding capital–output ratios.

Taking into account also foreign capital, the supply of capital was not a serious constraint on the growth of the industry. Even during that period when Chinese investors were least willing to provide equity capital for coal-mining enterprises, investment was fairly freely available from foreign sources. As will be discussed in more detail in Chapter 7, this investment, which increased rapidly in the period up to 1913 (see Table 5), took the form of capital for developing foreign mining concessions or Sino-foreign companies and also of loans for Chinese-owned enterprises. Even though virtually no new concessions were granted after 1904 (except in the admittedly important case of Manchuria) and indeed some of those already granted were redeemed, capital was still being imported into China up to 1914 to develop existing concessions. Meanwhile many of the largest

Table 5. *Foreign capital invested
in major Chinese coal mines,
1899–1913*

Year	¥'000 invested
1899	1,527
1900	11,517
1901	12,286
1902	13,973
1903	15,990
1904	14,295
1905	15,437
1906	14,282
1907	29,047
1908	39,740
1909	42,946
1910	45,889
1911	50,686
1912	58,930
1913	63,163

Note: These figures, which refer to the
Kailuan, Peking Syndicate, Fushun,
Benxihu, Zichuan, Fangzi, Jingxing and
Yantai mines are crude, and give only an
approximate picture.
Source: Wang Jingyu, 1957, p. 37.

Chinese-owned mining companies were seeking loans from foreign banks in
order to finance expansion. The total supply of capital from all sources was
adequate to fuel a very rapid growth of mining in the first fifteen years of the
century.

After the outbreak of the First World War, the main sources of capital for
the expansion of coal mining in China were either the reinvestment of
profits from existing projects or new commitments by Chinese investors and
Chinese banks. While the exclusion of new foreign capital may possibly
have resulted in a higher cost of capital, it did not result in a shortage that
seriously hindered growth. Chinese mining companies, many of which
made large profits out of the boom in the East Asian coal market between
1916 and 1920, were able to increase their subscribed capital and to finance
the repayment of foreign loans. The more successful were able to finance
these repayments from profits, though their less fortunate counterparts had
to take out new loans from Chinese banks. Whether from retained profits,
share capital or bank loans, however, many companies succeeded in raising

large amounts of capital to finance their operations during the golden age of the industry between the mid-1910s and mid-1920s.

Not surprisingly the financial crisis undergone by the industry during the civil wars reduced profit expectations and thus the ease of raising equity capital. But the banks were still prepared to make large loans to mining companies – and not only to those with a record of high success. The Liuhegou Company, regarded by the management of the Sino-British Kailuan Mining Administration (KMA) as a bad risk,[33] was nevertheless able to raise several million yuan in bank loans in the late 1920s and 1930s.[34] The availability of Chinese funds in such difficult circumstances and for mines with only moderate prospects does not suggest that the supply of capital was, at the levels of activity then attained, a major constraint on the general development of the industry, although difficulties were experienced under certain circumstances.

Labour

Even in countries with large unemployed or underemployed populations it is not necessarily easy to recruit a stable industrial labour force. In India, for example, managers often complained about the difficulties of doing so.[35] These difficulties showed up in seasonal variations in the labour supply and in high rates of labour turnover as well as in overall labour shortage. In China, however, the supply of labour was in general adequate to meet the demands of the growth of the industry.

Several estimates have been made of the numbers of workers in Chinese coal mines, but all are far from satisfactory. Coverage of small mines is both patchy and unreliable. For large mines more figures are available but there is still no estimate covering all modern mines for a single year. Surveys generally suggest a total of between 150,000 and 220,000 workers in modern coal mines in the late 1920s and early 1930s. A probably reasonable estimate of an output of 100 tons per worker-year also suggests a workforce in the early 1930s of around 200,000, rising to close to 300,000 on the eve of the war.

For other mines no reasonable estimate can be made, as the output figures are valueless and as figures for productivity vary widely. A minimum estimate for the number of full-time equivalent workers engaged in small mines in the early 1930s would be 100,000, and the number may have been considerably higher. As many of the workers were actually part-time and seasonal workers, there were probably several hundred thousand engaged in coal mining at some time of the year.

The 200,000 or so workers in modern coal mines made up one of the largest groups of modern industrial workers in China. Cotton spinning mills also employed about 200,000 workers, though the textile industry as a whole accounted for over 500,000. The Kailuan and Fushun mining complexes, each employing around 40,000 or more workers, were among the largest single employers in China.

The recruitment of this workforce made little dent in China's overall working population of 260 million, over 80% of whom worked in agriculture;[36] many of these were underemployed for at least part of the year. Indeed total factory and mining employment was well under 2% of the workforce, and thus made a very small impact on total employment. In such circumstances it is unlikely *a priori* that serious difficulties would be encountered in fulfilling the coal mines' demand for labour.

Manchuria, exceptional also in many other ways, provides the main instance where the supply of labour was at least temporarily inadequate. The general pattern in the region was of development fuelled by massive immigration, and coal mining was no exception. From the start coal mines were dependent on immigrant labour[37] and, when output especially at the South Manchurian Railway Company's (SMR) Fushun mines was expanding very rapidly to meet boom demand in the late 1910s, the company was unable to find sufficient labour. As a result it was forced to ration sales in the profitable export market. In order to attract labour it raised money wages and also expanded a system of recruiting offices in Hebei and especially in Shandong which was to stay in operation for over a decade.[38]

Although the success of this recruiting drive meant that shortage of labour did not again directly limit the level of output, continuing very high turnover rates indicate that the problem was not completely solved. In as far as the instability of the labour force was caused by the movement of workers between the mining and other sectors rather than just between mines, it led to lower levels of skill and productivity and so constituted a problem for management. In the early 1920s turnover rates (expressed as the percentage ratio of the average of arrivals and departures of workers at the mine to the average number at the mine at any one time) for Chinese hewers (admittedly the most mobile category) at Fushun were very high, at over 400 in the late 1910s, while at the Benxihu mine, also in Liaoning, in 1920 the turnover rate was 434.[39] Labour turnover in Manchuria remained high throughout the 1920s: Fushun's rate was still 312 in 1929, but fell sharply to 96 in 1931 and, after a brief and slight rise, to 73 in 1936.[40] Although some of the turnover was accounted for by workers going on leave and then rejoining the workforce, there was certainly great instability in the coal-mining workforce in Manchuria up to the late 1920s.

Figures for length of service also suggest that labour turnover at both

Table 6. *Length of service of workers at Fushun, 1928 and 1934*

Percentage of workers at the mine	1928	1934
Less than 1 year	60.3	38.0
Less than 2 years	82.1	61.4
Less than 5 years	97.1	83.8
Less than 10 years	99.9	96.0
Less than 15 years	100.0	99.1
Less than 20 years	—	100.0

Sources: MMT, rōmuka, 1931, pp. 54–5; MMT, keizai chōsakai, 1936a, p. 27.

Fushun and Benxihu was high but falling. In 1925 85% of the workers at Benxihu had been at the mine for less than one year, but in 1930 the proportion was only 54%.[41] Table 6 shows in more detail a similar trend at Fushun.

These labour turnover rates for mines were substantially higher than that in manufacturing industry in Manchuria, which was just over 50 in 1925,[42] and reflected the slower development of a permanent labour force in the mining sector. The rates were probably also higher than those in mines in other parts of China, since the Manchurian economy as a whole still had the characteristics of the frontier, with a less-settled population than elsewhere.

Outside Manchuria, Kaiping in north-east Hebei (China's first successful modern mine, established in the early 1880s) experienced some early difficulties in recruiting a regular workforce, but had largely overcome them by the 1890s.[43] Although figures for labour turnover do not exist for mines outside Manchuria, by the twentieth century the major problem was that of seasonal variation in the supply of labour. All mines experienced a sharp fall in employment and output over the Chinese new year. The KMA, which ran the Kaiping mines from 1912, recognized the inevitable and closed the mines entirely over this period,[44] but as this was a holiday period – not one where the workers sought alternative employment – it is not a case of true seasonality.

More important was the phenomenon whereby workers left the mine to work in the fields at harvest and other agriculturally busy times. Most small unmechanized mines in all areas of China operated only sporadically throughout the year – the smallest working for only a few winter months, larger ones for perhaps half the year: for instance, mines in southern Sichuan worked only between October and March,[45] those in the Fenhe basin in Shanxi closed in spring and summer and others in the same province operated only between the ninth and first or second lunar months.[46] This seasonality was not, however, due solely to shortage of labour. Climatic and demand fluctuations also played a part: some mines in Guangdong closed in summer because there was too much rain, others because gas became too great a problem.[47] Similarly in Shanxi households used very little coal in summer, thus reducing demand and adding a further incentive for mines to close during that season.[48]

Even large mines were affected to some extent, especially in the first two or three decades of the twentieth century. In the 1920s the KMA's chief manager complained of a steep fall-off in labour supply at harvest time.[49] At Baojin in Shanxi between 1920 and 1922 on average 50% more shifts were worked in December and January than in June, though the seasonal pattern involved was not entirely constant,[50] and at Liujiang in north-east Hebei output dipped each year between 1916 and 1922 in the high summer months of June–September.[51]

Most mines suffered more or less seriously from seasonality of labour supply in the 1910s and 1920s. By the 1930s, however, data on seasonal labour supply and output back up the evidence from Manchuria of a more stable labour force. In Jiaozuo, Henan, the Zhongyuan Company's output showed no seasonal pattern at all in the 1930s (with the exception, as always, of a fall-off in February),[52] while in Shandong fluctuations in the output of Zhongxing's mines were not seasonally regular.[53] Other mines, especially the less well-established ones, still exhibited a strong seasonal pattern in their output and employment. In north Shanxi the mines operated by the Jinbei and the Baojin companies produced much more coal in winter than in summer.[54] Even Kailuan at least in the early 1930s showed some falling off of output in the summer.[55] This was only very slight, however, and seasonal variations in the output of modern mines were much less important than fluctuations caused by changing demand for coal.

An indirect way of studying the adequacy of the supply of labour is through the behaviour of wage rates. In a competitive market a shortage of labour supplied to the industry as a whole would lead to rising wages relative to those in the rest of the economy, while a shortage of skilled in relation to unskilled labour would lead to high wage differentials.[56] Even if the labour market was not perfectly competitive, as it obviously was not, in the absence of strong counter-indications these factors are likely to provide useful information on the supply of labour.

From the very fragmentary data on wages, the conclusion emerges that the level of money wages was fairly stagnant, except for a brief period in the late 1920s, when there was a widespread, though not universal, rise in money (and probably real) wage rates. The only series covering a

Table 7. *Wages of unskilled workers at Zhongxing coal mine, 1917–31*

Year	Average monthly wage (¥)	Mine output ('000 tons)
1917	7.84	428
1918	7.98	519
1919	8.09	569
1920	7.64	695
1921	7.46	668
1922	7.70	781
1923	7.96	788
1924	7.97	866
1925	8.01	822
1926	7.90	603
1927	8.78	260
1928	9.42	nil
1929	10.82	150
1930	11.53	356
1931	13.02	763

Source: Liu and Shi, 1932, p. 63.

reasonable number of years is one for wages at Zhongxing between 1917 and 1931, which suggests (see Table 7) a rapid rise in wages in the late 1920s: wages in 1931 were 65% higher than in 1926, whereas the north China wholesale price index had risen by only 23%. Another report ascribed the economic difficulties of the Liuhegou Company in Henan also to a rapid rise of wages in the late 1920s.[57] These instances tend to back up the assertion by the Geological Survey of a general rise in mining wages across China in that period.[58]

Table 7 also suggests, however, that this rise in wages was not due to any pressure on the supply of labour: there was no rise at all in those years when the growth of output was most rapid and necessitated hiring increasing numbers of workers. Indeed the general wage rise took place at a time of dislocation for the industry, when many companies, including Zhongxing, had to close down or drastically to curtail their operations, so that demand for labour actually fell. Wages rose rather because the miners became more organized in the wake of the Nationalists' Northern Expedition, and were able to take advantage of the temporarily favourable political situation to win limited wage rises. In the 1930s, the Nationalists became less favourable to the labour movement, while the economic depression following on their earlier difficulties made it impossible for most companies to pay wage increases, so that the rising trend was halted.

Apart from this episode, the causes of which lie in the field of political history, a generally stable wage rate suggests that there were no major difficulties with the labour supply – Zhongxing doubled its output in seven years without needing to pay more for labour. Nevertheless the particular geographical and seasonal difficulties described above did also affect wage rates. Where small mines still operated in the summer months, they often had to fix wages according to the local supply and demand at any particular time, as had those in Mei xian, Guangdong, and in Hancheng xian, Shaanxi.[59] Most large mines had, however, fixed scales of wages (and of contract prices where the work was put out to contractors) so that seasonal variations were small, but the contractors even at the medium-sized modern mine at Jiawang in Jiangsu had on occasion to resort to paying higher wages in summer.[60] Wage rates in Manchuria also reflected the particular situation of labour supply there, with steep rises in money wages as the SMR attempted to boost output in the late 1910s, and with year-to-year fluctuations of as much as 25% in the 1920s.[61] Even in an area notorious for surplus labour like Shandong, a sudden boom in coal mining could lead to a temporary shortage of labour and a subsequent rise in wages to try to counteract it: this happened in Boshan xian both in the late 1910s and in 1931.[62]

In contrast to the general sufficiency of unskilled labour, skilled labour – both supervisory and technical – was in very short supply throughout most of the period. To circumvent the shortage of trained supervisors, most mines both recruited and managed their labour through contractors.[63] In this way they were able to take advantage of the abundance of small-time commercial entrepreneurs which existed in many pre-modern Asian societies. This abundance allowed the industry to expand quite smoothly, albeit at the cost of adopting an institution that was to prove to have long-term disadvantages.

The shortage of technicians, on the other hand, was more directly reflected in the structure of wages, through generally large differentials for skill. In the late nineteenth century wages were very high for the skilled mechanics imported from Shanghai or Guangzhou: in the 1880s the highest wage at Kaiping was at least seventeen times as high as that for completely unskilled work.[64] Data for north China mines in the 1920s and 1930s suggest that the skill differential (average skilled wage: average unskilled wage) was approximately 2:1. At the Jingxing Company's collieries in south Hebei in 1928 the ratio of the wages of fifty-eight engine drivers, foundrymen and other skilled workers to those of 101 miscellaneous unskilled workers was 2.25:1.[65] Workers paid by the month (generally skilled workers) at Kailuan's Linxi colliery received an average of 91% more than did daily paid workers (although at the same company's Zhaogezhuang colliery they received only 65% more).[66] Finally, eighty mechanics employed by the Datong Mining Company in Anhui received 135% more than 500 or more hewers and ordinary workers.[67] Skill differentials appear on the whole to have been somewhat higher than those pertaining in Shanghai, which Howe estimates at an average of 1.77 : 1 in 1930.[68]

As in other respects, Manchuria presents a somewhat different picture of wage differentials. Mechanics at Fushun were paid only 50% higher wages than were miscellaneous workers,[69] a finding that tallies with Howe's conclusion that differentials were lower in Manchuria than elsewhere in China.[70] Two possible reasons for this come to mind: first, that the shortage of skilled workers in Manchuria was less, *relative* to the supply of unskilled workers, than in the rest of China; second, that one of the factors easing any shortage was a level of employment of foreigners (here Japanese) far higher than in mines elsewhere in China.

Indeed the more or less complete lack, at least up to the 1910s or 1920s, of Chinese engineers trained to take the highest responsibility, coupled perhaps with some prejudice in favour of foreign abilities, meant that mining companies looked mostly to foreigners for the technical skills needed to chart the overall direction of the mines. As early as 1874 the director of the Fuzhou Navy Yard asked the inspector-general of customs for help in finding a foreign engineer to run the coal mine he proposed to open at Jilong in Taiwan, and David Tyzack (who arrived on the island in 1875) was only the first in a long line of Western engineers working in Chinese coal mines.[71] The English engineer at Kaiping, Claude Kinder, was responsible for building China's first surviving railway, thus making a great contribution to the country's modernization.[72] Although one or two semi-modern mines prided themselves on their reliance on Chinese technicians, up to the 1910s all the mines aspiring fully to modernize their operations employed at least one foreign engineer, with the Germans especially prominent at Pingxiang, Jingxing, Zhengfeng (the Chinese-owned neighbour of Jingxing), and Zhongxing.[73]

Salaries for these foreigners were substantially higher than those of Chinese in equivalent positions. The Chinese general manager of Jingxing received only half the salary of Henneken, his German counterpart.[74] Similarly the Belgian engineer in charge at Kailuan's Zhaogezhuang colliery was paid twice as much as his Chinese colleague at the same company's Majiagou colliery.[75] The growing, though still small and inadequate, stream of Chinese engineers trained on the job or at university no doubt reduced costs in this sphere. Some Chinese companies, such as Zhongxing, appointed Chinese chief engineers in the mid-1910s and reduced their dependence on foreign labour. Nevertheless the fact that

Zhongxing reverted to the employment of a German engineer when it embarked on a new period of modernization and expansion in the 1930s suggests that the greater technical expertise of the foreigners may have compensated the companies for the extra expense.[76]

The need to use foreign staff imposed higher costs on the industry and, therefore, meant that sales, and so output, were lower than they would otherwise have been. But these extra costs were not great in relation to the size of the industry, and on the whole the supply of all the factors of production, land, labour and capital, was highly elastic as the industry expanded. None of the factors therefore constituted a major obstacle to the growth of coal output, but nor did the price of any fall to an extent which might have led to substantially lower coal prices and thus greater sales.

3

MODERNIZATION AND DUALISM: THE TECHNOLOGY OF THE PRODUCTION AND DISTRIBUTION OF CHINESE COAL

Since the supply of the factors of production was sufficient to preclude any steep rise in their price but did not promise any steep fall, any chance of a substantial cut in the cost and price of coal in the main markets lay in technological change either in mining or in transportation. The rise in coal output from large mines outlined in Chapter 1 is some measure of the application of at least some modern mechanical methods to coal mining, but the determinants of the pace and nature of this change were highly complicated, as is indicated by the survival of a large unmodernized sector. While a spectrum of technologies was used in all countries, the non-mechanized sector was (and remains) more important in China than elsewhere. The reasons for this lay in the respective advantages of each type of technology in local conditions and point to the importance of the concurrent revolution in transport technology as a major influence on mining modernization.

The continued viability of traditional technology

Alongside the growth of a modernized mining sector from the late nineteenth century, production of coal by mainly traditional and unmechanized methods continued, showing little if any sign of an absolute decline and even clearly increasing in some areas.[1] Small mines using this sort of technology were found in every province, and indeed were the only type of mine in most areas outside north and north-east China. While the aggregate output in most provinces using this technology was generally estimated at between 50,000 and 100,000 tons, in some it was much larger: both Sichuan and Hunan, where modern mining methods only just began to appear on the eve of the war, probably produced as much as 1 million tons annually from a multitude of such small mines.[2]

The continued survival of pre-modern methods in the provinces of west and south-west China – and in the remoter areas of north China – requires no elaborate explanation, since the high cost of transporting coal gave natural protection to such mines, enabling them to sell coal at costs which would have been prohibitive in the major mining areas or in areas penetrated by cheap railway transport. Mines serving local industries in Guangxi or Yunnan had little need to fear competition from cheaper north Chinese coal. The point is well illustrated by the rise and decline of the traditional-style mines at Tahe in Henan: they were able very profitably to supply local demand when the blockage of the railways in 1929–30 raised the price of coal by 400%, but they could not successfully compete when the railways began again to bring in cheap supplies from outside.[3] The obverse of this argument is that this very isolation which protected local mines also limited the market and thus made small-scale unmechanized production the most logical choice.

It was, however, by no means only in such areas that traditional technology continued to flourish. While the data for outlying provinces tells little about trends in production, rather more reliable information describes the continued survival of mines using non-mechanized methods in the very areas in which modern mines also operated. There they were able to take advantage of that expansion of the market permitted by cheap transportation which lay behind the growth of modern mining. The most outstanding example was the small-scale mining industry of Boshan in central Shandong, where government figures show that output (up to the 1920s all from mines using at most steam engines to raise the coal and water) grew by 8.6% annually between 1902 and 1936. If the output of the two mines that modernized their operations in the 1930s is excluded for those years, the rate of growth falls to a still considerable 7.8%.[4] Moreover, after the mid-1910s growth in Boshan was more rapid than that of the modern Sino-Japanese mine just down the railway at Zichuan.

In districts like Mentougou in the Western Hills outside Beijing there was no such continuing growth among the many small mines, but estimates for output were much the same for the 1930s as for the 1920s, and small mines were able to continue to exist in competition with the modern mine run by the Sino-British Zhongying Company.[5] The nearby mines of Fangshan were, however, affected at least temporarily by the expansion of Mentougou, though by the mid-1930s they were recovering earlier levels of output.[6] A third area of concentrated small-mine production was Shanxi. There were large numbers both in Pingding in the east of the province, where the partly modernized Baojin Company had to coexist with many small mines which produced over 60% of output,[7] and at Datong in the north where the two modern mines in the district produced only 40% of the area's output, the rest being accounted for by over twenty-nine traditional mines.[8]

In some localities small unmodernized mines were run by the main mining company or by contractors leasing the rights from the company, but the large mine remained in a predominant position. At Yixian the Zhongxing Company operated several small mines alongside its modern pits; in the early 1920s they contributed about 20% to total output.[9] At Jiaozuo many small mines operated under licence in the area of the Zhongyuan Company, by contract obliged to sell their output at a fixed price to the company, but in practice always tempted to undercut the company's prices on the open market.[10] Again, when the KMA closed its Majiagou colliery in 1936, the miners who lost their jobs opened many small pits in the area, which the administration tried to get the local authorities to close.[11]

Such mines, directly contiguous to mines using modern technology, enjoyed none of the natural protection that benefited their counterparts in outlying provinces, and had instead to compete directly on cost. Production costs differed little between the two groups, although it is not clear in all cases whether the figures cover the same items. At Boshan a Japanese source put costs for the traditional mines at between ¥2 and ¥2.4 per ton. Although a Shandong government report put the figures a little higher they were still below the ¥2.7 to ¥3.8 costs for the modern mine at neighbouring Zichuan.[12] Even figures at this level of aggregation do not exist for other coalfields, but the very phenomenon of a multitude of small mines coexisting with a large one militates against any very large cost differential: in Pingding many small mines were profitable at prices determined by the Baojin Company, but during the depression of the 1930s, their output and profits declined more sharply than did those of Baojin, and many were forced to close; this may suggest that their costs were a little higher than those of the more modern mine.[13]

Some authors have suggested that the lower wages paid in traditional mines enabled them to produce at costs comparable to those of modern mines.[14] This implies that while the commodity market was competitive within the area the labour market was not. Whereas in cotton spinning adolescent female labour with an opportunity cost close to zero could be used to compete with more highly productive factories,[15] mining companies employed adult males in very strenuous work, so that even in off-peak seasons the opportunity cost must have been substantially higher than zero. So *a priori* it would be surprising if large wage differentials existed between the same jobs in the same area in different mines.

There is nevertheless some evidence for the existence of just such a differential. The *Mining Weekly* reported that wages in the modern mine at Mentougou were 40–50¢ for an eight-hour shift, in the traditional mines 30–40¢ for a twelve-hour shift.[16] Likewise in Datong in north Shanxi wages for underground workers in the three largest mines were 50¢, in most of the smaller mines 30–40¢.[17] This apparent differential can, however, to some extent be rationalized as the price the modern mine had to pay to keep a year-round labour force, while the small mines only operated at times when the opportunity cost of labour was lower. Indeed in Boshan, where most mines worked more or less on a year-round basis,[18] there is less evidence for any differential: wages at the Zichuan mines were between 60¢ and 70¢ for a twelve-hour shift, those in Boshan about ¥1.20 for a twenty-four-hour shift.[19] So non-competitive labour markets offer at most only a partial explanation.

Hou Chi-ming argues that, even with no wage differential or difference in the price of capital, it is still possible for two different techniques to produce at the same unit cost.[20] The implication of his argument is that output per unit of capital is lower in a more modernized mine, that per worker higher. Torgashev's study of figures for output per worker appears to bear out at least that part of the theory: he concluded that output per man shift in native mines was between 50 kg and 100 kg, as against between 300 kg and 400 kg for the best modern Chinese mines, and attributes reports of higher productivity in small mines either to deliberate misrepresentation or to the figure referring to output per underground worker or per hewer, quoting evidence from several parts of China to back up his case.[21] In the present context, however, the problem is just that wide selection of evidence: the question here is how productivity differed between different technologies on the same coalfield. In that case geological conditions, while of course differing at different depths, would be at least comparable, while productivity differences between a modern mine in Hebei and a traditional mine in Hunan might be due mainly to different geological conditions.

Within the same coalfields the weight of the data indicates no great differences in crude output per man between the different types of mine. In central Shandong, the modern mine at Zichuan recorded an output per man per shift of 0.44 tons; twenty-three out of thirty-three small mines in neighbouring Boshan claimed a higher productivity.[22] At Mentougou 2600–2700 workers at the modern mine produced 1500–1600 tons, 2600 workers in the small pits 1300 tons, a small differential in favour of the modern mine.[23] In Datong thirteen out of twenty-eight small mines reported an output per man-year (a measure which would favour the modern mines, which worked more steadily throughout the year) higher than the average of the three largest mines.[24]

These measures are crude, in that no account is taken of the quality of output. Although no breakdown – for instance, into lump coal and slack – is available for the output from different types of mine, Chinese mines using pre-modern technology in the nineteenth century were unable to compete in the coastal markets because their lower prices were more than outweighed by their poorer quality, in terms of less lump coal and of a high admixture of other matter with the coal. In the twentieth century, however, Boshan coal was of sufficiently good quality to sell in Shanghai. So, while the crude output figures must be read with caution, they cannot be ignored entirely.

Rather than any of the above explanations, each of which may have been valid in certain circumstances, the particular economic conditions pertaining in an extractive industry – that is the inevitability of diminishing returns – best explain the survival of small mines in the vicinity of large modern ones. Exploiting seams close to the surface meant avoiding the escalating expenditure on haulage and other auxiliary activities that was unavoidable in a large modern mine. Small mines were in that way able to use the abundant resources to produce coal as cheaply as was possible with modern technology. In Britain nineteenth-century technological improvements were less a means to greatly increase output per worker than an attempt to ward off diminishing returns.[25] As these technological advances were the very ones which were the basis of mining modernization in China, it is not surprising that older methods could survive in a country with far more abundant and less heavily exploited coal resources – and thus far less down the road of diminishing returns – than Britain.

Perhaps the question should be not why traditional technology survived, but why modern methods were introduced. The story of modernization will be told in the next section, which will show that even in the 'modern' sector a wide range of technologies coexisted. The key was scale: large-scale production or at least loading facilities were needed to take full advantage of the economies of scale in railway transportation. Large-scale production implied long-term production in order to make full use of fixed capital investments, and it was in the longer term that the external diseconomies of small-scale working became apparent. While low-cost in the short-term, these methods meant that the field was worked in a disorganized and, in the long-term, uneconomic way. When the deposits accessible to this type of technology had been exhausted, and the field had to be worked by a deep modern mine or not at all, the legacy of the past emerged in a myriad of small pits penetrating the strata, often full of water and gas, causing serious problems for the deep mine and great danger to its workers.

The introduction of modern mining technology

Despite the survival of a large unmechanized sector, the Chinese coal industry as a whole was transformed from 1895 by the introduction of basic modern technology from the West, and the sector using this technology at least for certain operations came to dominate production. As suggested in the last section the introduction of this technology was less important in directly reducing costs than in permitting a much greater scale of production so that rail transport could be used with reasonable efficiency. So modernization, hesitant and uneven always, was most thorough in those aspects of operations where the use of mechanized methods and non-animal power was most necessary for the functioning of a large-scale mine. It was most uneven where substitution with other factors was easy without affecting the overall operation. Other factors, most importantly local geological conditions, but also the social organization of work and the ideas brought by the mine managers from their country of origin, also contributed to the wide diversity of technology employed even within the modern sector of the industry.

Coal-mining technology began to be transformed with the introduction of the Newcomen engine for draining pits in England in the early eighteenth century. This opened the possibility of much deeper and larger pits than had been feasible earlier. From the 1780s Newcomen and Watt engines were used for winding the coal – now the biggest production bottleneck – but the next major breakthrough came in the mid nineteenth century with the use of guide rails and cages in the shafts, which greatly increased winding capacity. Other improvements were more gradual: the shift to long-wall working, the move to the use of ponies and then of mechanical means of haulage, and the slow accretion of knowledge about gases and means of ventilation. All the major inventions making possible the modern mine were, however, available by around 1850, and certainly by the 1880s when China began to adopt Western technology. The next revolution of technique, the mechanization of coal-face work and loading, began in the early twentieth century in the United States, but was only fully adopted in Europe after the Second World War; it had little importance in China up to 1937.[26]

From the late 1870s Chinese entrepreneurs and officials began to use selected parts of this technology in their fledgling modern coal-mining industry.[27] Most of the so-called 'modern' mines were only modern in the most rudimentary sense. Often the only change made was the replacement of human with mechanical power in the operation of the winding engine. Water was still usually raised in leather buckets rather than by pumps.[28] Cages and guide rails were not used and operations underground were still entirely along traditional lines. The Jilong mine in Taiwan was slightly more advanced: it used steam-operated pumps as well as winding engines and a Guibal fan to provide ventilation. It also had a manually operated tramway from the mine to the water's edge, but it always remained on a relatively small scale and output never much exceeded 50,000 tons.[29] Before 1895, indeed, Kaiping in Hebei was the only really modern mine in China. Not only did it have all the major features of a large modern colliery – using mechanical winding and pumps, cages and guide rails in the shafts and artificial means of ventilation – but over the fifteen years after its opening its management constructed first a canal and then a railway to carry the coal to market.[30]

With the construction of a wider railway network, other modern mines were established, and by the 1930s China had more than two dozen colliery companies operating mines with at least the basic features of a modern colliery. Even then a wide range of technologies was used in some aspects of the work, and geology, factor prices and substitution, and even national proclivities all played their part in determining the particular methods used in any one mine.

Even within the large-mine sector, scale of output varied widely, with two companies having production capacities of over 5 million tons in the 1930s. The largest colliery complex, that at Fushun, was capable of an output of almost 10 million tons. Two other colliery groups were producing over 1 million tons in the early 1930s, and another eight over 500,000 tons. More important from a technological point of view was the size of the individual collieries, and here too Chinese collieries tended to be large by world standards. Not surprisingly the largest were those operated by the Kailuan and Fushun complexes: Fushun's open-cast mine had a capacity of over 3 million tons per annum, and at least one of its underground pits a capacity of over 1 million tons.[31] Kailuan's Zhaogezhuang colliery, with a capacity of around 2 million tons, was China's largest underground colliery, and indeed, according to the company's management, the largest outside the United States in the early 1920s.[32] Kailuan had two more collieries capable of producing over 1 million tons per annum,[33] while Zhongxing's single colliery at Zaozhuang in southern Shandong was expanding to close to 2 million tons by the mid-1930s.[34] Statistics for other complexes are often insufficiently clear to allow us to distinguish how much coal came from individual collieries run by the combine, but collieries with capacities of between 250,000 and 500,000 tons were common among the medium-sized mining companies of China.

The physical form of mines of this, or any other, size depended mainly on geological conditions rather than on economic considerations. Only in Manchuria did these favour open-cast mining, with 30–40% of Fushun's output coming from the massive Guchengzi open-cast pit, and large strip mines also at Zhalainuoer and Hegang in Heilongjiang.[35] But 90% of China's coal was produced from underground mines.

Only at a few sites did conditions permit the use of horizontal or sloping drift entrances: in Liaoning, some of the entrances to both the Benxihu and Fushun mines were slope mines, and other examples can be cited from large mines in Hebei, Shandong and Jiangxi.[36] Most mines were shaft mines, and even those using drifts generally had a shaft entrance to the mine as well. The abundance of resources and the relative youth of the industry meant that the mines did not have to be very deep – at least by European standards – in order to sustain a large output. The deepest shafts in each of twenty-one collieries operated by the ten most important mining companies varied from 90 metres to 496 metres, with the average being 210 metres;[37] another twenty-seven collieries run by fifteen smaller companies had deepest shafts on average of 126 metres.[38] Over the total of forty-eight collieries, which include nearly all the largest in China, the average of the deepest shaft in each colliery was 163 metres. These depths were comparable to, or even a little greater than, those in the United States, but European mines were far deeper. In Great Britain 43% of mines in 1944 were deeper than 270 metres, while the deepest approached 1800 metres; mines in the Pas de Calais region just before the Second World War varied between 300 and 800 metres deep.[39] China's shallower mines needed to use less power, equipment and labour for winding, pumping and ventilation, so that productivity in Chinese mines compared more favourably with that in Europe than it would have been the case had the mines been of equivalent depths.

Also in the main geologically determined was the system used to work the coal, which in most mines was some version of the room-and-pillar system; of the major collieries only Zhongxing used mainly long-wall.[40] While in Britain the switch from room-and-pillar to long-wall working was often an indicator of modernization, room-and-pillar remained more suitable where seams were thicker, and continued to be the predominant method of working in the United States.[41] Since Chinese conditions were in some ways more similar to those in the United States, room-and-pillar was also mostly used there, and the relative advantages of each system were well recognized, with some mines – for instance Pingxiang in Jiangxi and Benxihu in Liaoning – using both methods according to the seam concerned.[42] Elsewhere, however, as in the Zichuan mine in Shandong, the use of room-and-pillar even where geological conditions favoured long-wall did, according to the provincial government, imply technical backwardness.[43] Moreover, after 1949 the exigencies of face mechanization led to a rapid increase in long-wall working at the expense of room-and-pillar.[44]

Natural conditions also determined in some respects the level of mechanization of the mines, which in others was more a function of relative factor prices and substitution. The degree of possible substitution in the case of pumping and ventilation equipment was limited, and factors such as the size and depth of mine, and the amount of water and gas determined the capacity of pumps and fans that had to be installed; naturally, some flexibility remained, depending on how far the company was prepared to cater for the comfort and safety of its workers.

Most smaller mines were still able to rely on natural ventilation, as was the situation in Japan.[45] How far this term encompasses also the use of furnaces is not clear: all the pits operated by the Baojin Company used natural ventilation, only in one case is a furnace mentioned.[46] At the medium-sized mine of Bodong, certainly larger than the Baojin pits, there were no dangerous gases and so natural ventilation was thought sufficient, although this was aided mechanically in one area of the mine.[47] Many other mines producing up to 100,000 tons per annum also relied at least predominantly on natural ventilation.

All the larger mines needed at least some mechanical aids to ventilation. According to a Japanese observer five major Chinese mines in the 1930s had fans averaging 3000–4000 cubic metres per minute capacity,[48] while the huge size of the operations at Kailuan and Fushun is reflected in the 20,000 and 40,000 cubic metres per minute capacities of their pumping systems.[49] At Fushun provision for ventilation had been inadequate up to the 1910s, and it took the explosions and fires of 1917–18 to force the management greatly to improve its equipment; over the next years it installed several very large fans at its main pits, including two with capacities of 8500 cubic metres per minute at its Ōyama and Tōkyō pits,[50] as large as any but the very biggest in Japan.

Some mechanical means of pumping out the water was also essential in a large modern mine. Some of the smaller modern mines raised water not only by pump, but also in the leather buckets common in traditional and semi-modernized mines.[51] But steam or, less commonly, electrically powered pumping equipment was installed at all the large mines. The capacity installed was far greater than the average load on the equipment, because the amount of water varied greatly between seasons: at Zhongxing's mines it varied between a minimum of 200 tons per hour and a maximum of 1250 tons.[52] In some of the north-east mines, moreover, the methods of filling in areas already mined created further amounts of water which had to be removed by pumps.[53] The scale of pump used tended to be smaller than the largest in Japan, with those at Kailuan, for instance, only having half the capacity of the large pumps at Miike.[54]

Other aspects of underground operations, of which the working of the face and the haulage of the coal were the most important, were more susceptible to economic decisions made on the basis of the relative costs of labour and capital, permitting the use of either manual or mechanized methods without greatly interfering with the overall work of the mine. The handling, sorting and loading of coal after it had been brought to the surface could also be undertaken using any of several levels of mechanization.

The general response of mining companies to these decisions was wherever possible to adopt manual methods, to substitute labour for capital, as is shown by the small amount of power used in Chinese mines. Whereas in Britain and the United States even before the First World War, around 2.8 hp was employed for every worker,[55] in China not even the most advanced mines measured up to this average even in the 1930s. Fushun, employing 60,000 workers, devoted 80,000 kW of generating capacity for use within the colliery complex, and in addition some 37,000 hp of steam winding capacity; that is, under 2 hp per employee.[56] Zhongxing, with about 6000 workers, employed 6000 kW generating capacity and used a 500 hp winding engine, in all just over 1 hp per worker.[57] In smaller mines even less power was used per worker; at the Shuidong mine in Anhui under 100 hp power capacity was used for well over 300 workers, and this was far from untypical for smaller mines.[58]

Hardly any mechanical power at all was applied to the actual cutting of the coal, nearly all of which was done by miners wielding pickaxes, as indeed it was in most of Great Britain up to the 1930s.[59] This was the area where it was most difficult to mechanize, and where the most complicated and expensive machinery would be needed. The first step towards mechanization was the use of electric or pneumatic drills to undercut the coal: 0.5 hp electric drills were commonly used in the underground mines at Fushun. The next step, the use of mechanically powered coal cutters, got no further than the experimental stage in prewar China. In the mid-1930s Fushun was conducting such experiments,[60] while Zhongxing was also using Flottman chain coal cutters and shaking conveyors,[61] but these remained very much the exception in China.

Factor costs were not the only reason why so few mines used mechanical methods at the face. The cutting of the coal was generally under the control of labour contractors, and the contract system had implications for the type of equipment used, as did the modernization of equipment for the survival of contracting. While work was parcelled out in small units, small-scale unmechanized technology was most suitable, and the use of expensive machinery belonging to the mining company by people only indirectly responsible for it was clearly unsatisfactory for that company.

Haulage of the coal from the face to the pit-bottom admitted the widest variety of techniques, ranging from manually dragging the coal in baskets to a system of tramways and electric locomotives. Few mines had a completely integrated system, and methods differed according to the size of the roadway. All modern mines had iron tracks in the main roadways, though not necessarily in the side ones, but even in the 1930s mechanical means of propulsion were the exception. Much of the haulage work was also put out to contractors, again discouraging the installation of expensive modern equipment, but relative factor costs were probably a more important determinant of the level of mechanization of haulage. No simple deduction can be made, it is true, from cheapness of labour to the adoption of unmechanized techniques, but that this was the way mine managers saw the matter is clear from the comment made by one of the KMA's Belgian directors in 1948: 'The general level of the underground workings does not compare with modern American or European standards (due to the cheapness of labour in China at least before the war).'[62] Another factor that probably influenced companies to keep the level of mechanization low was the high risk of capital investment due to China's chronic political instability. If the mine had to close temporarily because of a blockage of transport, a large investment in mechanical equipment would lie expensively idle, while if the same functions were fulfilled by human labour, it would be easier to lay off workers and thus reduce outlays.

So, Kailuan, whose collieries produced more coal than those of any other company in China except the SMR, used in its mines a system of manual hauling of trucks to the main roadways, on which mules took them to the shaft-bottom. There were 1100 mules kept underground in 1929, 620 in the Zhaogezhuang colliery alone in 1920.[63] The Jingxing and Liuhegou mines also used mainly animal power,[64] but Pingxiang had used an electrically powered rope system from the 1900s.[65] The Japanese-owned mines were the most advanced in this respect, as in several others: Benxihu used an electrically powered rope system, while from 1924 Fushun switched from the use of pit-ponies to electric locomotives in its major underground mines.[66] The Sino-Japanese Luda Company also modernized its Zichuan mines in the 1930s and introduced electric locomotives.[67] This was possibly the result of the experience of the Japanese managers in their own country, where underground haulage was relatively highly mechanized and the use of animals for haulage had disappeared from the mid-1920s. In Great Britain, on the contrary, there were still over 50,000 pit-ponies working in the late 1930s.[68]

Less is known of surface arrangements, but there too relatively labour intensive methods were used. Coal was mostly sorted by hand, often by child labour.[69] Again the KMA made explicit the considerations it took into account in such decisions in the 1920s: 'It is the general experience throughout the Far East that mechanical loading devices will not compete with Chinese manual labour, and the Administration finds it advantageous to employ Chinese coolies for the loading and bunkering of ships.'[70]

As mechanical power comes to be used in greater amounts and for more purposes, the advantages of the flexibility and reliability offered by the use of electricity rapidly lead to the supersession of steam by electric power.[71] In China, however, most mines still used steam power, though there was a clear trend towards electrification in the largest mines.

The threshold above which it became economic to replace human or animal power with steam varied according to the type of district involved. In areas like Boshan, where many mines were concentrated and where there was a wide and expanding market, only the very smallest did not use steam.[72] In remoter areas the threshold was probably higher: only the two largest (though still small by national standards) mines in Bishan, Sichuan, used small steam winding engines.[73] Such engines sometimes generated as little power as 10 hp: nine of the seventeen small pits operated by the Pingxin Company in Jiaozuo, Henan, used 11 hp engines, the rest other small engines of up to 45 hp.[74] These small engines could only wind up to 100 tons per day. When such small amounts of power are used it can be more economic for a large number of small mines concentrated in one area to purchase electricity generated elsewhere than to produce their own power in any form. Although never general practice, there had begun a trend in Boshan in this direction.[75] Where the supplier was a monopoly producer, any advantage of large-scale power generation could be negated, and the Jin'gou mine in Liaoning was forced to look to its own power generation rather than buy expensively from Fushun.[76]

In larger mines steam engines were mostly the first type of power installed in the 1900s, even at a time when the switch to electricity was in full swing in England. Steam remained the predominant form of power, especially for the concentrated amounts needed by winding engines, where the advantages of steam were greater than for other operations: small mines which bought electricity for most other purposes often still employed steam for winding.[77] In Japan in the early 1930s, two-thirds of the winding engines in the major mines were still steam powered,[78] and the proportion was still higher in China. Even the Huainan mine, opened by the government in the 1930s, installed steam winding engines.[79] Except in the largest half-dozen mines, the engines varied from around 100 to 1000 hp, and raised between a few hundred and 2000 tons per day; the relationship between power and winding capacity depended of course on the depth of the mine; Luda needed 700 hp and 900 hp engines to raise the same amount of coal from its 300 metre shafts at Zichuan as Liuhegou did with 100–150 hp engines at its 100 metre shafts.[80]

Nevertheless the trend towards electricity both for winding and for other purposes was clear, as it was in Japan, where all new mines opened after 1919 used electric winding engines.[81] Thus Zhongxing's first shaft, completed in 1913, had a steam winding engine; its second and third, opened in 1921 and 1934, used electricity.[82] Similarly Kailuan's two most modern collieries at Zhaogezhuang and Tangjiazhuang used electrically powered hoists[83] but, despite intentions of changing the older engines to electricity, the heavy investment required for this meant that the quite serviceable steam hoists earlier installed at the company's other collieries continued to be used up to the war.[84] Many mines used a mix of methods; the Jingxing mines in Hebei used steam for winding, and almost as much power in the form of compressed air as in that of electricity for other purposes.[85]

The Japanese-run mines in the north-east had progressed furthest towards the adoption of electricity. This was largely a matter of scale, as Fushun was the largest mine in China, and one of the largest in the world. Its power station produced over 460 million kWh in 1935,[86] though as much as 40% of this was sold to outside users. Its huge collieries used some of the largest engines anywhere: when the East Ryūhō mine was opened in 1936 the 5400 hp electrically powered Koepe-type winding engine capable of lifting 650 tons per hour was reported to be the world's biggest.[87]

Chinese mines had thus come a long way since the earliest beginnings of modernization at Jilong in the 1870s. While by no means necessarily allowing production at a cost much cheaper than allowed by the old technology, mechanization, by warding off diminishing returns, did enable far more coal to be mined at more or less constant cost than would have been possible otherwise. It was also a necessary concomitant if the industry was to take full advantage of the opportunities offered by the other revolution in technology that took place in China mainly between 1895 and 1915 – the cheapening of transportation by the construction of the railways.

Transportation

While not in itself the subject of this book, the construction of the railways played such a vital role in the growth of the coal industry that at least the outstanding parts of the story must be told.

In pre-modern China, as in Britain,[88] the high cost of traditional transport, especially over land, was the crucial determinant of the size and pattern of the coal industry. In China land transport costs ranged upwards from around 6¢ per ton km, the cost of transport by cart in Shandong; where coal had to be carried by wheelbarrow the cost was generally around 10¢, by pack animal as high as 15–20¢.[89] While the cost of transport by junk or inland waterways was much lower – as little as 0.2¢ per ton km on the Yangzi, more normally around 2¢,[90] most of China's coal deposits were in the north, where water transport was less available. Thus coal produced at a cost of 100 cash per picul, 15 km south of Qinghua in Henan, cost 250 cash in the city;[91] even this rate, whereby the cost of coal doubled over 10 km, was less extreme than the situation in England, where the cost doubled after only 6.5 km.[92]

Rail transport could reduce these costs to under one-fifth of the previous level for land transport. While rates varied considerably according to the line used, the amount of coal carried, and even the season, most coal was carried for less than 1¢ per ton km. Because of coal's great bulk and low value per unit of weight, the cost of transport is inevitably of almost decisive weight in final cost at all but pit-head markets. So this technical innovation in transport was by far the most important factor in bringing down the final cost of coal in urban markets.

Apart from the abortive Wusong railway, the first line in China was built in the 1880s to carry Kaiping coal to the nearest point of shipment for water transport.[93] The extension of that line as far as Tianjin and the building of a short railway in Taiwan were the only projects undertaken before 1895, but in the last decade and a half of the Qing the railways that were to remain the core of China's network up to and beyond 1949 were constructed. In Manchuria the Russians built a line (the Chinese Eastern Railway) running from north-west to south-east linking Siberia to Vladivostok, with another running at right angles from it linking Harbin and Dalian (from 1905 the stretch from Changchun to Dalian became the South Manchurian Railway). The Kaiping line was extended to become the Bei–Ning, linking Shenyang and Beijing, which was linked in the other direction also to Hankou. That line (the Jing–Han), one of the two major north–south lines, also had feeders, mainly coal carrying, to Taiyuan (the Zheng–Tai) and between Daokou and Qinghua (the Dao–Qing). The other major north–south line (the Jin–Pu) ran from Tianjin to Pukou, while a railway (the Jiao–Ji) also ran from Jinan through central Shandong to the port of Qingdao.

In all over 9500 km of railway was built up to 1911 (see Table 8), but after that construction slowed, and over the whole of the republican period up to 1937 only about 11,500 km were built. The major projects were the extension of the Jing–Han to Guangzhou (the Guang–Han), and the gradual construction of the east–west line (the Long–Hai) linking Xi'an to Lianyungang. In addition further construction was carried out by both the Chinese and the Japanese in Manchuria, which came to have by far the most complete network in China.

Table 8. *Growth of railway transport in China*

Year	Approximate length of network (km)	Freight traffic (thousand million ton km)
1895	360	n.a.
1911	9,620	n.a.
1915	9,740	5.8
1920	11,030	8.9
1928	13,040	10.9
1936	21,036	17.8

Sources: Network: Yan Zhongping, 1955, p. 180; Chang Kia-ngau, 1943, p. 46; traffic: my own calculations from various sources.

Some simple calculations illustrate the importance of the railways in greatly reducing the final cost of Chinese coal, and thus increasing the scope for expansion of Chinese mines. Assuming that imported coal from Japan cost about ¥9.00 per ton in the coastal ports in 1913, and that production cost in China was about ¥3.00,[94] the economic radius for the production of coal was about 75 km if carts were used to carry the coal, but well over 500 km if railways were used. The actual saving in costs in various cities depended on the distance of the mine from the market. Thus, had carts been used instead of railways, Kaiping and Jingxing coal would each have cost more than three times as much as they did in Beijing, while Mentougou coal, mined only 44 km away from the city, would still have cost a substantial 50% more.

The same factors also acted, at least in theory, to open up the interior to imported coal, but penetration was in fact very slight. Anyway, the coastal market was growing the most rapidly, so Chinese coal reaped the greatest benefit from the transport revolution. Thus the modernization of transport, coupled as it had to be with the opening of large modern mines, made an immense contribution to the growth of the industry. How great it is impossible to estimate, but by the 1930s the total amount of coal carried by the railways was roughly equal to the total output of modernized mines. Without the railways the cost of most Chinese coal in the cities would have been much higher, and therefore sales and thence output much lower.

Cheaper coal in the main markets

Only pit-head consumers reaped no benefit from the reduction in transport costs. In other areas the price of Chinese coal fell by amounts depending on the distance it had to be carried over land, as well as on the availability of competitive coal or of substitutes. While it is impossible to disentangle the various influences at work in the statistics, this fall in price must in itself, apart from any autonomous increase in demand, have led to greater sales of Chinese coal, either at the expense of foreign coal or as part of an increased total consumption.

North China's cities, most dependent on land transport, benefited most from the transport revolution. Even in Beijing, situated almost astride a coalfield, the use of railways to bring coal to the city resulted in a considerable fall in the price of coal briquettes, especially in relation to the cost of living. Table 9 shows three periods when the real cost of briquettes clearly declined: 1905–8, 1909–12, and 1915–17. Many factors were no doubt at work, and the detailed price and sales figures necessary to make a full analysis are not available. But the first two falls at least took place at times when new transport facilities were opening up coalfields near the city. In 1906 the opening of the Jing–Han made coal from the fields just to the south of the city more cheaply available, while the railway between Beijing and its main coalfield, Mentougou, was built between 1906 and 1908.[95] In 1910 the overhead wire transport linking the coal mines at Tuoli to the Jing–Han at Liangxiang was completed; at its period of maximum operation, this facility was carrying 180,000 tons of coal per annum.[96] The 1915–17 fall in prices is less easy to explain this way, though a light railway did improve the transport situation within the Mentougou coal field from 1914.[97] The continuing importance of rail transport for the Beijing coal market is also shown by the failure of camel transport to avert a coal famine in 1928 when wars blocked the rail lines.[98]

In cities further from their source of supply than Beijing the fall in price was greater. A Japanese observer reported a 60% fall in the price of coal in Jinan after the completion of the Jiao–Ji linked the city to the Boshan coalfield, 157 km away.[99] Prices must have fallen similarly in rural areas along the railway lines, but no figures are available.

Discounting any autonomous increase in demand, price elasticity determined the effect this fall in prices had on sales. Scattered qualitative references suggest that elasticity was quite high. The reduction in the cost of Kaiping coal, after modernization had countered the effects of diminishing returns, led to the revival of native industries which had earlier languished because of the high cost of fuel.[100] Later the KMA's chief manager reported on the effect cheap water transport had on the sale of the company's coal:

> The consumption of coal, more especially by the native industries, shows a continuing tendency to increase year by year and coal as a commercial fuel is now being used in the far-off inland districts in

Table 9. *Cost of living and coal briquette prices in Beijing, 1900–17*

Year	Index of cost of living (1900 = 100)	Index of briquette prices (1900 = 100)	Index of real cost of briquettes (col. 3 ÷ col. 2)
1900	100	100	100
1901	84	96	114
1902	94	97	103
1903	104	96	92
1904	96	93	97
1905	93	94	101
1906	102	94	92
1907	107	93	87
1908	110	94	85
1909	110	98	89
1910	111	93	84
1911	123	88	72
1912	126	85	67
1913	123	84	68
1914	115	82	71
1915	109	80	73
1916	119	72	61
1917	126	68	54

Sources: Recomputed from Meng and Gamble, 1926, pp. 59, 72.

much greater quantities than hitherto [. . .] Native boats laden with export cargo, after discharging at sea ports, take back coal inland at very cheap rates of freight, and so distribution of coal becomes general all along the many waterways. There are no signs whatever of the former native fuel being reverted to, the native consumption of coal has come to stay and will probably continue to increase.[101]

In Jinan the increase of the coal trade subsequent to the opening of the railway is shown by the fact that nearly all the fifty-six coal traders trading there in 1917 were located in the newly constructed commercial quarter of the city. Moreover Boshan interests, using the Jiao–Ji to bring coal to the city, almost completely displaced the formerly dominant Shanxi coal merchants.[102]

Even in the ports, where the construction of the railways may not have led to any increase in total sales, Chinese coal was now able to compete with foreign coal on more favourable terms, and in north China imports practically disappeared from the market. In Tianjin imports dwindled almost to nothing by the end of the 1880s as cheap Kaiping coal, carried by rail, barge and ship, became available. Later the customs commissioner in Qingdao reported that the building of the Jiao–Ji had had the same effect there, although the statistical picture is less clear.[103]

Shanghai depended almost entirely on water transport to bring in its coal, and China's lack of tariff autonomy together with the geographical position of this, China's largest market meant that even after the building of the railways Japanese coal could compete on equal terms with Chinese. Since Japanese coal exercised price leadership there up to the 1930s (for instance the price of Chinese coal rose in 1931, when the exchange rate kept that of Japanese coal artificially high),[104] the growing availability and competitiveness of Chinese coal showed up mainly in a larger share of the market. Table 10 shows that the share of imports in the sum of imports plus output from modern Chinese mines (a passable proxy for the national market) declined rapidly and sharply between the early 1900s and the early 1920s, the period of the construction of the railways; the sole five-year period in which the trend was reversed only proves the point – it was then that railway disruption prevented the shipment of Chinese coal to the ports, leading to a partial reversion to the previous state of affairs. Similarly in Shanghai the share of Japanese and other imported coal declined steadily. The growth of a coal industry in China capable of producing and transporting coal at a competitive price was the chief, although not the only, cause of these trends.[105]

In rural areas the possibility of import substitution was virtually non-existent, but the high price of other fuels may well have meant a high elasticity of demand for coal if its price was cheap enough, so that quite large amounts of coal could have been sold in places where it was virtually unknown before. On the other hand, costs rose steeply with distance from the station, and in any case the peasants purchased only a small proportion of their fuel, so that the price would probably have had to be very low indeed for them to buy coal instead of using other fuel which they could themselves collect on the farm or elsewhere.

To some extent the effects of modernization in the mining and transport sectors were part of a continuing process: as new lines opened up new areas, demand for the now-cheaper coal might increase in those areas, while new coalfields might have the opportunity to compete in a wider market. In more important ways, however, the impact can usefully be seen as an essentially one-off shift in the supply curve for coal that took place in the first two decades of the century. By 1920 railways already served enough coalfields to meet demand at the current levels, while the creation of a coal-consuming industrial base in new areas of the interior would require a far more drastic level of action than just the construction of new railways. Moreover, while pressure continued from mine owners for lower freight rates and others talked of excessive production costs at the mines, in neither case was it likely that any large savings could be made, certainly nothing

Table 10. *Share of imports in the Chinese coal market, 1901–37*

Year	Share of imports in (imports and output from modern mines – Percentage)	Average share of imports in total shipments of coal into Shanghai by sea (Percentage)
1901–05	55	80
1906–10	33	70
1911–15	19	58
1916–20	11	44
1921–25	10	38
1926–30	13	33
1931–35	6	22
1936–37	2	10

Sources: IMC, *Returns and Reports*, 1900–19; IMC, *Annual Trade Report and Returns*, Shanghai 1921–6; MMT, chōsabu, 1937e, pp. 543–4, 634; Hsiao, 1974, pp. 43–4. These figures are only approximate because of changes in the basis of customs reporting in the 1920s and 1930s, both in respect of exported bunker coal and in the classification of Manchuria as 'foreign' from mid-1932. These difficulties do not affect the overall trend shown by this table.

compared to the effects of their original construction. So, once these effects had largely worked through, demand became the main determinant of the rate of growth of the industry.

4
THE GROWTH AND COMPOSITION OF DEMAND

Demand for coal in China increased continuously from the mid nineteenth century up to the anti-Japanese war. It originated in three categories: industrial, household and export. Demand from industry grew mainly with the growth of coal-using industries, but technical progress economizing in the use of coal, substitution for imported coal and competition with other fuels also affected the level and trend of that demand. Household demand increased to some extent as China's population grew, and rose or fell along with income levels and to a greater extent with fluctuations in the price and availability of alternative fuels; but urbanization was the most important factor influencing the long-term increase in the use of coal as a household fuel. Finally, the proximate determinant of the demand for exports (almost all to Japan) was the relative price of Chinese coal in overseas markets. The high elasticity of supply of Chinese coal at this time meant that the limited quantity and quality of Japanese coal reserves and the strong, though uneven, growth of Japanese manufacturing and metallurgical industries mainly determined the level of exports from China.

There were very few years in which increased industrial activity, larger urban populations or expanding coal markets abroad did not add to demand at a given price. Modern industry (including transportation) constituted the most dynamic source of demand, and gradually accounted for a growing proportion of total consumption. Even in the early years when that proportion was still low, specific backward linkages from modern industrial or transport enterprises into modern coal mining attest to the key role of this sector.

Demand from transportation and manufacturing industries
The growth in and transformation of demand began in the mid nineteenth century. Previously (see Chapter 1) coal consumption – by both industrial and domestic users – had been mainly scattered and on a small scale, and concentrated largely in coal-producing districts. But from

around 1850 there emerged centres, mainly in the treaty ports, of large-scale consumption by industry and shipping which were not able to rely on local supplies and which were able and indeed obliged to seek coal from many distant sources.

Shipping

Steam-powered shipping was the main source of this increasing demand, and was central to changing patterns of demand also in other countries.[1] The first steamship appeared in Chinese waters in 1835[2] and, despite a brief heyday for the famous clippers, by the early 1870s steamships accounted for over 80% of the shipping recorded by the Maritime Customs.[3] The total tonnage of steamers entered and cleared rose fairly steadily at about 6.7% per annum from under 6 million tons in 1871 to over 28 million in 1895 and over 80 million in 1910. This created a *potential* demand for coal which grew a little less rapidly than the total amount of shipping, but still at 4.7% per annum – from around 300,000 tons in the early 1870s to over 1 million tons by the turn of the century, and then almost doubling in the course of the next decade.[4]

Chinese coal was the obvious candidate to supply this potential demand. It was substantially cheaper than the main alternatives in the 1850s and 1860s, British and Australian coal. In late 1866 coal from Taiwan cost under 6 taels per ton in Shanghai; that from Britain or America over 10 and that from Australia about 8.5.[5] Early in the next decade, Swires reported that they could buy native coal at half the price of Cardiff coal.[6] This induced shipping companies to try to develop this source of supply, and the earliest foreign interest in Chinese coal had been shown by a P & O contract in 1847 to buy 700 tons of Formosan coal for its fleet.[7] Interest continued and in 1869 the Shanghai Steamship Navigation Company switched to Chinese coal, thus considerably reducing its expenditures.[8] The extra freight costs incurred in carrying imported coal up the Yangzi made native coal an even more attractive proposition in the river ports, and led to brief coal booms in some cities.[9] Considerable interest was also shown in north Chinese coal, such as that produced near Beijing, as fuel for the Tianjin–Shanghai run.[10]

Nevertheless the price advantage of coal from unmodernized Chinese mines proved illusory as it was more than outweighed by its poor quality. Quality was a vital factor because the relatively low efficiency of fuel consumption by steamships in the mid nineteenth century meant that a substantial part of their carrying capacity had to be given over to bunker coal, and any saving on the bulk of coal could be used to take on more cargo.[11] Pre-modern Chinese mines were poorly placed to meet this demand for high quality lump coal. Traditional methods produced a high proportion of dust, while the total absence of washing or screening facilities left a product of very uneven quality.

Backward linkages from the shipping industry were crucial in the early development of China's modern mining sector. It was the demand from their shipping that stimulated British interest in Chinese coal, and as early as 1864 John William Howell requested permission to open a mine at Jilong.[12] When, a decade later, the Chinese authorities did open a semi-modern mine there, the aim was at least partly to provide bunker coal,[13] and the shipping market was the main target of the establishment in the 1880s of the semi-modern mines at Jingmen in Hubei and at He xian in Guangxi.[14] Kaiping's first manager anticipated that coal from the mine would be able successfully to compete with foreign coal in the coastal market, and to supply coal to bunker the China Merchants' Steamship Navigation Company ships, expectations that were at least partly borne out by Kaiping's success in driving foreign coal off the Tianjin market and in beginning to win a stake in the Shanghai market in the late 1880s.[15] Kaiping was the only success story, however, and coal from the other, less-thoroughly modernized, mines proved to have the same problems of uneven quality that had restricted sales from mines using traditional technology. Since output from Kaiping was far too small to satisfy the market, customers had to look elsewhere for their coal.

Because of the failure of Chinese mines to satisfy the growing demand for bunker coal, foreign coal dominated the Chinese coastal market through-out the nineteenth century. The excessive cost of Australian and British coal was countered not by the development of Chinese mines but by the rapid increase from the 1870s of coal imports from Japan. Geographical proximity made Japanese coal much cheaper than British or Australian and it came on to the market very little, if any, more expensive than Chinese coal.[16] While there were also quality problems in early shipments of Japanese coal,[17] it came to offer a better mix of price and quality than did Chinese, Australian or British coal, and dominated the coastal market well into the twentieth century. Indeed the Chinese bunker market played a vital part in the early development of the modern Japanese coal industry, taking up to half the output from the two modern mines at Takashima and Miike in the early 1880s.[18]

A consequence of the dominant position of imported coal in the coastal market was that shipping preferred, where possible, to bunker in Japan, where Japanese coal was cheaper. Rather than take on Chinese coal of poor quality and irregular supply, steamers would go on to Nagasaki to take on Japanese coal.[19] Thus the actual sales of bunker coal in China were far below their potential level as part of the demand was transferred abroad.

Shipping companies nevertheless bought considerable amounts of coal, and constituted the most important, sometimes almost the sole, market in the ports. In Yantai (Chefoo), a treaty port on the north coast of Shandong, the few thousand tons of coal imported annually from the 1860s to the 1890s all went to fuel steamships.[20] Steam launches were also important in the rather small markets of the inland Yangzi ports: in Hankou all the coal noticed by the customs was sold to shipping,[21] while both Jiujiang and Yichang enjoyed brief periods as coaling ports.[22] By far the most important ports on the China coast were Shanghai and Xianggang (Hong Kong), the latter of course falling under British jurisdiction. According to a Japanese source, about 65% of Xianggang's 600,000 tons coal market was accounted for by shipping.[23] As that port handled about 80% more shipping than did Shanghai, an estimate for Shanghai of 150,000–200,000 tons bunker sales in the late 1880s and early 1890s, calculated indirectly from the customs figures, is probably close to the mark.[24] By 1913, 31% of an estimated 2.3 million tons total market in Shanghai was used by shipping.[25]

While shipping in the nineteenth century merely created a potential source of demand for Chinese coal in the ports, in the twentieth century Chinese mines began increasingly to supply that market. Moreover, Chinese ports were now attracting business away from other East Asian coaling stations by offering cheap coal. This category of demand was always more price elastic than others because of the relative freedom of ships to take on coal at different locations. By a vigorous programme of price-cutting and sales promotion, the SMR attracted more shipping to Dalian in the early 1920s and increased bunker sales by 170% between 1919 and 1922, although the trade of the port fell by 19%.[26] From this time Dalian became the most important coaling port in China, selling 600,000 tons or more per annum.[27] Unlike Dalian, Qinhuangdao was not a major port in its own right, but its function as an outlet for Kailuan coal meant that it sold around 200,000 tons per annum. Other ports, especially those of central and south China, had no nearby mines, and ships preferred to take on coal in cheaper locations if possible. Nevertheless, because of the large amounts of shipping, especially at Shanghai, the bunker market remained substantial. At Shanghai around 500,000 tons were sold to shipping companies, and Guangzhou and Hankou each sold about 100,000 tons.[28]

From the 1910s, however, the growth of the total bunker market in East Asia slowed down, although China was getting a bigger share. The war diverted much shipping to other uses, and, after a brief spurt in the early 1920s, growth in shipping using Chinese ports slowed, coming practically to a halt in the 1930s, reflecting the overall downturn in world trade. Even though improvements in fuel economy were probably slower in fact than in the mid nineteenth century, they still reduced the amount of fuel needed per unit of shipping by about 2.25% per annum in the twentieth century.[29] This appeared all the more threatening when the total amount of shipping was stagnant or in decline. From the 1920s, in addition, the world's major shipping fleets began to turn to the use of fuel oil instead of coal to power their ships. By the mid-1930s, demand for bunker coal had been reduced by the fact that 20% of shipping was oil powered.[30] So, although bunker sales in China were around 2 million tons by the mid-1920s, and remained at a similar level until the mid-1930s, thus accounting for around 7% of the total market for modern coal mines, from the early twentieth century this sector was overtaken as the most dynamic source of demand by a new form of transportation that was rapidly developing in China.

Railways

In the first decade of the twentieth century the newly constructed railways came to constitute an important source of demand for coal, although their role as coal carriers was of even greater significance for the industry (see Chapters 3 and 5). Just as with the growth of shipping, this new source of demand created specific backward linkages into coal mining as railway companies sought directly or indirectly to guarantee their sources of fuel supply. In Manchuria the SMR operated the Fushun mines partly with this in mind, although they also had a much broader development strategy. In 1901 the Chinese Eastern Railway opened Zhalainuoer (China's largest lignite mine) in Heilongjiang to supply fuel for their operations.[31] In Hebei, the Jing–Han took a very active part in the development of the Lincheng mine, with the expectation of reducing its fuel costs from the level necessitated by the use of Kaiping coal.[32] Even for mines where no direct investment was made by railway companies, the nexus remained very close, especially in the early years of the century, as the railways were generally the most important single customers of the mines (see Table 11).

Very broadly, consumption of coal increased in line with total traffic. Unfortunately no total traffic figures exist for years before 1915, but Table 12 summarizes the later figures, which show continuing growth in traffic, though much slower in the late 1920s and early 1930s than at other times. The table indicates that by the 1930s locomotives consumed some 2.3 million tons of coal, while railway workshops and other auxiliary enterprises used about another 20%, raising total consumption to around 2.8 million tons. Rapid growth of railway transport resumed on the eve of the war, raising total consumption to well over 3 million tons per annum.[33]

Table 11. *Importance of sales to railway companies for some modern mines*

Mine	Period	Percentage of total sales going to railways
Zhalainuoer	1913–15	88
Fushun	1907–10	43
Jingxing	1912–13	36
Kaiping	1906	16
Kaiping	1911	12
Zhongxing	mid-1910s	12

Sources: Horiuchi, 1967, p. 739; Manshikai, 1964–5, vol. 2, p. 67; MMT, 1919, pp. 605–8; Gu, 1916, 8:57; IMC, *Returns and Reports, 1906*, part II, vol. 1, p. 27; *1911*, part II, vol. 1, p. 155; SKJ 27 (October 1914): 59.

Table 12. *Growth of rail traffic and use of coal in locomotives*

Period	Average annual passenger traffic (thousand million passenger km)	Average annual freight traffic (thousand million ton km)	Average use of coal in locomotives ('000 tons)
1915–19	3.44	6.97	1,176
1920–24	4.94	9.75	1,707
1925–29	5.54	10.72	1,910
1930–34	5.84	12.78	2,291
1935–36	7.42	17.79	3,511

Note: This table covers *all* Chinese railways, not just the Chinese National Railways; it is compiled from data from many sources and where data are not available, estimates were made on the basis of tons/passengers carried, revenue, or sometimes interpolation (see also note 33).

Although the connection between mines and railways was never again quite as close as it had been in the 1900s and 1910s, it remained important. Sales of coal to railways kept pace with growth in traffic, and the growth in freight traffic paralleled that in modern mine output, for coal was by far the most important single item of freight, by weight, for most railways. It is not therefore surprising that from the mid-1910s the symbiotic growth of the two industries led to a roughly constant proportion – around 10% – of modern mine output being used by railway companies.

The parallel growth of traffic and coal used by locomotives was disturbed mainly by technical progress in fuel efficiency. Figures for the SMR show that each year it used on average 2.1% less fuel for each unit of traffic than in the previous year.[34] There was, however, no such trend for the Chinese National Railways. The diversion of equipment to military use during the civil wars led to a very inefficient use of railway resources, and also depleted the financial reserves necessary to buy new equipment. Throughout the history of the railways the rate of replacement of equipment was very low, so that much of it was obsolescent by the 1930s.[35] As a result there was no improvement in fuel consumption per unit of traffic, although the buoyant effect of this on the coal market was very small compared to the fall of consumption when traffic declined during the civil wars.

The role of the railways as a leading sector in coal consumption was inevitably restricted by the dependent relationship of railway traffic on coal output. So, once the basic network had been established, other sectors took over the leading role.

Manufacturing, metallurgy and electric power

Modern industries began to use coal from the time they emerged in the ports in the mid nineteenth century. The government armament factories provided the most substantial demand. Twenty-nine arsenals were established by Qing officials between 1861 and 1895, although by no means all operated at the same time.[36] The largest were at Shanghai, Nanjing, Tianjin, Fuzhou and, from 1890, Hanyang. In the 1880s the Jiangnan (Shanghai) arsenal used 10,000 tons of Taiwan coal annually, and may have bought coal also from other sources.[37] This suggests that the government arsenals used at least 50,000–100,000 tons of coal a year at that time. Like shipping and the railways, this infant arms industry generated specific backward linkages. The officials in charge of the arsenals disliked having to use foreign coal both because of their economic nationalism and because of its high cost.[38] This was the main stimulus behind their interest in modern coal mining. The Tianjin arsenal used coal from unmodernized Chinese mines from 1874,[39] and several of the early modern mines were opened to meet this demand. The Jilong mines were first developed in order to supply fuel to the Fuzhou dockyard as well as to shipping,[40] while both the Yi xian and the Kaiping mines were intended to supply coal to the Tianjin and Nanjing arsenals.[41] The Yi xian mine certainly did supply coal to the Nanjing arsenal, although this was probably not its most important market.[42]

Numerous foreign industrial enterprises also sprang up in the ports before 1895, but their legality was uncertain,[43] and so their number and size – and therefore their demand for coal – was limited. Nevertheless the Shantou (Swatow, Guangdong) sugar refinery used over 15,000 tons of coal a year,[44] while the pioneer silk filature at Shanghai and the bean mill at Niuzhuang in Liaoning also used considerable amounts of coal.[45]

After 1895 the growth of modern manufacturing industry in China accelerated, and the use of coal in order both to provide heat and power for general manufacturing and to supply necessary raw materials, for instance for the metallurgical and cement industries, began to assume major proportions. The most important determinant of the extent of this demand was the level of activity of the coal-using industries, and Chang's figure of 9.4% per annum industrial growth rate between 1912 and 1936 probably approximates the growth in coal-using industries over the whole period.[46] But this growth was uneven between industries and between regions, something that had a major effect on the structure of industrial coal consumption.

The general characteristics of China's industrial growth in this period were reflected in the composition of coal consumption. That is, the heavy and metallurgical industries were relatively unimportant, the light industries, especially textiles, comparatively developed. Apart from the metal industries, the only producer-goods industry that required substantial amounts of coal was cement; it used around 50,000 tons of coal in 1912, but around 400,000 tons in 1936, as the construction boom in Manchuria led to a rapid increase of cement consumption there.[47]

Iron and steel played a central role in the growth of the market for coal in many economies. In his history of the British coal industry, Buxton goes as far as to say: 'The outstanding feature of the Industrial Revolution was the extent to which the consumption of coal became so intimately bound up at all points with that of iron . . . The evolving technology of the iron industry and its growing demand for mineral fuel were primarily responsible for the rapid expansion of coalmining output.'[48] The iron industry took about 30% of coal output in 1870 and even though the proportion declined thereafter, it remained an important customer.[49] It gained this position first because of the switch from using charcoal to using coal as a fuel,[50] and then from the strong growth of output of iron and steel themselves, thus necessitating the use of increasing amounts of fuel. In continental Europe, too, the history of the two industries was closely entwined,[51] and under conditions of socialist heavy industry-oriented industrialization the story has been the same: in China since 1949, 20% of coal has been used by the iron and steel industry.[52] Even in Japan – and even in 1928, before the boom in heavy industry – the metallurgical industries took about 10% of coal sales.[53]

In prewar China, the iron industry was much less important, although in Manchuria its role was closer to that in other countries. Indeed the experiences of Manchuria and the rest of China were so different that they really require separate treatment. The greater development of a heavy industrial base in Manchuria was one of the salient differences between the two economies, especially by the mid-1930s.

China's iron industry got off to a relatively early start: Zhang Zhidong's Hanyang ironworks were opened actually before the Japanese state steelworks at Yawata. The search for fuel was a major early problem, eventually solved by the opening of the coal mines at Pingxiang, primarily to supply the ironworks.[54] Early growth was relatively rapid, and by 1916 the ironworks produced almost 150,000 tons of pig iron and over 40,000 tons of steel. In 1908 the two enterprises were merged together with the Daye iron mines to become the Hanyeping Company. Other companies also invested in both coal and iron: in Shanxi the Baojin Company opened an ironworks in 1917, six years after opening its coal mines, but had to buy coal from Hebei as the local product was unsuitable.[55] Later, the Liuhegou Company in Henan bought up an ironworks, although the coal mine remained the core of the enterprise.[56]

Despite this promising start, serious problems arrested the development of the industry. As Table 13 shows, output rose until the late 1910s, after which it fell sharply, never again reaching those levels. Crippled by the difficulty of raising the large amounts of capital needed, and by the harsh terms imposed for Japanese loans, the industry was never able to develop;[57] indeed the pioneer Hanyang ironworks actually closed in 1922.[58] Metallurgy never became a major customer for Chinese coal.

Manchuria presents a different picture. Despite a much later start, output grew strongly throughout the period. By the 1920s, pig-iron output exceeded that in the rest of China, and the gap was to widen (see Table 14). The Japanese were willing and able to invest the large sums needed, and continued to back iron and steel production even though the SMR lost money on its iron-making operations in all but two years between 1919 and 1932.[59] Output came from two major companies. The Benxihu Coal and Iron Company opened its ironworks in 1915, after running coal mines for four years,[60] and the SMR opened its Anshan ironworks in 1919[61] – this was established as a separate company, the Showa Steelworks, in 1933.[62] As a result of this much stronger development of iron- and steel-making in Manchuria, that industry used 13% of all the coal sold in Manchuria in 1933, 17% in 1936.[63] It accounted for 20–30% of coal used by industry in the early 1920s, 30–40% in the late 1920s.[64] The two major ironworks were run by the largest coal producers in Manchuria, and both industries formed an integral part of the Japanese plans for the development of an industrial base in the region. So the place of iron-making in the history of the coal industry was a much greater one than was the case in the rest of China.

Table 13. *Iron and steel output by modern methods in China outside Manchuria, 1901–35*

Period	Average output ('000 tons)		Estimated use of coal ('000 tons)
	Pig iron	Steel (Hanyang)	
1901–05	30.9	—	74.2
1906–10	74.6	30.1[a]	203.0
1911–15	91.1	37.6	256.2
1916–20	147.8	31.3	386.0
1921–25	91.4	(46.8)[b]	228.6
1926–30	8.7	—	20.9
1931–35	39.0	—	93.6

Note: [a] 1907–10 only
[b] 1921 only
Sources: Quan, 1972a, pp. 4–5, 108, 191; Yan Zhongping, 1955, pp. 102–3.

In the rest of China, and indeed in China as a whole, general manufacturing industry, and particularly textiles, were more important consumers of coal than they were in other countries. Cotton-spinning mills used directly around 300,000 tons of coal in the early 1910s, and just under 1 million tons in the 1930s.[65] The latter figure, especially, understates their importance, because an increasing proportion used coal indirectly, through the purchase of electric power; around three-quarters of the power used for newly installed equipment in Chinese-owned mills in the 1930s was electric, and that proportion was around 95% for Japanese-owned mills. This was a way of achieving greater output per unit of power, one aspect of the technical progress which inevitably reduced the growth of industrial coal consumption in China, as elsewhere.[66]

In the 1910s silk filatures used almost as much coal as did the cotton mills, but their consumption was relatively stagnant up until the 1930s, when the disastrous depression in the world silk market made its effects felt. Even in the 1930s, however, the Shanghai silk filatures all used coal to provide both hot water and power, as well as electricity for lighting,[67] and the seasonality of their operations, peaking in May–July, was important in the short-term fluctuations of the Shanghai coal market.[68]

In China proper other manufacturing industries used about as much coal as did textiles, but here too Manchuria was different. Statistics are far more complete for that region, and so not directly comparable, in that they detail consumption by small industries which would in the rest of China merely be part of the aggregate category 'rural use'. Nevertheless the textile industry clearly occupied a much less prominent place in Manchuria, and in 1933, for

Table 14. *Iron and steel output by modern methods in Manchuria, 1911–37*

Period	Average iron output ('000 tons)	Average steel output ('000 tons)	Average use of coal ('000 tons)
1911–15	29.5[a]	—	—
1916–20	73.3	—	—
1921–5	106.7	—	259.5
1926–30	265.7	—	713.3
1931–5	440.5	136.8[b]	1023.0
1936–7	697.8	385.5	—

Notes: [a] 1915 only; the Benxihu ironworks was opened in that year.
[b] 1935 only.
For most years Benxihu is assumed to have used as much coal per ton of output as did Anshan.
Sources: Quan, 1972a, pp. 4–5; MCG 15.5 (May 1935): 16–17, 15.7 (July 1935): 109; Sheba, 1937, pp. 831, 834, and 1938, pp. 801, 803.

example, a long list of industries, such as the distilling of alcoholic beverages, oil-pressing, brick-making, engineering, glass, gas and weaponry, all consumed more coal than did cotton spinning mills, and in many years oil-pressing and brick-making used over 100,000 tons, as did in some years the distillers.[69]

Electricity generation was the most rapidly growing source of demand for coal in China (see Table 15). The amount of electricity generated in China grew at 17.5% per annum from 43 million kWh in 1912 to over 2500 million kWh in 1936.[70] Production was highly concentrated: almost 60% of output outside Manchuria in 1936 was generated in Shanghai, and the Shanghai Power Company alone produced more electricity than did all the Chinese-owned plants in the industry. Manchuria was the other major centre of production, but net output of electricity for sale only amounted to about the same as Shanghai Power Company output in 1936, and was considerably lower in earlier years. The largest plant was at Fushun, but only half of its output was sold, the rest being consumed within the mining and industrial complex.[71]

Increasing amounts of coal were needed to generate this electricity: consumption rose from about 100,000 tons in 1912 to almost 3 million in 1936. The Shanghai Power Company (before 1929 the Riverside Power Station run by the Shanghai Municipal Council) was China's largest single purchaser of coal: by the mid-1930s the company used 600,000 tons of coal per annum.[72] Since it was located in Shanghai, many mining companies in both China and Japan competed for a share in this contract, and the tender prices offered a barometer of the way the coal market was going.

Table 15. *Growth of electricity output and coal consumption by public utilities*

Period	Average annual net output of public utilities (million kWh)	Estimated average annual consumption of coal ('000 tons)
1912–16	94	174
1917–21	292	464
1922–26	723	979
1927–31	1,335	1,535
1932–36	2,015	2,324

Source: Wright, unpublished paper; methods for estimating coal consumption in Wright, 1976, pp. 338–42.

Although this coal consumption has been classified in the 'industrial' category, it should more properly be said to be consumed indirectly by households or by other industries: in Shanghai, 78% of the Power Company's output was sold to industry.[73] In the rest of the country, this proportion was probably lower – in 1936 40% of electric power sold in China proper was used for lighting, 60% for power, although some of that sold for lighting may have been for industrial plants.[74] Moreover, the growth of demand for coal from the power industry represented only in part an increase in net demand, being in part also a switch by consumers from direct to indirect use of coal.

Although this rise in the general level of industrial activity and power generation was the most important single factor acting on the industrial demand for coal, other influences, such as substitution between coal and other fuels and between Chinese and foreign coal, were also at work. Since the Second World War, and earlier in the West, increasing competition from other fuels, most notably oil, has been a major factor depressing coal sales. But in China up to 1937, although bunker demand was beginning to fall for this reason, industry as a whole was still overwhelmingly dependent on coal. Since at least the 1910s liquid fuel had been an alternative to coal, especially for small plants, and many small electric light plants used oil-engines to generate their power. As is shown in Tables 16 and 17 however, although many small utilities in Jiangsu used oil, by far the most electricity was generated using coal, while industrial power plants almost all used coal. Nationally 92% of electricity generated between 1932 and 1936 was produced using coal, a percentage which if anything was slightly increasing over the period.[75] Competition from liquid fuel was, therefore, not a major depressant of the demand for coal from industry in pre-1937 China.

Table 16. *Fuel used by electric utilities in Jiangsu, 1930s*

Fuel used	Plants		Capacity		Average capacity
	Number	Percentage	Kilowatts	Percentage	
Coal	38	29	213,721	93	5,600
Oil	91	68	16,205	7	184
Both	4	3	—	—	—

Notes: Four plants are excluded because the fuel used is not known; where a plant used both fuels, capacity is divided in proportion to the number of generators using each fuel; the foreign power stations in Shanghai accounted for a large proportion of capacity in both cases, but the percentages are unchanged if these are omitted; a few of the plants using coal generated electricity by gas rather than steam.
Source: China, shiyebu, guoji maoyi ju, 1933, 8:1126–38.

Table 17. *Fuel used by major industrial power plants in Jiangsu, 1930s*

Fuel used	Plants		Capacity	
	Number	Percentage	Kilowatts	Percentage
Coal	33	97	70,039	100
Oil	1	3	75	Neg.

Note: One plant is omitted as the fuel used is unknown.
Source: China, shiyebu, guoji maoyi ju, 1933, 8:1136–9.

For Chinese coal specifically, substitution between it and imported (nearly all Japanese) coal was a much more important concern. The building of the railways opened the coastal market to Chinese coal, and for two decades or so it competed in Shanghai on more or less equal terms with Japanese coal. Sales of Chinese coal increased in the short term when high freight charges or exchange rate fluctuations raised the price of imports; sales of foreign coal increased when the civil wars cut off supplies of Chinese coal at competitive prices.

Overall the trend up to the early 1930s was for the *share* of Japanese coal in the market to fall, but the absolute level of imports to remain, apart from temporary fluctuations, relatively constant; Chinese coal merely took the largest share of the increment in an expanding market. Despite this, imported coal was often blamed by Chinese coal companies for their difficulties, and in May 1933 the government raised the tariff on coal from ¥1.6 to ¥3.5 per ton, thereby increasing the price of the cheaper Japanese coals by 25% or more. The elasticity of demand for a particular type of coal over this range proved to be such that the tariff almost removed foreign coal from the market. Total imports fell from over 2 million tons in 1933 to just over 500,000 tons in 1936; during the same period the share of Japanese coal in the Shanghai market fell from 15.7% to 4.8%.[76] Industrial firms were forced to abandon the now too-expensive Japanese and Manchurian coal even though the inconsistent quality of the Chinese alternative caused a pollution problem in Shanghai.[77] In all probability 1 million or more tons were added to total demand for Chinese coal by the tariff, a substantial increase when compared to consumption in the modern sector.

The other major influence on the level of industrial demand was the trend towards greater thermal efficiency in the conversion of fuel into power and greater economic efficiency in terms of output per unit of power used. Technical progress in fuel economy was probably most rapid in the nineteenth century,[78] but most figures cover the twentieth century and the depressing effect of improving fuel economy was felt particularly in the West between the wars, when it added to other structural problems of the coal industry. Increases in thermal efficiency, for which statistics are more easily available, were especially marked in the electric power industry, because of the very rapid expansion of that industry. United States power stations increased their thermal efficiency by over seven times between 1882 and 1942, about 3.4% per annum,[79] while in Japan improvement was even more rapid – 6.3% per annum between 1914 and 1932.[80] These advances in electric power generation also benefited other industries which used or switched to electricity, but progress was much slower in general manufacturing: in the United States other manufacturing industries increased output per unit of fuel by only 25% between 1909 and 1929, as against a 200% increase in the electric utilities.[81] Efficiency also improved in the metallurgical industries: in Japan the amount of fuel used per ton of pig iron fell by 4.6% per annum between 1920 and 1932.[82]

In China these effects were disguised by the rapid growth of industrial activity, but improvements in fuel efficiency were incorporated in new investments in every sector, reducing the growth of coal consumption. The Shanghai Power Company increased its output per unit of fuel by 4.2% per annum between 1915 and 1931.[83] Progress in the first decade and a half of the century was even more rapid: if technique had been frozen at the 1915 level, only 50% more coal would have been used in 1931 than was actually used, but at the 1901 level ten times more coal would have been needed. The Shanghai Gas Company also succeeded in increasing output per unit of fuel, but only by 1.6% per annum in the 1920s,[84] while the Onoda cement works registered a 2.2% per annum improvement between 1906 and 1930.[85] No series is available for general manufacturing industry, where there were three ways of increasing fuel efficiency: by more efficient use of their own steam engines; by switching to electricity (assuming that the utilities were more fuel efficient than the original plant); and by improving organization so that output increased per unit of power used. It would be surprising if fuel economy had not improved by 2–3% per annum, so that in 1936 industry used little more than half the coal it would have used had technique been frozen at the level of 1912.

Increases in fuel economy also sustained coal sales in at least two ways. They reduced the incentive to switch to other fuels, and improved the competitive position of coal. Moreover, they reduced the price of the final product, and thus, depending on price elasticities, increased sales of that product so that the industry could expand its output and thus its use of coal. Yet it is perhaps unlikely that these two effects counterbalanced the more direct reduction in the growth of the demand for coal brought about by technical progress.

Rural industry

While plausible estimates can be made of the consumption of coal by modern industry, we know much less about that by unmodernized industries in rural areas and small towns, which the statistics lump together with rural and even urban household use. Nevertheless rural industry, most importantly 'native' iron-making and ceramics, probably accounted for the bulk of rural consumption and was very important for the survival of many small mines in remote areas. Such a nexus often long predated the modernization either of mining or of industry.

The native iron industry was concentrated in Shanxi where there were abundant resources of coal and iron.[86] Well into the twentieth century this traditional iron industry provided the most important market for Shanxi coal: in the early 1910s, 1000 small furnaces in the Pingding area alone used around 80,000 tons of local coal a year, and coal was also sent to other iron-producing areas in the province. But the market was not expanding, and the paradox was that if the local iron industry expanded and modernized, local coal would no longer be suitable, and so the local coal industry would decline.[87] Other areas also worked scrap iron where coal was available: in the early twentieth century there were flourishing ironworks at Boshan in Shandong using scrap iron originally from Shanxi.[88] In Manchuria, too, many small ironworks produced native pig iron,[89] and other centres of traditional iron production included Sichuan, Guangdong and Henan,[90] of which the first especially may well have used charcoal rather than coal.

In north China in particular the ceramics industry flourished mainly in coal-mining areas. In Boshan ceramics production expanded after the construction of the railway, only later to decline when affected by competition from neighbouring Zichuan.[91] Both major centres of ceramic manufacture like Ci xian in Hebei and lesser centres such as Yu xian in Henan tended to be situated in coal-mining areas in order to ensure a supply of cheap fuel.[92] The nexus was less close in south China, where alternative fuels were not quite so scarce, and the potteries of Jingdezhen mostly used wood, switching to coal only after 1949;[93] in nearby Raozhou, on the other hand, the pottery works opened in the early 1910s soon replaced firewood with coal from neighbouring mines.[94]

Iron and ceramics were probably the most important coal consumers in rural China, but they were far from the only ones. The traditional glass industry, of which Boshan was again a major centre, also used a lot of coal.[95] In Peng xian, Sichuan, the glass factory was a customer for coal, though in other areas of the province, non-mineral fuel was used.[96] Lime-burning was another largely rural industry that provided a market for coal mines; especially in the remoter areas of the south-west the existence of coal mines sometimes depended on this market.[97] Coal was used less commonly than vegetable fuels, however; in Hunan only two counties producing a small part of the province's lime output used mainly coal as a fuel.[98] In some areas other industries, such as brick-making, the distilling of alcoholic beverages and sulphur-burning, also accounted for considerable quantities of coal.[99]

In Japan the salt industry had been the largest consumer of coal in the traditional sector,[100] but this was not so in China. Because the major salt-producing areas did not have large coal reserves, when the exhaustion of timber resources forced the adoption of different methods on the salt panners, they moved rather to the use of solar power. This was especially true of the Liang–Huai salt area in Anhui and Jiangsu, which was China's major producer of salt.[101] Only in Sichuan was coal readily available to the panner, and a close nexus linked the two industries there: the mines of Weiyuan, for instance, depended almost exclusively on the salt pans for their market.[102]

A rural coal-using industry that developed in the twentieth century was tobacco-drying. Whereas the traditional Chinese tobacco industry had dried the leaves in fresh air and shaded sunlight,[103] the bright leaf tobacco introduced in various areas of north China by British–American Tobacco and Nanyang Brothers required the use of fuel, mostly coal, in the little drying sheds that dotted the countryside in tobacco-growing areas.[104] In some areas such as Henan these sheds provided the incentive and the market for small mines to open in the neighbourhood. The prosperity thus brought to these small mines was, however, fragile, and varied very much with the price of tobacco on world markets.[105]

While rising costs of alternative fuels induced some extra use of coal as a substitute – for instance in Yunnan, where the growing scarcity of charcoal led to increased demand for coal from the metallurgical industries[106] – the fate of the industries themselves was the more important determinant of the long-term demand trends in this sector. On this point it is difficult to generalize, for widely differing industries in many areas of the country were involved. Industries, such as lime-burning, which served agriculture in remote areas were probably only slightly affected by market trends, as were the coal mines dependent on them. More typical were those that suffered from the instability inherent in market forces. During the First World War traditional coal producers in Xinhua county, Hunan, enjoyed a boom because of heavy demand from the antimony smelters in the area. When the price of antimony plummeted after the war, the coal mines also went into a decline.[107] Many of the small-scale industries of north China benefited greatly from the expanded markets opened up by the construction of the railways, but later suffered when the north-east was practically closed to Chinese goods from 1931 and when cheap foreign goods flooded the Chinese market during the depression: the industries of Boshan offer a good example of this cycle.[108]

Overall then, trends in this category of demand depended on the general fate of rural industries, a controversial subject in itself. Nevertheless no one seriously contends that, even taking into account the tobacco industry, there was any substantial net increase in rural industrial activity in China between 1895 and 1937, and so there was at least no great growth in this type of coal consumption.

Household consumption of coal

The second major category of demand was that from householders using coal for cooking or heating. Average per capita use of coal for these purposes in the countryside was almost negligible; it was used only in those areas, mainly in north China, that were close either to a mine or to a railway station. Most of the peasants' fuel was collected rather than purchased, and the low opportunity cost of peasant labour in slack times meant that coal would have to be very cheap before it was worthwhile for peasants to buy any,[109] though in some areas coal might feature in their gathering activities.[110] In Buck's 1921–4 survey coal was bought in any but negligible quantities in only two out of thirteen districts studied, and the survey did not cover south or west China where the use of coal was less common than in the north.[111] Not even in Manchuria was the use of coal by rural households common,[112] and the situation described in 1922 in Gansu was probably typical of much of north China: only government buildings and the rich burned coal itself. The ordinary people close to a mine might take a pack animal to bring away some slack to mix with mud or dried dung for fuel, but peasants living away from a mine still used mostly firewood, charcoal or dried grass.[113] In general only if they lived close to a railway could peasants not living in a mining area use coal, and even then its cost rose sharply with distance from the station.

Nevertheless in China many small purchases added up to a considerable total, and coal was widely used in mining areas and where railways offered cheap transport. So in Shanxi, where coal was plentiful and wood scarce, many – some sources say all – households used coal.[114] Travellers in the province and in neighbouring Shaanxi reported that the main fuel used was coal, which was often a poor-quality product from local mines.[115] In the 1930s about 1 million tons of coal – excluding that mined and sold locally – was sold along the Jing–Han between Zhengzhou and Beijing alone.[116] In some districts near the railway, like Xinzheng xian in Henan, the use of coal was widespread: 99% of the families surveyed by Buck in that county used coal. Even there, however, it made up only 25% of the total value of fuel used by the households.[117] In another county along the railway, Ding xian in Hebei, coal accounted for only 12% of peasants' fuel bills.[118] The greater role of industry even in rural consumption is shown by the fact that even had the whole of Ding xian followed the consumption pattern of Gamble's survey families (which is unlikely) household consumption would have accounted for less than 50% of the 20,000 tons imported annually into the county.[119]

Among the influences acting on the level of autonomous demand from rural households were, in theory, total population growth and its distribution between regions, rising or falling incomes, and changes in the price of other fuels. Not all of these, however, had an important impact in the actual situation of prewar China.

Total population growth, which Perkins estimates at 0.6–0.7% per annum between 1893 and 1933,[120] did little to raise household demand in the early twentieth century. There was practically no increase at all in the population of the north-west and a much smaller than average increase in the major coal-producing provinces of north China. Most of the increment in population was concentrated in south China, where little if any coal was used. The number of people living in Manchuria did, it is true, grow by seven times over the period, but still remained less than the population of either Henan or Shandong. Moreover, at least in earlier years, other fuels as well as coal were abundant there, and so the effect on coal consumption was limited, although not negligible.

What was happening to rural incomes before the war is a highly controversial subject in itself. While John Lossing Buck and more recently

Ramon Myers argue that rural standards of living were constant or even gradually rising, other scholars have seen the situation in the countryside in crisis terms.[121] Whatever the precise trend, incomes did not rise sufficiently to induce the peasants to buy coal rather than to collect fuel.

The rising cost of alternative fuels was probably the most important influence on household demand in rural areas. The great expansion of coal mining in the eleventh century had been due to the exhaustion of the forests and thus rising prices of timber and charcoal. Over a long period the exhaustion of the timber of north China had been one factor behind the shift of the centre of Chinese civilization towards the south. Urbanization and increased economic activity meant still higher demands for timber in the Ming, so that by the end of that dynasty the crisis in supply came to cover the whole country, and the expansion of population to the north China uplands in the seventeenth and eighteenth centuries further reduced the areas available for forest. Although this shortage was dealt with primarily by adopting low-energy solutions to ecological problems,[122] coal was available as an alternative in many areas of north China and there was now an increased incentive to use it. Despite consumer resistance to the smoke and pollution caused by burning coal,[123] relative prices were generally decisive in the end, as when in Hu xian, Shaanxi, the local magistrate sent a servant in 1885 to open a coal mine after wood had become scarce in the district.[124] Similarly in Yunnan householders turned to using coal as the forest retreated.[125]

The twentieth century saw no amelioration of the problem. High prices of firewood encouraged the use of coal near Wuhu,[126] and in the north the building of the Jing–Han, by allowing the peasants to switch from the cultivation of sorghum to the more profitable cotton, reduced the amount of sorghum stalks available as fuel, while at the same time enabling the import of coal to fill the gap.[127] In Manchuria, too, rising prices of timber caused a switch to coal.[128] Although in the short term substitution could go the other way, as when the falling price of firewood in Guangzhou in late 1930 led to its being used in place of coal, or when higher prices of Shandong coal in 1932 caused consumers to burn grass and firewood instead,[129] the trend was gradually towards the use of coal. The increased demand generated in this way was, however, less important than the rise of industrial or even urban household demand. Although Buck saw the use of coal as one way to solve the fuel crisis in the Chinese countryside,[130] the day was and still is far off when coal burns in the grate of every Chinese peasant's home.

Accelerating urbanization and population growth in the cities were, unlike total population growth, very important factors in the expansion of the demand for coal. City-dwellers, being mostly unable to collect their fuel,

Table 18. *Household consumption of coal in major Chinese cities in the mid-1930s*

City	Household consumption ('000 tons)	Per capita (kg)
Changchun	268	740
Shenyang	265	340
Dalian	230	360
Beijing	500	320
Tianjin	300	250
Shanghai	500	140
Wuhan	200	160
Guangzhou	50	50

Sources: MCG, 15.7 (July 1935): 104; KYZB 393 (7 August 1936): 142; KYZB 394 (14 August 1936): 152; CEJ 6.2 (February 1930): 196–8.

were much more likely than their rural counterparts to buy coal.[131] Table 18 shows figures for total and per capita household consumption of coal in some major Chinese cities. These compare with corresponding levels of per capita consumption by rural households which could not have been much more than 10 kg.[132] Obviously per capita consumption was higher in the northern cities, where there was both more coal and a colder climate, than in those of the south. In Beijing coal – mostly in the form of briquettes of mud and coal-dust – was by far the most important household fuel.[133] Only around 20% of Shanghai households, on the other hand, used coal; coal and charcoal together accounted for only 12.3% of household fuel expenditure, as against 24.5% for kerosene and 42.6% for firewood.[134] Use of coal itself (rather than briquettes) was very much concentrated in the higher income levels,[135] with foreign-style dwellings and particularly foreigners taking a disproportionate share: the Japanese in Manchuria, less than 1% of total population, used about 33% of household coal.[136]

During the early twentieth century the number of these urban coal consumers, both Chinese and foreign, was growing rapidly. The population of Chinese cities increased by about two-thirds (that is, by about 1.6% per annum) between 1900–10 and 1938 and, in contrast to the growth of total population, the increase occurred mainly in the north, where most coal was used. Urban population in Manchuria increased about fourfold, that of Shandong threefold, while the population of Beijing doubled. The foreign population grew even more rapidly – at about 11% per annum between 1895 and 1929.[137] The concentration of urban growth in coal-consuming areas and the more rapid expansion of the foreign population meant that coal consumption grew considerably faster than did total urban population.

Relative fuel prices also influenced the demand for coal by urban households. Between 1900 and 1920 the reduction of the price of coal due to the construction of the railways was probably greater than that of other fuels, and so improved the competitive position of coal and increased its consumption. After that there is little evidence of major secular shifts in relative prices which might have increased the demand for coal. There was, however, some short-term substitutability, especially between coal, firewood and charcoal, but because kerosene required different equipment to burn, there was less short-term substitution between it and coal.

Exports

The export of Chinese coal, almost all to Japan, increased very sharply in the early 1910s, as the output of Chinese mines came on tap, and again, after a period of stagnation because of the scarcity and high cost of shipping, in the early 1920s. Exports continued to grow even in the late 1920s (see Table 19) as the major exporters were less affected by the civil wars than were many other mines. From mid-1932 exports from Manchuria were no longer counted by the Chinese customs, and separate figures must be given (see Table 20).

The proximate determinant of the demand for exports was the relative price of coal in China and Japan, which in turn depended on their respective demand and supply conditions. In the 1930s Japanese coal reserves were estimated at about 8000 million tons, of which much was of poor quality and very little suitable for making metallurgical coke.[138] Chinese reserves were over 200,000 million tons. Of the other necessary resources labour was also more expensive in Japan.[139] The rapid growth of Japanese industry and of its coal consumption meant that the stage of rising costs had been reached there, while in China supply was still highly elastic.

China exported two types of coal to Japan. The inadequacy of Japanese supplies of coking coal forced steelworks to use at least some imported coal, so that imports of Kailuan coking coal were welcomed by all sections of Japanese business.[140] Ordinary fuel coal, mostly from Fushun, competed with Japanese coal, however, solely on cost per calorific unit. While its import was encouraged by coal consumers as a way to reduce industrial costs,[141] Japanese coal producers, particularly those on the margin (like the small mines of the Chiku-Hō region), saw cheap imported coal as a threat to their existence, and demanded restriction. As early as 1921 the SMR agreed with the Japanese Coal Owners' Association to limit shipments to Japan.[142] The agreement was renegotiated annually until sales and profits of Japanese producers plummeted during the depression of 1930, when the Chiku-Hō mine owners led a campaign to ban the import of Fushun coal

Table 19. Exports of Chinese coal, 1901–30

Period	Average exports ('000 tons)	Value of exports (¥ '000)
1901–5	33[a]	335[a]
1906–10	110	941
1911–15	1,164	8,385
1916–20	1,609	12,350
1921–5	2,715	27,180
1926–30	3,722	44,202

Note: [a] 1903–5 only
Source: Hsiao, 1974, pp. 92–3; Haikwan taels are converted to yuan at the ratio of HKT1 = ¥1.558.

Table 20. Exports of coal from China and Manchoukuo, 1931–6

Year	Exports from China		Exports from Manchoukuo	
	'000 tons	¥ '000	'000 tons	J¥ '000
1931	3,583	48,388	—	—
1932	2,014	17,945	—	—
1933	573	5,074	3,941	40,277
1934	797	6,267	3,697	36,047
1935	852	6,525	3,538	34,195
1936	1,304	10,615	2,977	27,909

Note: For 1931 and the first part of 1932 exports from Manchuria were included in the figures for China.
Sources: Hsiao, 1974, p. 93; Manzhouguo, caizhengbu, 1935, pp. 88–91; Manzhouguo, jingjibu, 1937, pp. 100–1.

altogether. Although they did not get their way, there was a reduction in the agreed quota for Fushun imports. Nevertheless, so long as Fushun coal remained cheaper than its Japanese competitors, sales to Japan tended to increase unless restricted by special agreements, and imports reached a new peak in 1933.[143]

Sales to Japan, therefore, were of considerable importance, especially for Manchurian coal mining. Fushun was run by the SMR, in turn controlled by the Japanese government, but, rather than putting the supply of fuel to the home country as the main priority, company policy was first to meet demand in Manchuria. The export market was always secondary, although as much as 30% of the company's output went to Japan in the mid-1920s. Even when demand in Japan reached unprecedented levels in the mid-1930s, sales there of Fushun coal actually fell because of rising consumption in the Manchurian market.[144]

There were no mines in China specifically catering for the export market as did some British mines in the late nineteenth and early twentieth centuries.[145] Even Kailuan exported only a small proportion of its output to Japan: about 10% in the mid-1920s, and, despite a steep drop in the early 1930s, about the same proportion again by 1933–4.[146] China remained by far the most important market for Kailuan and for other mines. Among other mines, only the Japanese (later Sino-Japanese) mine at Zichuan sold as much as 10% of its output to Japan, and that only in periods of exceptionally high demand.[147]

In the mid-1930s the rapid development especially of heavy industry in Japan, coupled with the reduction in exports from Manchuria – now split off from China – impelled the Japanese again to look to China for sources of supply. In 1934 they bought 60,000 tons of high-quality coking coal from Zhongxing for experimental purposes.[148] Nihon Kōkan bought 150,000 tons of this coal in 1936 and planned to buy 320,000 in 1937.[149] Even the much less favourably situated mines at Jingxing in Hebei and Datong in Shanxi began to sell some coal to Japan as total exports from China doubled between 1935 and 1937. Ironically this coal went mainly to fuel the war industries which made possible the Japanese invasion of China and the seizure of all the major mines of north China.

Colliery consumption of coal

Finally, coal mines themselves used considerable amounts of coal. In other countries, about 5–8% of total consumption was used in the collieries themselves, except in the United States where the proportion was far smaller.[150] The Geological Survey of China estimated that 3% of the output of modern mines and 6% of that of semi-modern mines was used in the collieries themselves. Although these figures tally quite well with the post-1949 situation,[151] most estimates for individual mines before 1937 were higher than this: the Zichuan mine used about 10% of its own output, Zhongxing 8%.[152] Jingxing in the mid-1930s used 7%,[153] and even Kailuan 5%, although Fushun somewhat less.[154] Smaller mines probably used a little more and, according to the Chinese Economic Year Book, Shandong mines mostly used between 8% and 10% of output them-selves.[155] Over time any trend towards fuel efficiency (not of first importance for mines) was probably balanced by increased use of power in mine workings, so that it is reasonable to suggest a constant 8% of output being used in the mines.

Structure of consumption

The different growth rates of the various sectors of demand led to changes in the overall structure of consumption, and Table 21 provides estimates that illustrate the direction and to some degree the extent of these changes. It was almost a commonplace in prewar analysis to cite the high proportion of total consumption accounted for by household use as evidence of China's backwardness.[156] This was only partly true. First, it is incorrect to assign all of the 'rural use' category to household consumption; in fact at least half was probably used in small-scale rural industry. Second, the proportion of 'rural use' in total consumption was falling, although that of urban commercial and household use was fairly constant. Third, a large proportion of coal used for domestic heating is by no means incompatible with a high level of economic development. The estimates in Table 21 are recalculated in Table 22 to exclude exports and to assign half of 'rural use' to the industrial sector, and then to compare China's pattern of coal consumption with that of other countries. This indicates that China's pattern of consumption differed from the norm less than one might have expected. If household consumption actually took up as much as (and no more than) half of 'rural use', then it did occupy a larger place in total consumption than in other countries, but only amounted to one-third of total consumption as against one-quarter in the United States. Probably the most significant factors emerging in Table 22 are the very low place occupied by the metallurgical industries and the relative importance of non-mechanized industries in general manufacturing (nearly two-thirds according to our assumption).

The backwardness of the economy is suggested by the very low per capita use of coal and indeed of all forms of non-human energy in the economy. Table 23 gives estimates for per capita use of coal in various countries, and indicates that despite its large coal reserves and cold climate (in the north), China used less coal not only than the developed countries, but even less than India, which has little coal and little need for fuel for winter warmth.

This exiguous per capita consumption is another indication that the growth of the industry, fairly high in terms of annual percentages, can have had only a marginal effect on the economy as a whole. It is nevertheless true that demand was steadily increasing throughout the first three and a half decades of this century, first in the transport industries, later in manufacturing and the generation of electricity, while urbanization in north China also provided an expanding market for coal. Per capita use of coal was rising, albeit slowly, and the pattern of use was coming to be increasingly weighted towards industrial use. The growth of the coal-using industries and other factors, such as technical progress, which affected industrial demand were particularly important because from the mid-1910s the highly elastic supply of coal and the difficulty of effecting any further major cuts in costs meant that the growth of coal mining was primarily a function of changes in demand.

Table 21. *Estimates of the use of coal, by sector, 1915, 1923, and 1933*

	1915		1923		1933	
	Million tons	Percentage	Million tons	Percentage	Million tons	Percentage
Rural use	7.42	43.2	8.03	33.3	8.87	29.5
Urban commercial and household use	2.27	13.2	2.92	12.1	4.00	13.2
Industrial	2.46	14.3	3.77	15.7	6.53	21.5
Electric utilities	0.20	1.2	0.93	3.9	1.83	6.0
Iron and steel	0.96	5.6	0.95	4.0	1.45	4.8
Textiles	0.76	4.5	0.99	4.1	1.30	4.3
Railways	1.15	6.6	2.11	8.8	2.72	9.0
Bunker	1.48	8.6	2.18	9.1	1.97	6.5
Exports	1.32	7.7	3.11	12.9	3.95	13.0
Used at mines	1.08	6.3	1.96	8.1	2.27	7.5
Totals	17.18		24.08		30.31	
Output and imports	14.90		25.92		29.88	

Note: These figures are only intended to give an approximate indication of the magnitudes involved. The first line in particular is subject to a wide margin of error. That category could alternatively be estimated as a residual, thus eliminating the discrepancy between the use and supply of coal. This discrepancy could also be the result of changes in stocks, or of incorrect estimation of small mine output by the Geological Survey of China.

Source: Tim Wright, 'Growth of the Modern Chinese Coal Industry: An Analysis of Supply and Demand, 1896–1936', *Modern China* 7.3 (July 1981) 333: copyright (c) 1981 Sage Publications, Inc. Reprinted by permission of Sage Publications, Inc. A detailed list of the sources and methods of estimation used in the compilation of this table is available on request from the author.

Table 22. *Structure of coal consumption in various countries, 1930s*

Percentage of total consumption accounted for by	Country/year					
	Great Britain 1936	United States 1936	India 1935	Japan 1936	14 major coal consumers 1936	China 1933
Domestic heating	19.9	24.0	30.8[b]	9.7	20.1	32.0[a]
General manufacturing	35.6	29.3		40.1	26.6	29.2[c]
Electricity	7.7	10.1		8.3	7.1	6.9
Gas	10.1	1.2		5.4	3.5	—
Metallurgy	12.0	14.8	24.4	17.1	19.6	5.5[d]
Collieries	6.7	0.9	5.3		4.3	8.6
Railways	7.2	19.4	31.9	10.1	16.3	10.3
Bunkers	0.8[e]	0.4	7.6	5.4	1.6	7.5

Notes: [a] Table 21: urban households and half rural use.
[b] Only a very small amount of this was used for domestic heating.
[c] Table 21: industrial use (excluding electricity and iron and steel) and half rural use. This figure for China includes gas-making.
[d] Iron and steel only.
[e] Domestic trade only.
The fourteen countries are Germany, China, Spain, United States, France, Great Britain, Hungary, India, Italy, Japan, Holland, Poland, South Africa and the USSR. Between them these countries accounted for 88% of world consumption in 1936.
Source: ILO, 1938b, pp. 48–9; see also Table 21.

Table 23. *Per capita use of coal in various countries, 1936*

Country	Use of coal per capita (tons)
Great Britain	3.9
United States	3.5
USSR	0.8
Japan	0.6
Spain	0.2
India	0.1
China	0.07

Source: ILO, 1938b, p. 69.

THE GEOGRAPHICAL PATTERN OF GROWTH

Geographically uneven development has been a major feature of twentieth-century China. Since 1949 a major objective of the Communist government has been the reduction of regional disparities of income and industrialization. They ascribed the pattern they inherited to the distortion introduced by the impact of imperialism,[1] but the difficulties they encountered in fostering greater regional equality indicate that more powerful economic forces were also at work.

Like other industries, coal mining – and especially mechanized coal mining – was very unevenly distributed across the country and, after outlining the actual regional pattern of output, this chapter will attempt to explain that pattern. Theoretical considerations suggest it might have been the result of differential supply of the various factors of production, variations in the level and type of demand between regions, or differences in the ease with which coal could be transported inter- or intra-regionally.[2] In China, however, neither quantity nor quality of coal resources adequately explain the pattern of output, nor does the supply of other factors of production. The regional pattern of demand goes some way to explaining the concentration of production in Manchuria, but there was a clear imbalance between excess production in north China and excess demand in central and south China. The chapter concludes that the economics of transport, the cost of which made up the greatest proportion of the price of coal in most major markets, was the crucial determinant of the geographical pattern of coal production, and that the availability of rail or water transport and the mix between these two determined the relative success of coalfields and enterprises. In addition, primarily through their influence on these variables, the political situation in the various regions, the policies of the governments in control there, and the power and direction of the foreign presence were also important. Two case studies – of Shanxi and Manchuria – will be examined to see how the various factors interacted.

The regional distribution of output

Table 24 indicates that throughout the early twentieth century north and north-east China between them produced over 90% of large-mine

Table 24. *Geographical distribution of large-mine output in China*

Percentage of total output from large mines originating in	1912–16	1917–21	1922–6	1927–31	1932–6
North-east	33.2	29.5	39.1	50.2	42.1
Liaoning	30.8	27.5	37.3	37.3	38.2
North	57.7	61.9	55.4	46.5	50.8
Hebei	39.3	39.6	34.4	34.0	27.9
North-west	—	—	—	—	—
Central-east	9.1	8.5	5.5	2.9	5.7
West and south-west	—	—	—	—	0.4
South-east	—	—	—	0.3	1.0

Notes: North-east: Liaoning, Heilongjiang, Jilin, Rehe.
North: Hebei, Shanxi, Shandong, Henan, Chahar, Suiyuan.
North-west: Shaanxi, Gansu, Ningxia.
Central-east: Hunan, Hubei, Anhui, Jiangxi, Jiangsu.
West and south-west: Sichuan, Yunnan, Guizhou, Guangxi.
South-east: Zhejiang, Fujian, Guangdong.
The percentages may not all add up to 100 because of rounding errors.

output, and indeed the two provinces of Liaoning and Hebei alone contributed at least 65% – and often substantially more. The only other areas where any large mines of note existed at all were the lower and central Yangzi provinces. While Table 24 shows some trend over time for the share of the north-eastern provinces to increase, that of the rest of China to fall, the constant features of regional distribution are much more notable.

Two colliery companies, the KMA in north-east Hebei, and Fushun (owned by the SMR) in Liaoning, accounted for an extraordinarily large proportion of output, and to a large extent stand behind this overall pattern of distribution. No other coal industry of comparable size in the world had over half its output produced by just two companies. Yet in only three years between 1896 and 1936 did Kailuan and Fushun produce less than 50% of total large-mine output, and in 1927 they actually contributed 71% of the total. Nevertheless, while by definition the share of other regions is increased if one omits Kailuan and Fushun, north and north-east China still accounted for over 80% of output, although the share of north China alone was generally greater – mostly over 60%. So the same basic geographical characteristics still obtained.

Total output was slightly more evenly distributed than that from large mines but, as is shown in Table 25, the north and north-east still accounted for over 80%. The share of the north-east, where there were very few unmodernized mines, was lower, and that of the main native mining

Table 25. *Geographical distribution of total coal output in China*

Percentage of total output originating in	1926	1931	1936
North-east	34.7	33.9	34.8
Liaoning	31.1	28.3	30.4
North	47.5	51.7	49.4
Hebei	23.9	28.1	19.2
North-west	0.9	1.2	0.8
Central-east	9.2	7.5	8.3
West and south-west	6.2	3.5	5.1
South-east	1.1	1.9	1.1
Others (Qinghai, etc.)	0.4	0.3	0.5

Note: For definition of regions, see Table 24.
The unadjusted output figures from the various issues of *Kuangye jiyao* are used in this table, so that the figures must be looked at with some caution.

provinces – Shanxi, Shandong and Sichuan – was higher. Nevertheless over 50% of the coal was still produced in Liaoning and Hebei.

Resources

In explaining this highly uneven distribution of output, regional disparities in the supply of the factors of production play only a minor part. This is not surprising given the overall conclusion that supply tended to be relatively elastic, leaving demand as the major determinant of growth.

Coal reserves were unevenly distributed throughout China, but in a very different pattern from that of output. The two provinces of Liaoning and Hebei, which between them produced over 50% of China's coal, had, according to the state of prewar knowledge as shown in Table 26, under 2% of total coal resources. Even the share of north China, which superficially matches its share of output, was in fact very differently distributed within the region, with Hebei taking up only a very small portion, and Shanxi, whose large-mine output was less than that of Hebei, Shandong or Henan, enjoying almost all the north China reserves. On a macro level the correlation between the inter-provincial distribution of output and that of reserves was very small indeed.[3]

Nevertheless coal reserves are not homogeneous either in quality or in geological ease of access, and to some extent the nature and geological condition of the reserves did influence the pattern of output. Although supplies of coking coal, which have been short since 1949, were earlier adequate because of the still exiguous demand from the metallurgical industries,[4] there were other differences in the quality of different coals, most importantly those in the calorific value and ash content of the coal.

Table 26. *Distribution of
known coal reserves in China,
around 1930*

Total reserves in	Percentage
North-east	1.9
Liaoning	0.7
North	56.1
Hebei	1.2
Shanxi	51.2
North-west	31.4
Shaanxi	29.0
Central-east	2.4
West and south-west	5.4
South-east	0.4
Others	2.4

Note: For definition of regions see
Table 24.
Source: Hou Defeng, 1932, pp. 3–4.

Moreover, there were two almost entirely separate markets for anthracite and bituminous coal. So there emerged nodes of development at places not otherwise very favourably located, but with coal whose quality demanded a premium price: the coal mined by the Zhongxing Company at Yi xian, while not the best in China, had a higher calorific value than Kailuan and Japanese coal, its main competitors in Shanghai, so that the company was able to charge a higher price and to make a profit despite relatively costly transport.[5]

The huge development at Fushun partly, although not completely, depended on its exceptionally thick seams, the thickest in the world.[6] Some of the seams were close enough to the surface to permit strip mining, so that production costs were very low and Fushun was able to hold a large share of the coastal market despite the more than 400 km journey to its port at Dalian.

Obviously coal cannot be mined if it is not there, so the pattern of reserves did impose some constraints on that of output. But there is overall no evidence that the quality of coal mined in the eastern provinces or the more favourable geological conditions accounted for the concentration of production in those provinces.[7]

Of the other factors of production, there is little evidence that labour supplies had much influence on the pattern of development. The area where output grew most strongly was precisely that in which the recruitment of labour posed the greatest problems[8] and, while labour was possibly more plentiful in north China than elsewhere in the country, it is much easier to explain the concentration of coal output there in other ways.

Capital supply was a more important variable. While the regional pattern of the supply of indigenous capital cannot explain that of coal output, since in broad terms Chinese capital was more plentiful in south and central China, the inflow of Japanese capital into Manchuria was undoubtedly one factor behind the development there. As such it was part of an overall development pattern which came increasingly to differ from that in the rest of China, and will be discussed in a separate section (see pp. 89ff).

Demand

The growth and changes in demand since the late nineteenth century had the effect of creating a much-expanded market for coal in the coastal provinces and especially in Shanghai. While local supplies were available in the industrial areas of north and north-east China, the concentration of industrial output in the port cities of Jiangsu and Guangdong – areas where little coal was mined – ensured that the distribution of consumption differed markedly from that of output.

Some 62% of coal consumed in China was used in the north and north-east, where most coal was mined (see Table 27). Although small quantities of coking coal were imported into Manchuria in the 1930s,[9] imports into the two regions were almost negligible, and the mines of each region grew partly in order to fulfil this local demand. This was particularly the case for the one-third or more of total consumption that was not transported by rail, and therefore was mostly sold at or close to the pit-head. Even that shipped by rail from large mines was mostly used within the region where it was mined. The rapidly expanding steelworks, industries, power-plants and railways of Manchuria provided a growing modern-sector demand for locally mined coal. North Chinese modern industry was less developed, but the abundance and therefore cheapness of coal there allowed small rural industries to use large amounts, while the cold climate meant a strong demand also from households, especially in the cities. The development of the mines in Shanxi, west Hebei and Henan were particularly dependent on demand, often from outside the modern sector, originating within their own region; this was because their location greatly restricted their ability to compete in coastal and overseas markets.

The third major centre of consumption presents a strong contrast. As in Manchuria, demand in the ports of central and south China was mainly an industrial demand: about 67% of coal sold in Wuhan was used by modern industry, shipping or the railways, while in Shanghai the proportion was over 75%, in Guangzhou 80%. Other cities such as Nanjing had a smaller

Table 27. *Approximate figures for
the geographical distribution of coal
consumption in 1930*

Coal consumed in	Percentage
North-east China	26.4
North China[a]	36.0
North-west China[b]	5.6
Central and east China	22.9
West and south-west China	4.2
South-east China	7.9

Notes: [a] excluding Chahar and Suiyuan
  [b] including Chahar and Suiyuan
Source: Hou Defeng, 1932, pp. 91–2.

share of industrial consumption, but were also much less important coal consumers.[10] Yet very little coal was produced within the region. The strong demand did induce entrepreneurs to open mines in the lower Yangzi provinces: Changxing in Zhejiang underwent major expansion financed by Shanghai industrialists at a time when outside supplies were particularly hard to obtain.[11] Later, in 1929, the same basic imbalance of supply and demand in the region led the Nationalist government to open the Huainan mine in Anhui, which by 1936 was becoming a major supplier of coal to Shanghai.[12] Nevertheless, up to 1937 and indeed to the present, the region has been mainly dependent on supplies from north and north-east China and, up to 1933, from Japan.

The pattern of coal consumption in important respects mirrored China's prewar economic history, in the concentration of industrial growth in Manchuria and Shanghai, with other small centres in the coastal and riverine treaty ports. It thus influenced the pattern of output both through the growth of mining in north and north-east China dependent on a geographically protected market, and through the necessity to locate mines to facilitate the solution of what was and remains one of the central problems for China's transport system – the shipment of fuel for the operation of the lower Yangzi industrial complex.

The economics of transport

Transport costs, as we have seen, played a crucial role in determining the final cost of coal at the point of sale. This was because of coal's low value per unit of mass and the substantial distance between the major markets and producing areas. The importance of the Shanghai market, situated far from most mining areas, in particular ensured that transport routes would largely determine the location of at least many major mines. Only for coal from mines very close to their main markets, such as Mentougou coal in Beijing, did transport make up less than one-third of total costs, and it mostly accounted for half or more.[13] So a company's ability to minimize its transport costs was crucial to its competitiveness in all but local markets.

In their turn transport costs were determined, obviously, by the distance the coal had to be carried and by the unit cost of the carriage. Little needs to be said about distance, which was the reason why mining was concentrated very heavily in the coastal provinces of east China, and why even now there has been little development of the resources of the far west. The huge cost of constructing transport links to Xinjiang, and the continuing high running costs of such facilities, limit the potential of that region, just as they do for the USSR in Siberia.[14]

Among those mines with comparable locations in the eastern provinces, unit transport costs became the crucial variable, one over which the company had some, although still limited, control. Unit costs were also a function of two elements: the type and mix of transport used, and the rates charged for each type of transport. Both were important, but the first was probably the crucial determinant of success in the coastal market.

Overland transport was an almost insuperable bottleneck unless the coal could be carried by rail. Not all traditional methods of transport over land were equally expensive, however, and in Shanxi mines able to send their coal by cart were able to tap a wider market than those dependent on pack animals or wheelbarrows.[15] In areas close to railways, mines with best access to the railhead had substantial competitive advantages: in Boshan in Shandong, mines in the Liangping area, which had to send their coal to the station on wheelbarrow or pack animals over winding mountain roads, failed to develop even though the actual distance was only short.[16] In the Western Hills one of the main advantages of the Sino-British Mentougou Company was that it could send its coal directly by rail to Beijing, while its competitors incurred transshipment and higher freight costs – 80¢ per ton to the main line, as against 44¢.[17]

Since even the shortest journey overland by traditional methods could be an insuperable handicap, even mining companies reliant mainly on water transport built short rail lines to their port of shipment. The first surviving railway in China was built between the Kaiping mine and Xugezhuang, whence the coal was shipped by canal.[18] Later the Changxing Company in Zhejiang operated a 26 km light railway with three locomotives to Wuliqiao, where it loaded its coal on to barges to take it to Lake Tai and thence on to the Yangzi.[19] In Hubei, the Fuyuan Company, though its mine was only 1 km from the Yangzi, still constructed a light railway to take its coal that far, such were the economics of overland transport.[20] Indeed any mine intending to modernize had to provide similar facilities, and there are several examples of much smaller mines building light railways: Shuidong in Anhui built a light railway to Shuangqiao whence its coal could go by river to Wuhu,[21] and in Hunan the Shichengjin mine at Liling, whose output was only around 30,000 tons per annum, had a 5 km light railway to Yangsanshi whence coal could be sent by junk or by rail.[22]

The trunk lines on which most companies relied to carry their coal were, however, built along routes determined by general commercial and strategic considerations – although the opening up of mining areas was one such consideration, for instance in the routing of the Jiao–Ji close to Zichuan and Boshan.[23] So in general the pattern of mining conformed to that of the railways, rather than vice versa; this was to be expected considering the relative abundance of coal and scarcity of cheap transport. In any event the railways came to carry around 65–75% of the coal mined in China (see Table 28), often over fairly large distances across the north China plain or in the north-east. The tonnage carried by rail was about the same as the output of modern mines, although of course some coal carried was from small mines.

In pre-modern societies transport by water was much cheaper than by land, and the ability to ship their coal by water had been a vital factor in the development of the Tyne coalfields in England,[24] and in that of the Leiyang coalfields in Hunan in China. Leiyang was able to take advantage of the cheap junk transport on the Yangzi riverine network to develop an almost national market, even though production costs were around five times higher than those in land-locked Shanxi.[25] In modern times, too, many mines in west and south China still relied on traditional river transport to ship their coal, since they had no access to railways: up to 300,000 tons came down the Lei and Lu rivers to Changsha, while over 100,000 tons a year was carried on other rivers in Hunan, on the Tuo in Sichuan and on the Han river in Guangdong.[26] Even in north China some coal was sent along the rivers of Henan and Hebei, notably by the mines at Jiaozuo.[27]

Even after the building of the railways, water transport was still often the cheapest method: in the 1930s most railways charged around 0.7¢ per ton km, steam ships on the ocean or major waterways generally under 0.5¢, and for Kailuan, which owned its own fleet, the cost was only just over 0.1¢.[28] So large mining companies attempted to maximize the extent to which their coal was carried by water, and the degree to which they succeeded was an important factor in inter-enterprise competition, especially in Shanghai, where most of the coal arrived by ship.

Table 28. *Coal carried by railways in China, 1932–6*

Year	Millions tons carried by			Output (million tons)	
	Chinese national railways	Manchurian railways	Total	Large mines	Total
1932	11.4	7.8	19.2	19.0	26.4
1933	10.5	9.7	20.2	20.9	28.4
1934	13.0	11.2	24.2	24.3	32.7
1935	12.3	10.8	23.1	25.7	36.1
1936	14.4	11.2	25.6	29.4	39.9

Notes: The figures for Manchuria are for April of the given year to March of the next. The 1936 figure for the Chinese National Railways is 12/11 times the coal carried between January and November.
The total output figures are from the Geological Survey of China, and, as shown in Appendix I, at best represent rough orders of magnitude.
Sources: *Tongji yuebao*, various issues; Sheba, 1938. p. 750.

Kailuan was the company best fitted by its location to furnish for itself a favourable transport mix, and its strength on the Shanghai market was due to the fact that its coal only had to be sent 100 km or so to the port whence it could be shipped for only a fraction of railway costs. The importance of minimizing the length of railway transport is shown by the efforts of the Zhongxing Company to construct a line of easy access to the new port of Lianyungang. After the opening of the Jin–Pu, Zhongxing sent its coal to Shanghai via a 439 km rail trip to Pukou and thence a 390 km trip down the Yangzi to Shanghai. In 1935, however, it built a line to the Long–Hai at Zhaodun, whence the coal was carried to Lianyungang. Although the length and costs of the journey from Lianyungang to Shanghai were greater than those from Pukou, the 250 km shorter rail journey was estimated to save the company ¥1 million a year and, by promoting sales, to increase profits by more than that.[29] Similarly the Huainan mine was in a much stronger competitive position after the completion of a line to Wuhu allowed water transport to take more of the burden of carrying the mine's coal.[30] There is in general a closer correlation between length of rail journey and sales in Shanghai than there is between total distance from Shanghai and those sales.

The other way of improving one's competitive position by reducing unit transport costs was to negotiate lower freight rates, often through the use of political influence. Other things being equal, transport was cheaper for large mines. Not only were they able to take full advantage of the cheaper rates available for the shipment of whole train-loads, but they were often the railway's main suppliers of fuel and thus in a good position to negotiate special terms. Exclusive contracts between coal mines and railway companies date back at least to 1901 when Herbert Hoover negotiated a concessional rate of 1¢ per ton mile (= 0.625¢ per ton km) for Kaiping coal carried on the Bei–Ning line.[31] As other modern mines were opened, mostly between 1905 and 1915, each attempted to negotiate special rates with its main carriers. The aim was not only to reduce the mine's own transport costs, but specifically to deny competitors the opportunity to do the same: in negotiations in 1910 over freight charges Kaiping asked for a guarantee that the same concessions would not be granted to other companies.[32]

In the 1910s most rates worked out at between 0.5 and 1.0¢ per ton km. The lowest rates were enjoyed for a short time by Lincheng, at 0.4686¢, but for most of the period the cheapest was the 0.5¢ charged to Zhongxing for coal carried to Tianjin and for that carried to Pukou when the price at Pukou was below a specific level.[33] In the late 1920s and early 1930s most railways attempted to raise their rates as a way of dealing with the disastrous financial situation they had fallen into during the wars.[34] Except for the longest journeys most rates were now over 1¢ per ton km.[35] Vigorous protests by the mining companies, made more strident – and more convincing – by the steep fall in coal prices in 1932 due to the flood of cheap imports, succeeded in getting a range of discounts applied to the official rates. The Jiao–Ji, for example, reduced their rates by 10% for coal sold within Shandong and by 20% for that shipped from Qingdao. The result of these and other discounts introduced on the Chinese national railways was to reduce charges close to the level of the 1910s: they brought down the costs to most mines, at least for the longer journeys, nearer to those of Zhongxing, that is 0.5¢ per ton km or slightly more.[36]

Shanxi's coal resources: a case of retarded development

With over 50% of China's known reserves, Shanxi's large-mine output amounted to under 4% of national output. The reasons for this discrepancy illustrate well the influences described above as acting on the pattern of the industry.

Coal reserves were scattered in almost every county of the province, and although inevitably some were of poor quality or lay in difficult geological positions, there were ample easily exploitable seams of high quality. Good-quality coking coal was available in the Taiyuan and Fenxi areas, and Yangquan's anthracite was as good as or better than any in the country. Datong's bituminous steam coal was also among the best in China, and was so easy of access that a 1950s' source said it needed only 75% as much fixed investment per ton of output as did other mines.[37]

An observer in the 1910s argued that the obstacles to the development of the province's coal industry lay mainly in the shortage of water (for use in steam engines) and of timber (for use as pit-props).[38] The *Chinese Economic Bulletin* in the 1920s claimed that shortage of capital hampered growth, and also led to working conditions so bad that no one except criminals or desperadoes would risk working in the mines, a situation which resulted in a shortage of labour.[39] Nevertheless it remains likely that if prospective profits had been high enough capital would have been forthcoming – to open mines and to attract miners – as it was elsewhere in China. In fact, the province's largest company, with mines both in Yangquan and in Datong, as well as in other areas of Shanxi, was never much of a financial success, barely recording profits even at the height of the wartime boom,[40] and most discussions of the problems of the province rightly lay the main emphasis on the difficulty of selling the coal, and particularly on the high cost of transporting it to the major coastal markets.

Most households in Shanxi used coal for cooking and heating, but that market held no great hope for expansion: population was fairly stable, there was little urbanization, and the high initial level of coal utilization left relatively little room for its spread to new households and areas. In any case, households tended to use cheap coal from small local mines, of which there were large numbers in most areas of the province. Poor internal communications within Shanxi also discouraged the construction of large mines aiming to supply the household market. Nevertheless the construction of the Tong–Pu railway did open new areas of the province to penetration by large-scale producers, by steeply reducing the price of coal in areas along the line.[41]

Much the same considerations limited the potential of coal use by the native rural industries, such as iron-making, which consumed much of Shanxi's coal output. Modern industry was virtually non-existent, although provincial governor Yan Xishan's Ten Year Plan in the 1930s did make a start.[42] To fuel this, Yan opened new coal mines, run by his Xibei Shiye Company. The main one was near the capital, Taiyuan, and its output increased rapidly in the mid-1930s to supply the growing industrial base in that city.[43] Moreover, the Tong–Pu ran through several other mining areas and permitted the modernization of some pits with a view to tapping the new industrial market.[44]

This was a development of the mid-1930s, and for almost all our period, any mine in Shanxi aiming at large-scale output and therefore sales had to look to other areas in east China, such as Shanghai, for its market. Since the province lacked any access to water transport, its hopes in the east depended entirely on the railways. The Peking Syndicate's early plans to exploit the coal resources of south Shanxi foundered on the rocks of political opposition and, more specifically, on their inability to get permission for a railway to carry their coal to Pukou for shipment along the Yangzi.[45] That left two areas, Datong in the north, with its steam coal, and Yangquan with anthracite in the east of the province, to try to develop a wider market.

Datong lay on the Jing–Sui 568 km from the port of Tanggu.[46] The Jing–Sui's rates tended to be a little higher than those of other lines – around 0.9¢ per ton km as against 0.7¢.[47] It was also subject to political and military disturbances, so that transport was not reliable: the charges made for carrying Datong coal depended on whether Yan Xishan or Jiang Jieshi controlled the line,[48] while in 1933 the Japanese incursions into Inner Mongolia increasingly disrupted the railway.[49] The length and cost of transport to the coast and the unreliability of that transport slowed down the development of this very promising mining area. Although on the eve of the war sales in the cities of north China were rapidly increasing and exports to Japan were being negotiated,[50] the potential of the area began to be realized only after 1937 under the Japanese, in a situation of rapid development of industry in north China and a heavy pressure on coal supplies. After 1949 the area was developed further, but the completely changed situation is illustrated by the fact that it supplied mainly, though not exclusively, the new industrial centres of Inner Mongolia and north Hebei.[51]

Yangquan was the main base of the Baojin Company, which had been established at the height of the rights recovery movement of the late 1900s and had thus become a focus for Chinese nationalism.[52] The area therefore was the chief concern in prewar discussions of the failure of Shanxi mining. It relied on the Zheng–Tai railway, whose freight rates were by far the highest of the north China coal carrying lines: as against commonly charged rates of about 0.7¢ per ton km, the Zheng–Tai had in 1933 regular charges of over 2¢ and, though special contracts with individual companies reduced the rates slightly, only for the Jingxing and Zhengfeng mines in Hebei were they below 1¢, and for coal from Baojin they remained over 2¢.[53] A more-complicated system was in operation in 1936, encompassing variations by season, by type of coal and by amount carried, but rates in summer still ranged between 1.2¢ and 1.8¢, and in winter between 1.2¢ and 1.9¢.[54] These rates were thus about double those paid by most other mining companies.

Chinese nationalists saw this as an example of the way in which the French managers of the Zheng–Tai oppressed Chinese enterprise. But even after 1932, when the loan agreement which gave the French control over the running of the railway ended and managerial power reverted to the Chinese, the same high-rate policy continued. The managers justified the high rates on the grounds that the line's operating costs were higher than those of other lines because of the difficult terrain it traversed; moreover the shortage of return cargoes to Shanxi raised the cost of transporting coal from that province, and possibly went some way to justifying the preferential treatment given to mines across the Hebei border. Finally, the short length of the line denied it the economies of distance available on other lines.[55] On the other hand, the Zheng–Tai made among the highest operating surpluses of all Chinese railways,[56] so there was certainly some justification in the complaints by Shanxi mines of unfair treatment, and some room for reduction of rates.

The high rates of the Zheng–Tai were responsible, so Yangquan coal interests argued in the 1930s as in the 1910s, for the poor financial performance and slow growth of the mines.[57] This interpretation was supported in part by the National Economic Council,[58] but it is doubtful if it was really more than a contributory factor to the industry's troubles. The Zheng–Tai ran only 121 km from Yangquan to Shijiazhuang. So a full 1¢ per ton km reduction in freight charges would have reduced the cost of Shanxi coal by just over ¥1.0 per ton. While this would have lowered the cost of selling Shanxi coal in Shanghai to just under the ¥17.20 selling price (in 1933–4),[59] thus removing any losses incurred, it would still have left it more expensive than other Chinese anthracite coals, and therefore in a poor position to compete with other cheaper kinds of fuel.

Apart from opening up communications within the province, the Tong–Pu, through its junction with the Long–Hai, offered an alternative route to the east for Shanxi coal.[60] Nevertheless transport costs inevitably and always would make up a large proportion of final cost at non-local markets. So long, therefore, as industry remained concentrated on the coast and so long as industrial activity there remained at a level that could be satisfied by other sources of supply, the development of Shanxi coal was likely to be slow. This basic factor far outweighed in importance the high freight rates of the Zheng–Tai or the unreliability of transport. When the province's output did greatly expand after 1949 (although still not to a level suggested by its share of coal reserves), it was on the basis of a new, or at least changing, industrial map, with industries and industrial cities growing up in the interior of China.

Manchuria: rapid development under Japanese auspices

In stark contrast to Shanxi, Manchuria, with under 2% of China's coal reserves and only about 7% of its population, produced in some years over 50% of its coal output. Moreover, between 1907 and 1936 output from large mines in the four provinces of Liaoning, Jilin, Heilongjiang and

Rehe,[61] grew at 10.9% per annum, that in the rest of China at 5.8%; if the starting date is moved forward to 1914, the rates are 7.5% and 3.6%. In large part this phenomenon can be explained in terms of the framework used above, but the Japanese ability and willingness to ensure continuity of production and transport was a further element of considerable importance.

The much higher per capita production (and consumption) of coal in Manchuria reflected an economy which both started from the beginning of the century at a higher level of development than the rest of the country and grew faster on that base. In the 1930s per capita gross domestic product in Manchuria was larger by at least 16%, and industry both accounted for a much greater proportion of total produce (19.7% as against 11.5%) and even more importantly was much more heavily concentrated in large-scale modern factory production as against handicrafts. In the same way per capita use of coal was twice that in the rest of the country, and a much larger proportion of coal (70–80% in Manchuria) was used in the modern sector.[62]

Many circumstances combined to bring about these different economic structures and growth rates. Considering Fushun (which accounted for most of Manchuria's output) in the light of the previous discussion, one notes first the exceptional geological conditions obtaining in the field, which allowed very low production costs. Chinese mines in the region were able to compete only when they could offer a better quality of coal, or when currency fluctuations meant their coal was temporarily cheaper than that of Fushun. Second, the SMR was prepared to invest and reinvest very large amounts of capital in Fushun: about J¥120 million up to 1936.[63] While it would be inconsistent to lay too much emphasis on this, given the argument that shortage of capital was not a major constraint in the rest of China, this remains a very substantial sum in terms of prewar China. Third, Fushun was able to take advantage both of a rapidly expanding local demand because of the expansion of other sectors of the Manchurian economy and, with the help of favourable freight terms from its owner, the SMR, of lucrative export markets in south China and Japan.

These factors suggest that conditions were in any case favourable to the development of mining there, but a further crucial element in the environment was the Japanese presence in the region. In addition to the sums they invested in the mines – sums that at first were dependent mainly on loans raised in the international money market – their influence was crucial in maintaining a degree of stability far greater than that in north China. Japan's, albeit reserved, support for the local warlord, Zhang Zuolin, ensured a much greater continuity of political power in Manchuria than elsewhere. More specifically, the Japanese were willing to act more directly than were other powers in the protection of their railways and other enterprises in China; this was made very clear in the Japanese attitude towards the rebellion of Guo Songling in 1925.[64]

The effects of this greater stability are clearly shown in the figures for railway freight and in those for coal output. Between the early 1910s and the mid-1920s Manchuria produced around 30% of China's coal, but in 1925–6 this proportion suddenly jumped to over 50%, as output in north China plummeted under the impact of the civil wars. Although in the 1930s output in China proper moved ahead again, only in 1932 – the aftermath of the Japanese invasion – did Manchuria produce less than 40% of total large-mine output. Its greater stability seems to have shifted the balance of output permanently (at least as far as the pre-1937 period is concerned) in its favour.

In the 1930s the Japanese, now in complete control of the region, embarked upon a much more active and systematic programme of economic development. That programme was by no means solely aimed at the extraction of Manchuria's raw materials for Japan's use, although that was the overall context in which Japanese policy operated. Even before 1931 the policy of the SMR regarding sales of Fushun coal explicitly put the satisfaction of demand within Manchuria ahead of the export of fuel to Japan. The same policy was in force in the 1930s, at a time when the Japanese planned to expand heavy industrial production in Manchuria as well as in Japan, thus establishing the region as an industrial base, and not merely as a source of raw materials for the metropolis. At this time, more than before, the basis of the growth of coal mining was the expansion of demand within the region, so that coal in Manchuria became in short supply by the mid-1930s, in sharp contrast to the rest of China, where, despite expanding exports, companies found it difficult to dispose of all their coal.

Conclusion

As one might expect, the locational pattern of Chinese coal mining reflected both the peculiarities of its prewar economic development and its geography and resource endowment. The lop-sided development of industry in Manchuria and the treaty ports greatly favoured the expansion of mining in Manchuria and in coastal provinces able to supply the Shanghai market. The exploitation of the massive resources of Shanxi, and to a lesser extent those of west Hebei and Henan, was limited by the exiguous development of modern industry in those regions; household demand in rural and urban areas, as well as small-scale rural industry, supported quite a large mining industry, but this market was expanding insufficiently rapidly to make up for the lack of access to the coastal centres.

Given that the geography of mining thus reflected the pattern of China's development as a whole, that pattern itself was only in part the result of the specific historical factors introduced by the unequal treaties and the foreign impact. The slow progress that the Communist government has been able to make in correcting this perceived imbalance of development indicates that other influences have also been at work. Most important among these was China's physical geography and the transport problems that caused. Other goods, like coal, more easily entered the national market if their origin was near the coast or along the lower Yangzi. This would have been true whatever the historical circumstances of China's economy and was the basic determinant of the geography of China's development.

6

THE TEMPORAL PATTERN OF GROWTH

China's lack of a national market makes any discussion of short-term fluctuations in the growth of the industry highly complicated. Not only geographical distance but also the use of different currencies meant that mines in one area might be less, or even oppositely, affected by a boom or slump. There were nonetheless several short-term factors that influenced either all or at least important groups of mining companies, reducing or inflating their profits and thus eventually having an effect also on output.

This chapter will first present some data on major economic variables in the coal industry – output, profits and prices – which will form the basis for the periodization of fluctuations in the industry. A chronological survey of the major short-term influences on these variables, taking account of the fragmentation of the Chinese market, will then distinguish two main types of fluctuations: those resulting, directly or indirectly, from China's (imperfect) integration into the world market, through the influence of exchange rates or world trade movements; and those caused by political disturbances in Chinese society. The second type, it will be argued, was the more serious for the industry.

Table 29 and Figures I to IV provide some of the basic information through which the working of these short-term fluctuations can be discerned. Profits are probably the best indicator of the financial health of an industry, and Table 29 presents profit figures where they are available for major mining companies over a number of years. Since figures for capital in prewar China are generally of limited value, the profits here are compared to revenue or to output. Moreover, the sources often fail clearly to specify how they are defining 'profit', particularly with regard to allowances for depreciation; while it is, therefore, not possible without further qualification to compare the figures in Table 29 between different companies, they do give a fair indication of the financial vicissitudes of the individual companies through time.

Figures I to III collate information on movements in coal prices for the Republican period. These are available in some detail for individual coals

Table 29. *Profits of various Chinese mining companies, 1907–36*

(i) Profits or losses (−) as a percentage of revenue

Year	Fushun	Zhongxing	Baojin
1907	37.3	—	—
1908	38.0	—	—
1909	30.6	—	—
1910	29.0	—	—
1911	33.7	—	− 33.8
1912	20.1	—	− 67.4
1913	12.5	—	− 36.4
1914	15.8	—	− 2.2
1915	15.9	—	n.a.
1916	13.2	—	− 5.4
1917	27.5	—	36.5
1918	19.9	—	8.3
1919	21.0	—	5.4
1920	9.4	—	6.3
1921	8.2	—	3.0
1922	12.6	29.5	1.6
1923	6.4	35.0	n.a.
1924	4.5	24.3	9.4
1925	9.4	10.0	8.4
1926	8.2	0.0	− 1.2
1927	11.8	− 31.4	− 6.4
1928	13.3	− 32.5	− 136.0
1929	14.6	− 33.6	—
1930	2.9	− 6.1	—
1931	nil	nil	—
1932	0.2	13.1	—
1933	7.1	15.0	—
1934	12.2	14.0	—
1935	13.7	13.6	—
1936	13.9	—	—

(ii) Profits or losses (−) per ton of output

Year	Fushun J¥	Kailuan ¥	Zhongxing ¥	Jingxing ¥	Liuhegou ¥	Baojin ¥
1907	2.37	—	—	—	—	—
1908	2.09	—	—	—	—	—
1909	1.74	—	—	—	—	—
1910	1.82	—	—	—	—	—
1911	1.58	—	—	—	—	—
1912	1.22	1.01	—	—	—	− 1.50
1913	0.79	1.44	—	—	—	− 0.74
1914	0.99	1.17	0.84	—	—	− 0.06
1915	0.90	1.07	—	—	—	n.a.
1916	1.03	1.33	—	—	—	− 0.17
1917	2.52	1.96	—	—	—	3.05
1918	2.72	1.84	3.75	—	0.76	0.61
1919	4.48	2.37	4.61	—	1.74	0.44
1920	1.89	1.66	4.17	—	1.90	0.50

Table 29. (cont.)

(ii) Profits or losses (−) per ton of output

Year	Fushun J¥	Kailuan ¥	Zhongxing ¥	Jingxing ¥	Liuhegou ¥	Baojin ¥
1921	1.19	1.06	—	—	2.07	0.19
1922	1.71	1.67	4.09	—	1.06	0.10
1923	0.81	1.63	4.61	0.80	1.33	n.a.
1924	0.55	0.72	2.46	1.34	0.60	0.48
1925	1.12	0.71	0.91	2.35	0.42	0.57
1926	0.83	1.68	0.01	1.23	1.23	−0.06
1927	1.37	2.27	−6.14	1.68	—	−0.31
1928	1.58	1.17	nil	−1.78	—	−1.87
1929	1.65	1.22	−6.91	1.72	—	−0.06
1930	0.26	0.76	−0.75	0.36	−3.33	−0.02
1931	nil	1.11	0.03	1.34	−1.29	0.89
1932	0.02	0.10	1.41	0.42	−0.20	n.a.
1933	0.69	0.06	1.69	0.50	−1.65	−0.36
1934	1.31	0.27	1.50	0.39	—	−0.08
1935	1.56	0.36	1.51	0.29	—	−0.18
1936	1.28	1.42	—	1.00	—	—

Notes: For Fushun the financial year ran from April of the given year to March of the next.
For Kailuan the financial year ran from July of the given year to June of the next; the figures are for net profit in this case.
For Jingxing the financial year ran from October of the previous year to September of the given year.
For Baojin the financial year ran from August of the previous year to July of the given year.
Sources: Fushun: SMR, 1936, p. 145; SMR, 1939, p. 143; Kailuan: Hebei sheng, 1930, diaocha, Table 1; Kuboyama, 1940, p. 436; annual company reports as published in The Times; Zhongxing: Zhang Huiruo, 1936, pp. 265–6; Jingxing: Xu, 1947, pp. 46–7; MMT, chōsabu, 1937d, p. 74; Dagongbao, 24 January 1937; Liuhegou: Xu, 1947, pp. 184–5; Baojin: Yu, 1926d, pp. 80–1; Yan Zhongping, 1955, p. 166; MMT, chōsabu, 1937c, p. 50; Hou Defeng, 1929, p. 56; Kuboyama, 1944, pp. 115–19; KYZB 150 (14 July 1931): 851–2.

and for the late 1920s onwards; for the 1910s and early 1920s more scattered information is used to provide an idea of the trend. The movements of fuel price indices, which also included other types of fuel, also provide useful information in the lack of any general coal-price index. Finally, Figure IV shows short-term fluctuations in the trend of output, by comparing output in a given year with the average of the previous five years.[1]

Because of the fragmentation of the market, no clear and unambiguous trends emerge from the information given in Table 29 and Figures I to IV. Nevertheless the major short-term influences can be discerned, at least from 1913 onwards. Figure IV shows first the clear break in the secular trend that occurred in 1913–14. After that, output, profit and price figures indicate that wartime demand created boom conditions at least in the south and

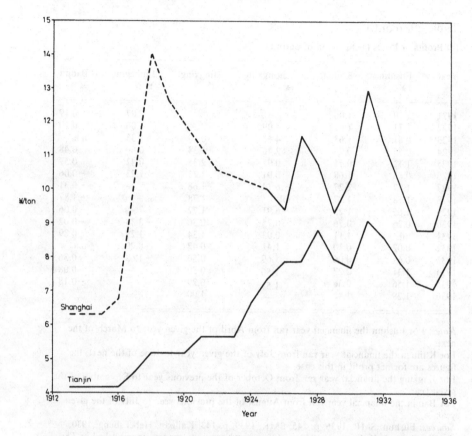

Figure I *Annual average prices of Kaiping No. 2 slack in Shanghai and Tianjin*
Sources: Zhongguo kexue yuan, 1958, p. 253; Nankai daxue, 1958, p.
81. Up to 1925 the dotted line for Shanghai represents only the most
approximate picture of price movements, culled mainly from NCH and
Yinhang zhoubao.

central Chinese ports; the boom was actually intensified with the release of
shipping capacity at the end of the war. Kailuan and Fushun, the major
Chinese suppliers of the Shanghai market, took the greatest advantage of
the boom, and were hardest hit when it ended temporarily in 1921–3.
Chinese mines in the interior were less affected by movements in the world
economy, continuing to prosper throughout the early 1920s. The civil wars
and consequent disruption of the railways in the late 1920s brought many of
these mines close to bankruptcy, but the foreign connections of Kailuan and
Fushun protected their lines of communication and allowed them to
continue to make high profits at the expense of the mines in the interior.
There were also conflicting trends during the 1930s, with the depression

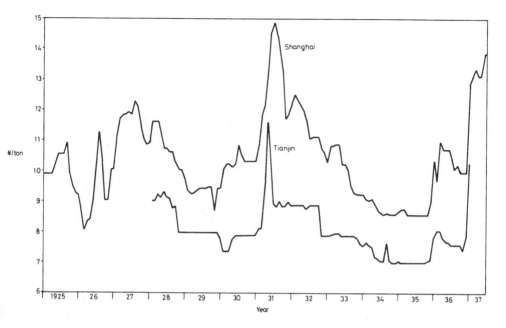

Figure II *Monthly average prices of Kaiping No. 2 slack in Shanghai and Tianjin*
    Sources: Zhongguo kexue yuan, 1958, pp. 253–7; Nankai daxue, 1958,
    pp. 108–10, 128.

hitting Manchuria in 1930 and the rest of China only in mid-decade; for many of the mines in the interior, however, the effects of this were more than outweighed by the buoyant influence of the restoration of railway transport.

Wartime and postwar boom

Traditionally the boom that took place in Chinese industry in the late 1910s has been ascribed to wartime conditions and to the consequent withdrawal of European economic power from East Asia. The decline in shipments of goods from Europe, scholars argued, created much more favourable market conditions for Chinese manufacturers both within China and in international markets.[2] Others have recently begun to emphasize other factors: David D. Buck shows that Jinan benefited from the boom despite increased Japanese economic activity in the area;[3] and Sherman Cochran also points out that the Nanyang Brothers' Tobacco Company's expansion at this time did not benefit from any reduction of competition from British–American Tobacco.[4] These scholars point to the expansion of the market resulting from the construction of the railways as an at least as important factor behind the boom. The two explanations are

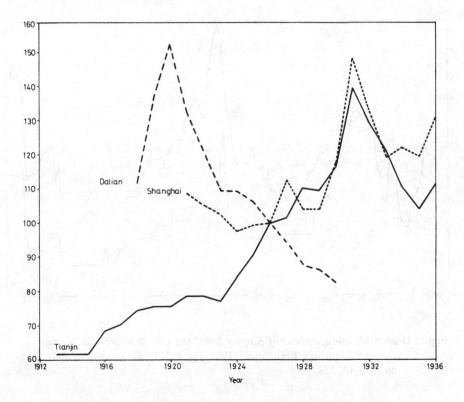

Figure III *Fuel price indices for Shanghai, Tianjin and Dalian*
   Sources: Zhongguo kexue yuan, 1958, p. 126; *Nankai Weekly*
   Statistical Service 3.32 (11 August 1930); Tokunaga, 1930, p. 116.

not, of course, mutually exclusive, and most agree that the railways contributed to the boom.[5]

Both influences were at work in coal mining, but the building of the railways was certainly the more important because of the dependence of the coal mines on them. The effects were felt as soon as the lines were completed – so that the great expansion of coal output took place before the war, and the break in the trend line occurred around 1913–14[6] – but they were still working through in the late 1910s, and contributed to the boom of those years. The Jin–Pu railway, for instance, was not completed until the end of 1912, so that its effects were not exhausted by 1914.

Wartime conditions also had considerable effects on both the demand for and the supply of coal, but the lack of integration of the market meant that these effects varied in different areas of the country. For the coal industry, three areas were of greatest importance – Shanghai, north China and Manchuria, in each of which market conditions differed radically.

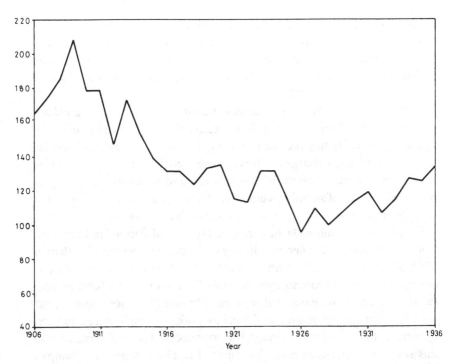

Figure IV *Percentage ratio of output in the given year to average of previous five years*
Sources: See Appendix A.

In Shanghai the growth of demand for coal almost certainly accelerated during the 1910s. Murphey suggests that the industrialization of the city from 1895 greatly increased its rate of population growth,[7] and that industrialization was most rapid in the 1910s. An upper limit to the rate of growth of Shanghai's industry is put by the sales of electricity to industrial consumers, which quadrupled between 1914 and 1918 and trebled again between 1918 and 1922.[8]

Whether or not there was any great acceleration, demand was certainly growing throughout the 1910s, but during the war years supply turned out to be highly inelastic. Up to 1914 Shanghai had depended mainly on Japanese coal, but booming industrial demand in Japan led to a shortage there, reduced the surplus for export and increased prices. Between 1914 and 1918 coal prices in Japan trebled,[9] and coal supplied to China was also much more expensive.[10]

Moreover the war in Europe put heavy demands on shipping, leaving an inadequate supply in East Asia. Freight rates from Japan to China increased sharply as a result – the rate per ton of coal from Moji to Shanghai increased from J¥1.15 to J¥8.60 between 1914 and 1918.[11] Although the effect of high prices in Japan and high freight rates was mitigated somewhat in China by the sharp rise of China's silver currency relative to the gold yen,[12] the price of Japanese coal on the China coast still increased steeply: Kishima lump, for instance, rose from ¥11.20 per ton in January 1916 to ¥28.10 in September 1918.[13]

This steep rise in the price of Japanese coal should have been a golden opportunity for Chinese mines. But because they were located in north China and so had to ship their coal to Shanghai by sea, they were as badly hit by the rising freight charges as was Japanese coal. Even Kailuan had its ships requisitioned by the British government, and so was unable to ship its own coal.[14] Costs of shipping Kailuan coal from Qinhuangdao to Shanghai rose sharply, from ¥1.15 per ton in 1915 to ¥8 in 1917.[15]

Rising demand and inelastic supply led to a 'coal famine' in Shanghai. Total shipments by steamer into the city were actually lower in 1918 than in 1913, although the trend between those years was very uneven. In this situation coal prices rose steeply, not only for Japanese and Kaiping coal (whose price more than doubled between 1916 and 1918 – see Figure I), but even for coal carried down the Yangzi by junk, although there had been little rise in the cost of junk carriage.[16] Fortunes could be, and were, made in this situation. Kailuan's Shanghai agent, Liu Hongsheng, for example, managed to charter several ships to bring Kailuan coal to Shanghai and sell it at a large profit. The nearly ¥1.3 million he made in this way in 1917–18 formed the basis of his fortune and of his future career as China's 'match king'.[17]

The response to the coal shortage included numerous complaints about the Shanghai Coal Traders' Guild, and allegations of squeeze.[18] More constructively, Shanghai interests began to pay increasing attention to the development of China's coal resources, particularly those in the lower Yangzi valley, and the *North China Herald* and the *Nongshang gongbao* (Gazette of the Ministry of Agriculture and Commerce) reported increased coal-mining activity in other areas of central China.[19]

Manchuria also experienced a shortage of coal, although there were significant differences from the experience of Shanghai. The region was also undergoing rapid population expansion, and growth in industry – and therefore in the demand for coal – up to 1919 was even more substantial than in the rest of China.[20] As in Shanghai, supply proved to be insufficiently elastic to meet the demand, although for different reasons. Ample coal resources were available within the region, but a shortage of labour prevented their full exploitation. While output grew throughout the period, in 1917 and 1918 it grew less than planned because of the SMR's inability to find enough labour for its Fushun mines. The after-effects of a massive explosion at Fushun in 1917 also held back the growth of output, and no doubt contributed to the reluctance of workers to work in the mine.[21]

Since Manchuria was a large net exporter of coal, most of the effects of the shortfall fell on exports, which declined by almost 40% between 1913 and 1920. There is no index for prices of coal sold within south Manchuria, but those of coal assigned to what were regarded as secondary purposes rose steeply: Fushun coal sold to shipping in Dalian rose from J¥9.50 per ton in April 1917 to over J¥20 for most of 1919–20, peaking at J¥25 in November 1919.[22] Similarly the price of Fushun coal in Harbin – and coal exports to north Manchuria were among those categories restricted by the SMR[23] – quadrupled between 1915 and 1919.[24]

The solution to the shortage in Manchuria was more within local control than was the case in Shanghai, and indeed an intensive recruiting campaign was launched in order to raise output. Nevertheless prices only came back to the level of the mid-1910s after depression sharply reduced demand in the region and more coal was diverted to the less-important sectors.

North China faced yet another situation. Less affected by the war than other areas, demand was still increasing because of urbanization, some industrialization and the expansion of the market as a result of the construction of the railways. But in this case supply was highly elastic, as the investments of the last few years of the Qing and the first of the Republic began to result in increased output. The shortage of shipping prevented coal being exported to other regions, so that Kailuan had problems disposing of its output during the war years.[25] In contrast to the steeply rising prices in other areas, therefore, coal prices in north China were relatively stable, with only small rises in the price of Kailuan coal in 1917 and 1920, at a time when its price was doubling in Shanghai (see Figure I). Even in north China, however, demand was pressing on supply and in Shandong there was reported to be a trend towards rising prices in 1917.[26] In addition companies selling in the lower Yangzi market were able to raise their prices: Zhongxing increased its prices from ¥3.80 to ¥5.00 per ton in 1917.[27]

Because they were unable to ship their coal to the most buoyant markets, Chinese coal mines, most of which were in north China, were unable fully to cash in on the boom. Nevertheless Kailuan still made over ¥1 per ton profit throughout the period (see Table 29) and, where figures are available, we find other mines also in a relatively healthy financial state: even Baojin, because of its location one of the less successful companies, managed to show a surplus between 1917 and 1922.

After peace was restored at the end of 1918, increasing availability of shipping allowed particularly those mines best situated to supply the coastal market to benefit from the continuing industrial boom. While Fushun was still occupied in supplying the Manchurian market, exports from Kailuan's port at Qinhuangdao rose by over 60% between 1918 and 1920, from 1.3 to 2.1 million tons.[28] In his report on the company year 1918–19, Major Nathan, the company's chief manager, enthused over the expansion of markets as the fall in freight rates allowed them to reduce prices; he spoke of having to drop contracts because of the shortage of coal.[29] Next year he said there was no sign of a fall-off in demand.[30] Company profits reached record levels in these two years, and dividends to the English shareholders reached 30% in 1919–20.[31] More fragmentary figures for other companies also testify to their prosperity: Zhongxing made profits of over ¥4 per ton in those years, the Japanese mines in Shandong even more.[32]

The slump of 1921–2

World-wide, the boom at the end of the war was very brief, soon to be succeeded by a slump which in many countries ushered in two decades of economic difficulties. For China's infant industrial sector, the underlying trend towards growth reasserted itself after a short hiccup – Chang's index of net value added fell in both 1921 and 1922, gross value of output in 1922.[33] Some industries nonetheless suffered a severe crisis, the effects of which were to echo for many years; in the cotton-spinning industry, for example, the weaknesses exposed in 1923 were to remain troublesome up to the outbreak of the Second World War.[34] But for coal mining there was merely a minor crisis of demand, one that affected most those mines on the coast and in Manchuria which had enjoyed the greatest benefits from the earlier boom.

The boom broke in Japan in March 1920, and over the next twelve months wholesale prices there fell by 40%, while coal prices dropped by 25% between 1920 and 1921.[35] Manchuria, whose economy was closely tied in with that of Japan, almost immediately followed Japan into recession. While not all industries in the region were equally seriously affected, the output of bean mills halved in 1920, and brickworks also cut back production, as an 8% profit rate for brick-making and related industries in 1919 turned into a 33% loss in 1920; overall the nadir of the crisis financially was 1921, when profits of seventy-seven major industrial companies were down 60% in 1920.[36] So demand for coal was sharply cut back and prices fell: the Dalian index of fuel prices, mainly reflecting the price of coal, fell by 14% between 1920 and 1921 (although the general price index fell even more sharply).[37] Coal prices were cut even more drastically in those sectors where the SMR had previously been rationing supplies: Fushun bunker coal prices halved between mid-1920 and mid-1921, while prices in Harbin fell by 47% between 1919 and 1921.[38] Despite this slashing of prices, sales of Fushun coal, reduced also by competition from Chinese mines benefiting from a fall in the price of silver relative to the gold yen, fell by 33%.[39]

Because of this fall in the value of China's silver currency, its industry continued to expand for most of 1920, and Kailuan maintained a high level of sales throughout that year.[40] Over the next three years, however, China did suffer a recession, although here again its timing varied in different sectors. The fall in industrial activity reduced the demand for coal in China's industrial centres, and the Shanghai fuel price index declined by 10% between 1921 and 1924.[41]

The dip in Chinese coal output in 1921 was nearly all the result of cutbacks by Kailuan and Fushun, the two mines most affected by the slump. The profits each gained from the coal trade fell rather more sharply, as they engaged in price cutting in order (with some success) to keep up sales. The SMR succeeded in 1921 in reversing the steep fall in sales in 1920, but at the cost of a profit level only half as high.[42] Kailuan, whose problems postdated those of Fushun by about a year, was able to sell almost as much coal in 1921–2 as in 1920–1, but profits were down 30%.[43] The limited effect of the slump emerged in Kailuan's annual reports, which were far more concerned with the disruption of railway transport than with any shortage of demand.[44]

Because the other mines of north China were not as dependent on the coastal market, they suffered less from the slump as they had benefited less from the boom. Unfortunately there exists only for Liuhegou a profits series covering each year between 1918 and 1924; this shows no real sign of the slump, as 1921 profits were steeply up, and 1922 profits only just below those of 1920.[45] More-fragmentary figures for other mines back up this picture, as do output and sales figures for these mines. Right up to 1937, internal disruption within Chinese society posed a more serious threat to these mines than did movements in the international economy.

The Chinese civil wars

The relatively smooth development of the industry up to the mid-1920s, only briefly interrupted by a fall in demand during the slump, was brought to an end by a different kind of crisis, one of supply, as political and military chaos blocked the transport of coal to market. Wars and political disturbances had caused troubles for the industry before. In 1900 the Boxer Uprising forced the closure of Kaiping and led to its loss to foreign interests, while fear of the Boxers drove foreign mining engineers from many areas in north China and put back the development of modern mines for several years.[46] Then in 1911 and 1912 the revolution interrupted the rapid growth of the modern coal-mining sector, affecting most seriously Pingxiang, the major Chinese-owned mine and the only modern mine south of the Yangzi: output plummeted and the company suffered serious losses.[47] Yet these incidents were relatively minor in comparison with the wars of the late 1920s.

Demand for coal grew throughout the late 1920s and early 1930s, although at a slightly lower rate than before. After the end of the 'golden age' of wartime conditions and as, from the early 1920s, supplies of raw materials from the interior began to be cut off,[48] the growth of other industries slowed, thus reducing the expansion of the demand for coal. Yet consumer-goods production still grew at almost 9% per annum between 1924 and 1933, electricity output at just under 11%. Imports of coal into Shanghai by sea also continued to increase rapidly throughout the late 1920s. Nor is there any evidence that the rate of urbanization, and thus of the growth of household demand, underwent any drastic reduction. It is true that coal consumption by the railways fell as traffic declined, and households and industries most directly affected by the fighting were no doubt forced to cut back their purchases. Total demand, however, continued to grow, and the source of the problems of the industry between 1924 and 1933 did not lie in demand.

Although the wars of the 1910s seem to have had little effect on the expansion of the industry, by 1920 there was growing concern over the unreliability of railway transport. Major Nathan in early 1920 stated that military control over the railways was the main constraint on the amount of coal Kailuan could ship to Qinhuangdao and thus on its total sales. From this time complaints at the effects of the civil wars on railway transport became a regular feature of the KMA's annual reports.[49] Other mines in Hebei and in Henan were also suffering from sporadic interruptions to railway transport, although not frequently enough to undermine the generally healthy financial situation of most companies.[50]

The increasing intensity of the civil wars in the mid-1920s led to the collapse of the railway system outside Manchuria, although even in the rest of China some lines escaped relatively lightly. Movements in overall freight traffic are depicted in Figure V. The problems were caused not only by the cutting of lines in the course of battle, but also by the depletion of the rolling stock, both by direct military expropriation and by the financial milking of the railways by the warlords. As early as 1923, before the fall in traffic volume, the British Department of Trade report on China described the 'deplorable' condition of the railways. Later reports chronicled the

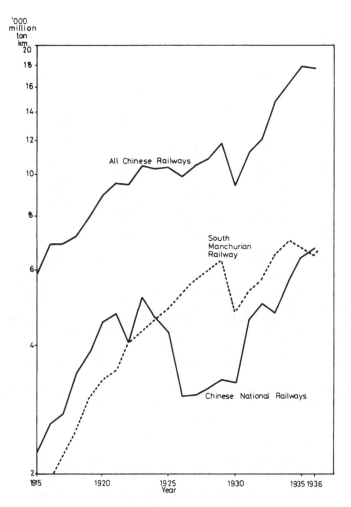

Figure V *Freight traffic on Chinese railways, 1915–36*
    Sources: See Chapter 4, note 33.

deterioration in their condition, and pointed out that even where there were no interruptions to traffic the stock continued to deteriorate and there was an increasingly serious shortage of rolling stock.[51] By 1925 the situation was described as one of 'utter disorganisation',[52] and this led in turn to a shortage of coal, thus further reducing railway transport.[53] The nadir was reached in 1926–7 when the division of the country between the Guomindang in central and south China and the warlords in the north cut in two the main north–south lines and brought traffic to a virtual halt, as Table 30 shows.

Table 30. *Goods traffic on major Chinese railway lines, 1923–36 (thousand million ton km)*

Year	SMR[a]	Jing–Han	Jiao–Ji	Jin–Pu	Bei–Ning
1923	4.33	1.57	0.44	0.85	0.82
1924	4.60	1.30	0.52	0.76	0.73
1925	4.84	0.85	0.48	0.56	1.02
1926	5.32	0.48	0.40	0.13[b]	0.81
1927	5.74	0.26	0.50	0.12[b]	1.32
1928	5.96	0.33	0.65	0.24[b]	0.79
1929	6.32	0.36	0.57	0.24	1.31[b]
1930	4.77	0.43	0.52	0.25	1.31[b]
1931	5.37	0.51	0.68	0.41	1.64
1932	5.70	1.00	0.61	0.65	0.90
1933	6.49	0.94	0.65	0.94	0.79
1934	6.97	1.37	0.85	1.11	0.91
1935	6.76	1.42	0.80	1.24	0.83
1936	6.41	1.36[b]	0.74[b]	1.13[b]	0.83[b]

Notes: From 1932, the Bei–Ning figures exclude traffic on that part of the line within Manchuria.
[a] The financial year of the SMR ran from April of the given year to March of the next.
[b] Denotes an estimate made from figures for tons carried or for revenue.
Sources: Manshikai, 1964–5, vol. 1, p. 301; Ping-Han tielu, 1932, p. 633; MMT, sangyōbu, 1938, appendix, tables, pp. 66–72; *Tongji yuebao*, various issues.

As a result of this collapse of railway traffic, shipments of coal from many mines declined sharply. When transport on the Jin–Pu ceased, Zhongxing was forced back to reliance on the Grand Canal, now silted up; sales in the lucrative Yangzi market plummeted and efforts to get coal out via Tianjin also failed.[54] The military confiscated even the locomotives owned by the Liuhegou Company on the Jing–Han, so that the company's main market at Hankou was virtually closed to it in the late 1920s;[55] it sent only 1200 tons of coal to Hankou between 1927 and 1929.[56] Table 31 shows the decline of coal transport on that line, and also illustrates how output fell in response.

Because of the failure of transport, coal prices in the cities of north China rose during the late 1920s. Even in Shanghai reduced supplies of Chinese coal led to record imports, although the availability of Japanese coal meant that the crisis had little effect on prices. In Tianjin, while the price of Kailuan coal rose by 50% in the late 1920s, that from mines along railways more severely affected rose more steeply: Fangshan coal by 115%, Shanxi coal by 127% between 1924 and the peak in 1928.[57] Areas solely dependent on the Jing–Han or Jin–Pu were more badly affected: in 1929 the price of coal in Baoding was ¥16 per ton, as against a normal price of ¥6 in 1935.[58] In the area of Tahe in Henan coal prices rose to five times their previous level when the railway stopped operating.[59]

Table 31. *Index of coal output along the Jing–Han and transport of bituminous coal by the railway, 1923–33*

Year	Coal carried	Output	Year	Coal carried	Output
1923	100.0	100.0	1929	26.7	45.8
1924	90.0	117.0	1930	27.5	49.2
1925	67.6	90.3	1931	46.5	83.9
1926	32.8	36.2	1932	—	90.4
1927	28.9	24.1	1933	—	99.9
1928	22.8	37.7	—	—	—

Note: The index includes output from the Peking Syndicate, Zhongyuan, Liuhegou, Jingxing, Zhengfeng and Lincheng mines.
Sources: Output figures, see Appendix A; transport figures from Ping–Han tielu, 1932, p. 191.

Severe coal shortages were experienced in some of the major cities during this period. On many occasions the citizens of Beijing were unable to procure the coal necessary to heat their homes, and the local authorities pressed the warlords, sometimes successfully, to let a few trains of coal through to the city.[60] Even Qingdao sometimes suffered, for instance during secret society disturbances in central Shandong in 1930.[61]

Recovery during the 1930s was slow because of the cumulative nature of the damage done to the railways. With the gradual restoration of order after the albeit incomplete Nationalist victory, Chinese coal began to return to the coastal markets,[62] but only in 1934 did transport on the Jing–Han reach the level of 1924, and right up to the war it never recovered the 1923 level. Throughout the 1930s mining companies along the Jing–Han and Jin–pu had to lease whole trains from the Bei–Ning to try to circumvent the lack of rolling stock on their home lines.[63]

The overall effect of the troubles clearly emerges from the output figures. Between 1924 and 1926 output from modern mines fell by 19%, and growth continued only very slowly up to 1933 (growth was only 2.7% per annum between 1924 and 1933, far below the trend rate). But the effects were unevenly distributed, largely because, as shown in Table 30, some railways were able to continue to operate, others had to close down almost completely: the SMR was hardly affected, and the Bei–Ning (over which British influence was strong) and the Jiao–Ji (in an area where the Japanese were prepared to use troops to maintain order) escaped much more lightly than did the Jing–Han or Jin–Pu.

The fate of different companies was largely determined by that of the railway upon which they depended, and the difficulties experienced by the Chinese mines along the Jing–Han and Jin–Pu created a very favourable situation for the big foreign mines of Kailuan and Fushun. Kailuan's net profit remained above ¥4 million between 1926–7 and 1931–2, and its manager was well aware that this situation was at least partly due to its Chinese competitors' inability to get their coal to market.[64] Similarly the SMR surpluses from their colliery operations remained at over 10% of revenue between 1927 and 1929.

Of the mines along the Jing–Han and Jin–Pu, Jingxing, which had a 25% German holding, escaped most lightly, only making a loss in one year. The company had special trains assigned to it, and although suffering still to some extent from shortage of transport capacity, it had a near monopoly for what coal it could ship.[65] Other companies suffered catastrophic declines in output and in their financial situation. Along the Jin–Pu, Zhongxing, which produced over 800,000 tons of coal in 1925, closed down completely in July 1927, and after its reopening in 1929 did not reach previous levels of output until 1932. The output of Jiawang in northern Jiangsu in 1927 was likewise under one-third of that of 1924, and did not surpass that level until 1934.

The financial situation was equally grim. Zhongxing, previously among the strongest of the mining companies, made losses of over ¥4.5 million between 1927 and 1930, partly as a result of the cessation of transport, partly because of direct payments the company had to make to the military – ¥740,000 in 1927 alone.[66] Profits foregone as a result of the civil wars amounted to at least as much as the actual losses. Liuhegou, which recorded profits every year between 1918 and 1925, suffered losses in the next three years as large as the profits it had earlier made, and in the succeeding years the debt burden incurred during the wars led to continuing losses.[67] From 1927 the Yili company in Ci xian made large losses, only getting back into the black from 1934.[68] The nearby Zhonghe Company broke even in 1927, but then suffered extensive losses.[69]

Coal mining in the world depression

The increasing integration of the Manchurian economy into the Japanese economic and monetary system meant that there were two histories of the depression in China; one for Manchuria, the other for the rest of the country. Whereas in Manchuria there was a relatively clear economic recession that affected mining companies through a fall in demand, elsewhere the situation was more complex: the onset of the depression was more gradual, and affected the industry only by stages, while the improvement in the supply situation with the recovery of the railways outweighed for many companies the decline in the level of demand resulting from falling levels of economic activity.

Japanese enterprises in Manchuria began to experience economic difficulties from the decline in the price of silver in mid-1929. This, combined with the collapse of Chinese paper money in the region, gave a competitive edge to Chinese enterprises working with depreciated currency. These enterprises continued to prosper even after the onset of depression in Japan in 1930. Nevertheless the predominance of the Japanese-owned enterprises in the region led to a steep down-turn in overall economic activity during that year and a consequent reduction in the demand for coal. Freight carried by the SMR fell by 25% in 1930,[70] leading to a similar decline in its use of coal, while coal sales to industry also fell by 9%. Even fierce price-cutting was insufficient to hold up Fushun's sales in Japan,[71] but a policy of active dumping enabled the company to maintain its level of sales in Shanghai despite the worsened currency situation.[72] To the effects of the depression were added in 1931 those of the disruption surrounding the Japanese takeover in Manchuria. Compared to the Chinese civil wars these were, however, relatively brief, and inflationary policies in Japan and Manchuria brought those countries out of recession long before the rest of the world, and indeed just as China was beginning to sink into it.

Chinese mining enterprises in Manchuria, like those in other sectors, took advantage of the fall in silver prices to promote their sales at the expense of those of Fushun. Despite the fall in local demand, 1929–30 was a golden age for Chinese-owned companies such as Muleng in Jilin and Beipiao in Rehe.[73] After 1931, however, not only did the yen fall in relation to Chinese currency, but most of these mines were closed or taken over in the course of the Japanese invasion; so all suffered a very steep fall in output between 1931 and 1933. Fushun's history was the opposite: between 1929 and 1930 sales fell by 10% and profits as a percentage of revenue fell to zero in 1931.[74] But the rapid reduction of the output of competitors in 1932 greatly improved Fushun's prospects in the later part of that year, and the expansion of the economy meant that demand exceeded supply by 1933, and indeed there was continuing pressure on supplies up to the war.[75] Profits also recovered their earlier levels by 1934. The Manchurian coal industry by 1933–4 faced a totally different situation from that in China, reflecting the by now almost complete separation of the two economies.

In the rest of China the timing of the various stages of the depression followed movements in the value of the country's currency. During 1930 and 1931, because of the depreciation of silver, most sectors of the Chinese economy were still buoyant, domestic prices remained stable, and exports were cheap in overseas markets. From late 1931 the abandonment of the gold standard by Japan and other countries ended China's immunity, and the rise of the silver yuan relative to other currencies opened China to foreign imports while making exporting more difficult. Three 'external' shocks also contributed to China's economic difficulties in the early 1930s. The Yangzi floods reduced peasant purchasing power in many areas, while the Japanese occupation of Manchuria was a further blow to sales prospects, particularly for the industries of north China. Finally, the Japanese attack on Shanghai in January 1932 virtually halted industrial activity there for several months, causing a 14% decline in the output of the Shanghai Power Company in 1932.[76]

Despite the attack on Shanghai, industrial production held up well until 1934; indeed Chang's index of industrial production rose year by year up to 1937.[77] The temporary prosperity enjoyed by the cities in 1933–4 was in part at the expense of the countryside, where deflationary tendencies were more severe as silver flowed from rural areas into the cities. From 1934, however, the appreciation of China's currency intensified as the American silver-purchasing policy raised silver prices and attracted a flood of the metal to leave China.[78] Urban areas now came to suffer almost as much from deflation as the countryside: prices had begun to fall in 1931, but reached their nadir in mid-1935, when Shanghai wholesale prices were 31% lower than they had been four years previously.[79] Consumer-goods output, more representative of urban industry than total industrial production, declined in 1934 and more steeply in 1935; even in 1936 it fell just short of the 1933 level.[80] Use of electricity, a serviceable proxy for industrial activity in Shanghai, also fell in 1935, only recovering in 1936 and exceeding previous levels in 1937.[81] Both the rise in wholesale prices in 1936 and 1937 to a level close to that of 1931 and the Bank of China report for 1936 suggest that by the second half of 1936 China was beginning to climb out of the recession.[82]

The history of coal mining during the period can be divided into two aspects: a sharp crisis in 1932–3 when a flood of imported Japanese coal threatened to drive Chinese coal off the market; and a more chronic difficulty with demand as the amount of coal used in the major cities hardly increased throughout the decade. Again the companies (notably Kailuan) mainly dependent on the coastal market were particularly severely affected.

Between January and October 1932 most Japanese coals in Shanghai fell in price by between one-third and one-half.[83] This led to strident protests by Chinese producers against Japanese dumping.[84] In fact, like Fushun,[85] Japanese companies had been dumping coal in China since 1930 as they cut yen prices in an attempt to counteract the fall in silver. It was only in 1932 when the value of the yen plummeted that their prices in terms of Chinese currency fell, thus precipitating the complaints of dumping.

As a result of the fall in prices, the share of Japanese and Fushun coal in the Shanghai market rose from 15% in January to 36% in August,[86] and this at a time when the Japanese attack on the city had caused a 20%

contraction in total sales. This overall contraction was a more-important reason for the decline in sales of Chinese coal than was the import of Japanese coal, which in fact on an *annual* basis occupied a substantially smaller share of the market than it had in 1931. Although its share in 1933 was slightly up on 1932, the imposition of a higher tariff from May 1933 permanently reduced the stake of foreign coal on the Chinese market, cutting the Japan and Fushun share of Shanghai sales from 29% in 1933 to 4% in early 1937.[87]

Chinese mines were still forced to cut prices, and therefore profits, to meet the Japanese challenge in 1932. Between January and October 1932, Kailuan cut the price of its lump coal in Shanghai by 39%, and of its slack by about 10%, and as a result its profits for the year 1932–3 were only around 35% those of the previous year. Zhongxing cut the price of its slack by 17%, and other mines made even more drastic cuts: Jiawang lump, for example fell by 40%. Overall the price of coal in Shanghai (including that of foreign coal) fell by 12% in 1932 and by a further 12% in 1933.[88]

For most Chinese mines the ability to resume sending at least some coal to market was more important than the market fluctuations caused by Japanese imports. So Zhongxing's profit in 1932 of ¥1.4 million was the best since 1924, and worked out at ¥1.4 per ton. Jingxing, too, had its best year of the 1930s in 1932, and, while Yili made a loss, it was much smaller than the one made in 1933.[89] As the KMA's chief manager pointed out, this return of Chinese coal on to the market ended Kailuan's quasi-monopoly in many markets and ushered in a new, more competitive, era; it was thus a more important cause of the company's losses than was Japanese dumping.[90]

Demand in general was fairly stagnant in the 1930s. Sales of coal in rural areas fell both because of the fall in agricultural prices, which reduced the peasants' incomes, and as a result of the after-effects of the Yangzi floods of 1931, which left wide areas destitute. In Anhui peasants affected by the floods switched to buying firewood instead of coal, thus reducing the coal sales of the Datong Company.[91] Peasants in Shandong and Hebei, whose incomes were cut by rural deflation, bought less coal during 1933 and 1934,[92] and in Shanxi both outside observers and the mine managers themselves saw the bankruptcy of the agricultural economy as one of the main problems facing companies in their efforts to recover financial viability.[93] Moreover, falling incomes induced some peasants to try to earn extra income by opening small mines, thus forcing down prices still more by bringing more coal on to the market.[94]

In the cities, too, there was no sign of rising demand, though the year-to-year pattern was not very clear. After a sharp fall in 1932, the figures for

Table 32. *Coal consumption in Shanghai, Hankou, Guangzhou, Yantai and Xianggang, 1930–6*

Year	Sales in 5 cities ('000 tons)	Coal imports into Shanghai ('000 tons)
1930	5,700	3,403
1931	5,810	3,617
1932	5,260	2,942
1933	5,100	3,323
1934	5,130	3,229
1935	5,585	3,303
1936	n.a.	3,240

Sources: MMT, keizai chōsakai, 1936b pp. 8–9; KYZB, various issues; MMT, chōsabu, 1937e, pp. 543–4.

Shanghai between 1933 and 1936 remained virtually constant, and at a level lower than that of 1930–1 (see Table 32). Nor did sales in the five major ports in 1935 reach the level of earlier years. In the data on shipments of coal by the railways (see Table 28), on the other hand, there is a clearer indication of an economic recovery in 1936.

Reflecting low demand, coal prices were weak throughout most of the 1930s, reaching their nadir in 1935, but beginning to recover in 1936; in north China, Kaiping No. 2 slack cost on average ¥9.07 per ton in 1931, ¥7.26 in 1934 and only ¥7.09 in 1935 before rising to ¥7.95 in 1936 (see Figure I). In Shanxi the price of Baojin coal fell still more dramatically, from ¥3.31 per ton in January 1931 to ¥1.58 in November 1934.[95] As shown in Figure I, the pattern in Shanghai was similar, although less pronounced.

This stagnation of demand in the main coastal ports led to intensified competition for a share of those markets. Total output continued to increase,[96] and Kailuan's chief manager wrote that for the foreseeable future he did not expect the East Asian coal market to be able to absorb all the coal produced there.[97] The established companies, of which Kailuan was now (after the loss of Manchuria) by far the most important, bore the main brunt of the recession: during 1935 and 1936 Kailuan adopted various expedients to cut back output, such as the cessation of all double-shift working, a reduction in the working week in 1935, and the closure of the Majiagou colliery in January 1936.[98] Kailuan's profits likewise remained at a low level up to the war: average gross profit for 1932–7 was under ¥3.9 million, the lowest of any quinquennium in the company's history.[99] Zhongxing, too, reported difficulties in selling its coal in times of industrial depression, but these appear to have had only a very slight actual influence on sales and profits – a 12% dividend was still paid for 1935.[100] Most other

Chinese mines also complained about the depression, but showed little hard evidence for its effects in their financial returns.

From mid-1936 the coal market began to pick up, as did Kailuan's performance; net profit for 1936–7 was almost four times as high as the previous year, itself the best since 1931–2.[101] Nationally prices began to rise, and figures for sales of coal in Shanghai for the first few months of 1937 showed a 23% rise on the corresponding period of 1936. With the very high elasticity of supply it is unlikely that the growth of demand would have been sufficient completely to solve the problems of the industry, especially those of the older mines. But the last year before the war was one of optimism for coal mining, as for other parts of Chinese society.

Conclusion

Two major themes emerge from this chapter. The first is the low degree of integration of the market. Different areas experienced entirely different market conditions at the same time. Partly this was because of geography and the rudimentary transport system, which prevented the sale of north China coal in booming Shanghai during the First World War; but after the end of the wartime shortage of shipping, price trends in north China and in Shanghai were fairly similar (see Figure I). More importantly, foreign penetration split up China, and Manchuria emerged as an almost entirely separate economy, reacting in large measure to movements in the Japanese rather than the Chinese economy and currency. As a result there is no single temporal pattern of growth for the industry, but rather an interwoven pattern of regional histories. The truth of this is highlighted by the fact that this whole discussion has focussed exclusively on the coastal provinces, while large areas of the interior were even less integrated into a national market.

Second is the prime importance of supply considerations – and thus of political stability – for all but the mines most closely tied to the coastal economy. The fortunes of the big foreign mines, Kailuan and Fushun, reflected the economic health of the Manchurian and coastal Chinese economies, both because a high proportion of their sales were to those economies, and because their location and their foreign connections protected them to a large extent from the effects of the transport disruption. For the majority of Chinese mining companies, which operated in the north China provinces of Shandong, Shanxi and Henan, and in the interior of Hebei, movements in the international economy were merely a distant clamour. Their concerns were far more with getting their coal to market in the first place, and so with the preservation of order and regular railway transport. Similarly in the cities of the interior, coal crises were ones of supply. The civil wars created a crisis of high prices and low output, not one of low prices and overproduction that until recently has typified crises under capitalism. The distinction is well made by Witold Kula in a reference to early modern Poland: 'In the feudal system crisis means a sharp increase in the general level of prices, whereas in the capitalist system (at least until 1939) it means a sharp drop in the general level of prices.'[102] The primacy of the non-economic over the economic in the tribulations undergone by most Chinese mines is an indication of the low level of development of China's society and economy and of the still limited integration particularly of the coal industry into the world economy.

PART 2
COAL MINING IN
CHINESE POLITICS AND SOCIETY

7

FOREIGN INVESTMENT IN THE COAL INDUSTRY

Most of China's coal was produced from mines owned by foreign or Sino-foreign companies. On this all scholars agree, but the implications of that fact can be read either as proving the contribution foreigners made to China's development or as exemplifying the degree of alien oppression of Chinese producers. In any country, indeed, the role of foreign capital is largely a political issue, and this was certainly true for China.

Nationalists were enraged at the dents foreign companies made in Chinese sovereignty, and no doubt this made them eager to attribute deleterious economic effects to those companies, even when those effects were in fact very difficult to calculate. Political issues such as sovereignty are, of course, of no less intrinsic importance than economic ones. Foreign mining companies did indeed impinge on Chinese sovereignty in many ways, although their interaction with Chinese governments and with Chinese society as a whole was a very complex one. One cannot, however, deduce even from the most outrageous piece of robbery practised against the Chinese people that the eventual net economic effect on China of foreign involvement even in that particular case would necessarily be harmful.

In any case, since the very distinction between different sources of capital is in large part political, the main questions arising about foreign investment in Chinese coal mining touch on politics. What environment enabled the foreign companies to acquire such a powerful position in the industry? How did they deal with the Chinese authorities and with their local collaborators? How did the multifaceted political relationships evolve over time? Such questions come at least as close to the concerns of those who have discussed the issue as does the highly complicated economic question of the net impact foreign investment had on the Chinese economy.

The foreign stake in Chinese coal mining
The foreign stake in the industry, as shown in the share of output coming from foreign mines, was very large indeed. In no five-year period

Table 33. *Share of foreign and Sino-foreign mines in total large-mine output*

Period	Percentage of output accounted for by		
	Wholly foreign mines	Foreign and Sino-foreign mines (i)	Foreign and Sino-foreign mines (ii)
1902–06	74.2	74.2	74.2
1907–11	70.6	76.4	73.5
1912–16	38.7	85.4	62.1
1917–21	33.4	73.5	53.5
1922–6	37.7	73.4	54.8
1927–31	38.5	77.3	57.3
1932–6	41.8	71.9	56.1

Notes: 'Foreign and Sino-foreign Mines (i)' includes all output of both wholly owned and Sino-foreign mines, including those in which a loan agreement gave effective control to foreign creditors.
'Foreign and Sino-foreign Mines (ii)' discounts the above totals for the Chinese share in Sino-foreign mines: 50%, except in the case of Jingxing after 1922, when 75% of the equity was Chinese owned, so only 25% of the output is counted under this head.

did the total output of wholly and partly foreign-owned mines contribute less than 70% of the total output of large mines in China.[1] Even if the output of Sino-foreign mines is discounted by the share of Chinese capital in the company, the foreign stake never fell below half. No very clear trend over time emerges from Table 33: it is clear that there was a fall in the foreign share in the late 1910s, reflecting a general growth in Chinese-owned industry and commerce, but before and after that the trend was very uneven. Within that total foreign stake, Table 34 shows that the British share steadily declined, while the Japanese rose. German investment, which made up most of the 'other' category, was important before the First World War, but declined steeply after the Japanese occupation of their mines in Shandong in 1914.

A very large proportion of all foreign output came from just two mines. Never less than 65% of output from Japanese-connected mines came from Fushun, never less than 70% of that from British-connected mines came from Kailuan. While other companies figured prominently in the political history of foreign mining, economically these two mines were of overwhelming importance, as much for the industry as a whole as for the foreign stake in it. The rising stake of Japan and Britain's decline is essentially the story of Fushun's outdistancing Kailuan as China's largest coal producer.

Table 34. *Share of enterprises connected with different countries in total foreign output*

Period	Percentage of total foreign output from firms associated with interests from					
	Great Britain		Japan		Others	
	(i)	(ii)	(i)	(ii)	(i)	(ii)
1902–6	89.0	89.0	—	—	11.0	11.0
1907–11	52.3	54.3	27.6	28.2	20.1	17.5
1912–16	44.1	34.8	38.3	49.8	17.6	15.4
1917–21	50.2	39.0	43.6	56.7	6.2	4.2
1922–6	38.5	28.6	55.5	69.1	6.0	3.3
1927–31	35.9	24.2	57.8	72.6	6.3	3.2
1932–6	33.4	21.4	62.8	77.5	4.7	2.1

Note: For the difference between columns (i) and (ii) under each heading see note to Table 33.

International rivalries and the establishment of foreign mines

From the start the weakness of China's sovereignty was central to the history of the foreign mines, and it was to be an issue of continuing concern. Consideration of the international rivalries in the penetration of China is indispensible to an analysis of foreign investment in coal mining. In tsarist Russia, by contrast, the state was strong enough largely to exclude such issues from business decision-making, and foreign investment was mainly in response to a perceived need of the recipient country.[2] In China, while in some mines the infusion of foreign capital was in response to such a need, diplomatic or even military pressure often forced the Chinese government to cede rights against its will; in most cases elements of both these factors were present.

Up to 1895 the Chinese government was strong enough to exclude all foreign investment from the mining industry. Whether or not that was a wise policy is not the issue here. The opposition of the Chinese bureaucracy to the concept of foreign mining is shown clearly in the secret correspondence of 1868, when all but one of the high officials canvassed for their views on treaty revision opposed allowing foreigners to work mines in China.[3] So, despite British expressions of interest in the Taiwan coal deposits as the amount of steamer traffic in East Asian waters increased from 1850, and despite continuing pressure from firms such as Jardines,[4] the only attempts to establish modern coal mining in China before 1895 were under Chinese control and used Chinese capital, although most employed foreign technicians.

In 1895 the Treaty of Shimonoseki cleared up the previously dubious position of foreign industrial enterprises in the treaty ports, and opened the way for an expansion of investment there. It did not in itself give foreigners the right to open mines (nor to engage in other economic activities that required the ownership of land) in the interior;[5] this still required a special licence from the Chinese government. Direct pressure from the foreign powers on a weakened China ensured, however, that such licences were often granted, and the financial burden of the indemnity to be paid to Japan was another form of indirect pressure on the Qing state to change its policies and grant licences in the hope of raising revenue from increased mineral taxes. Fears that Chinese capital would be insufficient to fund a large-scale expansion of mining led both central and provincial governments to encourage foreign investment for a short period.[6]

In the context of foreign investment, the last decade and a half of the Qing fell clearly into two periods. Between 1898 and 1903 the foundations of the foreign position in the mining industry were laid. They consisted of a series of contracts and agreements signed by the Chinese authorities at various levels, giving foreign interests the right to operate certain mines or to open mines in certain areas. As shown in Table 35, the number of these agreements peaked in 1898 at the height of the struggle for concessions, and again in 1902–3 as the Europeans returned to a still-weak China after the Boxer Uprising. Because the struggle for concessions provided the occasion for the foreign acquisition of mining rights, wider political considerations mostly determined the form and pattern of those rights. Whereas foreign investment in fully sovereign nations goes mainly to fund individual mining projects or specified mining areas,[7] in China the foreign powers saw mining rights as an important component of the spheres of influence they aimed to establish, and pressured the Beijing government to grant rights covering wide areas of territory, indeed in some cases whole provinces.

From 1903 China was beginning to recover its political will, and in the next eight years a revitalized government in Beijing and an increasingly assertive provincial and local gentry attempted to restore China's lost rights; such attempts continued to some extent the efforts of energetic officials even in the earlier period. As concern with the preservation of mineral and railway rights came to dominate the political scene, movements arose in several provinces. The number of new agreements tapered off sharply, and the Chinese did recover mining rights over wide areas. They failed in two vital respects, however – to recover mining rights that were actually being exploited, and to prevent the Japanese expanding their

Table 35. *Treaties and agreements allowing foreigners to mine in China,* *by year 1895–1912*

Year	Number of agreements allowing coal mining	Total number of agreements concerning mining
1895	1	1
1896	1	1
1897	—	—
1898	7	7
1899	2	3
1900	2	2
1901	2	2
1902	4	11
1903	3	3
1904	1	1
1905	3	3
1906	1	2
1907	2	2
1908	1	1
1909	1	1
1910	1	1
1911	—	—
1912	1	1

Source: Wang Jingyu, 1957, pp. 34–5.

position in south Manchuria after 1905 on the basis of claims on previous Russian interests. This general pattern can be seen in the history of many mining areas in China during this period.

Railway rights, themselves probably the most important components of the spheres of influence, frequently included a clause allowing the foreign concessionary to open mines within a specified distance (mostly 30 li, about 20 km) either side of the track.[8] This was especially the case where clearly defined spheres of influence allowed a greater consolidation of the foreign power's economic position. Russia's predominant stake in Manchuria up to 1904, of which the Chinese Eastern Railway and its branches were the main economic arm, also included mining rights along the railways at least in Heilongjiang and Jilin.[9] On the same basis they were also successful in extending their control, through loan agreements or other investments, to other mines in Manchuria, most notably Fushun and Yantai in Liaoning.[10]

After the Russians were driven out of south Manchuria by the Japanese in 1905, the Chinese attempted to reassert their position in the area, but without success. The Treaty of Portsmouth transferred the Russian rights there to the Japanese, who were to turn the area into a sphere of influence *par excellence*, with a far stronger position than that of any power in any other part of China. They had indeed much broader and more-comprehensive plans for the region than did any of the European powers in China, aiming to turn it into an economy complementary to Japan's, and even into a destination for emigration of Japan's surplus population.

The Changchun–Dalian line of the Chinese Eastern Railway was the most important of Russia's rights in south Manchuria to be ceded to Japan, and the SMR was formed in 1906 to run it. The mines at Fushun, in which the Sino-Russian Daosheng Bank had a stake, were also claimed by the Japanese under the treaty. Despite strong opposition by the Chinese, who stated that the mines were in fact Chinese,[11] the SMR went ahead to develop them, and invested J¥10 million between 1907 and 1912, raising output from 230,000 tons to just under 1.5 million.[12] Negotiations continued, the Japanese asserting that the company had clearly been Russian, the Chinese denying it, until, after the replacement of Yuan Shikai as foreign minister by Liang Dunyan, an agreement was signed in 1909 recognizing Japanese control over the mines.[13]

In addition the Chinese were forced to grant permission for a Sino-Japanese company to work the coal and iron deposits at Benxihu in Liaoning. Ōkura had been allowed to mine the area from 1905 by the Japanese governor of the Guandong Leased Territory, but this was strenuously resisted by the Chinese government. The agreement reached in 1910 provided for equal investment from the provincial government and from Ōkura, and the company officially started operations in January the next year.[14] So Japan had in five years moved from being merely a minor actor in the Chinese mining industry to being one of the two largest foreign investors.

Germany made a similar attempt to establish a sphere of influence in Shandong on the basis of the Jiaozhou agreement of 1898, which also granted it railway and mining rights. Here, however, the energetic Yuan Shikai inserted into the Chinese text of the 1900 mining agreement with the Germans clauses which were to allow the provincial authorities to undermine the foreign rights along the railway and which in 1911 led to the German retrocession of all rights except for those in the Zichuan and Fangzi areas which the Germans were already mining and also those in the potential iron-mining area of Jinlingzhen.[15]

Britain's interest in China was less concentrated and less geographically defined. But it, too, acquired rights stretching over large areas. In mining regulations agreed upon in 1898 between the Shanxi provincial authorities and the Peking Syndicate, an Anglo-Italian corporation, the Syndicate gained special mining rights across the main coal- and iron-bearing areas of south and central Shanxi, and a similar agreement signed with Henan later that year gave them rights to mine in Henan north of the Yellow River.[16]

These rights granted to the Peking Syndicate were the focus of some of the most important rights recovery activity. In Henan, Xiliang encouraged local competitors and tried to make the most favourable possible reading of the contract with the Syndicate in order to restrict foreign mining; as in Shandong, the foreign company eventually restored to China in 1909 most of the rights they had acquired, retaining only that area at Jiaozuo in Xiuwu county where they were actually mining. Resistance continued in Jiaozuo, as local gentry joined with coal interests in trying to prevent the Syndicate selling coal locally; these efforts, however, failed.[17] As will be described in Chapter 8, a Chinese company also bought back the Shanxi rights in 1908.

In south-west China, the Sichuan government likewise gave extensive rights to another British syndicate to mine across the whole of the province, although clauses within that agreement were such as to allow a more-assertive Chinese leadership to limit foreign penetration. The British never worked the rights, which were at least partly redeemed around 1910.[18] The French position in the south-west was recognized by a priority given to their interests in mining in the area from 1895, while an Anglo-French syndicate was granted wide rights in Yunnan in 1902. Again these rights were not actually exploited, and were later returned to Chinese control.[19]

Other agreements linked foreign interests with specific mines. Most seriously for China, Kaiping, the first and largest modern mine in China, was lost to foreign interests in the course of the Boxer Uprising. Increasingly reliant in the late 1890s on foreign funds, the mine had been made over, temporarily so the Chinese thought, to an Anglo-Belgian corporation in order to protect it from occupation during the foreign expedition against the Boxers in 1900–1. When the smoke cleared, however, the British had issued enough bonus shares to deprive China of control over its main modern mine. Partial success in a subsequent London court action was insufficient to enable the Chinese to end foreign control of the mine, and so Yuan Shikai, by now governor-general of Zhili, established the Luanzhou Mining Company in an adjacent area to try to force the British to come to terms. The British, however, had the better of a price war, and in 1912 the Kailuan Mining Administration was formed to mine and sell coal on behalf of both companies. Although there was to be a Chinese director-general, he had no real authority, which was instead vested with a chief manager who the rules provided indirectly would be a foreigner. In the division of profits, 60% of those up to £300,000 were to go to the Anglo-Belgian syndicate controlling Kaiping, 40% to the Chinese, although the division was to be equal over that figure. This arrangement continued despite the fact that output from mines originally opened by Luanzhou was from 1918 greater than that from the Kaiping mines.[20]

Other mines in north China also sought foreign funds to aid their expansion. Very soon after establishing his company – indeed so soon that some advance collaboration might be suspected – the owner of the Jingxing mine in Hebei accepted German investment in order to modernize. In 1902 the Jingxing Mining Company was officially established, with the Germans holding the real power, but the Chinese authorities were unwilling to accept the situation, and Yuan Shikai set up the Jingxing Mining Administration as a means to reassert Chinese rights in the area. After several years of dispute, these two organizations formed in 1908 an association called the Jingxing Mines, to be run by one Chinese and one German manager, with equal investment from either side.[21]

Also in Hebei, the owners of the Lincheng mine accepted in 1897 a loan from the company that was building the Beijing–Hankou railway, a loan whose terms gave the Belgian creditors a great deal of control over the mine's operations. An agreement in 1905 formalized the Belgian stake: during the term of the loan (fifteen years) the mine was to be worked jointly by the Chinese Lincheng Company and the Belgian Lu–Han Company, although the Belgian engineering manager had in practice the strongest say in company affairs.[22] In both Jingxing and Lincheng the Chinese government had had to recognize an already *de facto* foreign participation in a mining venture, although in both cases it achieved some success in limiting the extent of that participation.

Two other major mines also approached foreign interests in the years following 1895. In south Shandong the Zhongxing Company found itself obliged by the shortage of Chinese funds to seek German investment. Although that plan fell through, the company later took out a loan from a Sino-Japanese bank. In Jiangxi, Sheng Xuanhuai took out a German loan in 1902 for the development of the Pingxiang mine, but in neither of these cases did the loan agreement give the creditors managerial control over the company so there was less of a loss of China's sovereignty.[23]

Finally, one company, Liuhegou in Henan, resorted to the use of foreign capital even in the more nationalistic period of 1911. It had been set up in 1903, but found insufficient capital within China to modernize its operations. Therefore in 1911 it borrowed German funds through the agency of Li Hongzhang's confidant, Gustav Detring. This led in 1912 to the German manager of Jingxing, Henneken, being sent as adviser to the company, but in 1914 the Chinese manager took out a Belgian loan to repay the Germans, and as a result Lincheng's Belgian engineer came to direct Liuhegou's operations.[24]

In general the balance sheet for the rights recovery movement of the late Qing period was very mixed. Penetration in most of China was halted, and even in places rolled back, but Japan continued to press forward in Manchuria. Most telling of all, the Chinese failed to recover any mine that had actually been developed. Indeed the development of concessions won in the earlier period but which, during the chaos of the Boxer Uprising, had lain unexploited, coupled with the expansion of the Japanese in Manchuria, meant that the actual foreign investment in mining (see Table 5) increased most rapidly just at the height of the rights recovery movement. The political climate, on the other hand, was greatly changed, and for the rest of the prewar period foreign companies particularly outside Manchuria were put much more on the defensive.

After 1912, too, the foreign position in coal mining continued to reflect China's international situation. Virtually no new concessions were granted by the national government, but the Japanese expansion in and from Manchuria in the 1930s meant that many mines were lost to China. In the rest of the country, European companies in particular were more concerned with surviving the impact of the civil wars up to the late 1920s; and from 1928 the new Nationalist government, while under certain conditions welcoming foreign investment, was not prepared to grant control over resources in the way that had happened in the first few years of the century.

Only one important new mine was opened with the aid of foreign capital. In 1924 Russians resident in Harbin approached the Jilin government with a view to operating a mine at Muleng in the east of the province. The Russians invested ¥3 million, while the mine area was agreed to be worth the same amount and stood as the government's investment. While there were some disagreements between Russian and Chinese management, the mine expanded rapidly, producing 350,000 tons per annum in the late 1920s and making large profits.[25]

As during the rights recovery movement, the Chinese were able to regain control over some mines. At Liuhegou and Lincheng, the repayment of the foreign loans (even at the expense of taking out loans from Chinese banks) at the earliest possible opportunities in 1919 and 1920 respectively, led to the return of the mines to Chinese control.[26] Germany also lost most of its position in China during the war. The Zichuan mines were occupied by Japan after its declaration of war against Germany in 1914. For seven years these mines were run by the Japanese army, but after the Washington Conference a joint Sino-Japanese company, Luda, was formed to operate them.[27] The German stake in Jingxing was confiscated by the Chinese after their declaration of war in 1917. While the German investors recovered some of this stake in 1921, their share in the mines fell from 50% to 25%, so that Jingxing became the only mining company in which there was minority foreign participation.[28]

While the position of the European countries weakened slightly during this period, the Japanese were still eager where possible to increase their stake in Chinese coal. Not only was China central to Japanese imperialism, merely peripheral to European, but Japan also had an extra interest in the acquisition of raw materials from mainland Asia. Since the establishment of the state steelworks at Yawata, Japan had been dependent on imports for supplies of iron ore, and from 1899 the loans made by Japanese banks and other enterprises to the Hanyeping Company were made primarily with the aim of securing supplies of iron ore from Daye. Up to the First World War, Japan's coal reserves, although meagre, had sufficed both to supply the domestic market and to provide a substantial surplus for export, but the wartime shortage of coal was recognized as presaging a chronic deficit of fuel for the economy. Supplies of coal suitable for making metallurgical coke were particularly short, and in times of economic boom demand even for ordinary fuel coal outran domestic supply. So the supply of coal for the domestic economy became to Japanese investors, and more particularly to the Japanese government, an added incentive to invest in Chinese mining.[29] It most clearly operated in their policy towards north China, whereas in Manchuria the aim was primarily to build up a whole economy complementary to Japan and coal-use within that region was given priority.

As a result of these factors and of their comprehensive plans for Manchuria, the Japanese were always far less willing to retreat or compromise before Chinese nationalism than were the Europeans. Indeed the opposite was the case, as they advanced and occupied Manchuria in 1931, rapidly taking control of the major Chinese mines in the area. In October and November 1931, they took over the mines at Badaohao, Fuzhouwan and Xi'an, which had previously been run by the North-east Mining Bureau.[30] The takeover of privately owned mines was slower and less direct. They only reopened the Hegang mine in Heilongjiang using staff and workers from Fushun in 1933 after it had been closed for eight months.[31] As they advanced into Rehe and Hebei during the early and mid-1930s they took over or put pressure on the mines there. In Rehe the Beipiao mine was first forced to close by the cessation of transport on the railway between Jinzhou and Chaoyang, and later also occupied by the Japanese.[32] In early 1935 the Changcheng mine in north-east Hebei, which had earlier closed down, was reopened as a Sino-Japanese venture.[33] In the same area the Liujiang Company had long been involved in a dispute over boundaries with the neighbouring Sino-Japanese Taiji Company. On 4 May 1935 Japanese troops occupied the mine and, after protracted negotiations, it was merged with Taiji to become a Sino-Japanese company.[34]

By far the most important mine in the area was, however, Kailuan. There even the company's British ownership did not entirely protect it from Japanese pressure. This took several forms. Japanese companies, mainly the SMR, bought up Kaiping shares; there were several rumours of the mine's sale to the Japanese, and certainly an informal offer was made in 1935.[35] Moreover, after the Tanggu Truce excluded Chinese forces from the area, the KMA came increasingly to depend on the Japanese for the maintenance of law and order. On the other hand trouble-making activities by agents of Japanese military intelligence created unrest among the workforce.[36] The peddling of opium and other drugs by Japanese agents who were protected by the mine police, among whom Japanese influence was also strong, was seen by the mine management as one of their most serious problems.[37] So by mid-1936 the chief manager was talking of a likely need to admit Japanese into partnership.[38] Some first steps were taken that year with the hiring of Japanese advisers to work with the administration on security and labour matters.[39] While the mine remained under British control even after 1937, the need to consider Japanese interests acted increasingly as a constraint on company policy.

The Japanese were also keen to win a stake in other large north Chinese mines as part of a concerted policy to gain control over Chinese coal resources.[40] The main avenue through which they could do this was by making loans to mines in trouble in the depression. Thus loans were made to Liuhegou in the mid-1930s, although Chinese banks remained the company's main creditors, and talk of the mine falling into Japanese hands was premature.[41] The Zhengfeng Company, which was run by the family of the pro-Japanese Duan Qirui, had a ¥1.5 million loan from Ōkura, although Japanese sources said this was merely taken out to give the mine some protection against occupation by Duan's enemies.[42]

So by 1937 the Chinese had had some success in restricting European penetration. But in the 1930s the country was facing the most serious threat to its sovereignty since the 1898 crisis, and the coal industry was again involved, with the increasing Japanese use of Manchurian and north Chinese fuel to prepare their war machine for the invasion of China.

The politics of collaboration: foreign investors and their Chinese partners

Most of the foreign mines in China were at least in form Sino-foreign enterprises. The main (and very important) exceptions were the mines run by the SMR in Liaoning. But the British collaborated with the Chinese in the two joint sales organizations of Kailuan and Fu-Zhong (later Zhong-Fu); the Japanese joined with them to operate Luda and Benxihu, the

Russians in Muleng and Zhalainuoer, and the Germans in Jingxing. Why was this the predominant form?

The reasons were again primarily political, lying in the fact that the Chinese government retained formal sovereignty. Hou Chi-ming points out the advanced nature of even the early Chinese mining regulations, and suggests that they could well have acted as examples for more-recently independent countries.[43] While the exact provisions differed through the various versions of the mining regulations, all but one version stipulated Chinese participation, most of 50% and in 1931 of 51%. The later regulations in particular also stipulated Chinese participation in or even domination of administrative decision-making.

Early mining contracts generally specified some form of joint operation. The 1899 agreement for mining in Sichuan provided for a Chinese managing director and a foreign assistant director, and for the first 50% of the capital to be Chinese, the second foreign.[44] Other agreements, such as that with the Syndicat du Yunnan in 1902, made only vague references to Chinese participation,[45] and in this early period the Chinese partners often proved to be mere front men. The mines at Kaiping, Jiaozuo and Zichuan proved in practice to be completely controlled by foreign interests.

But the rise of Chinese nationalism, reaching a peak in the rights recovery movement and again in the late 1920s and early 1930s, made the joint company into an appropriate compromise between the Chinese and foreign positions. We have seen above how the Chinese set up competitors for the foreign companies at Jingxing and Kaiping-Luanzhou, forcing the foreign firms into a Sino-foreign form of organization. Similarly in Jiaozuo the Peking Syndicate joined in 1915 with its Chinese competitor, Zhongyuan, in a joint sales organization known as the Fu-Zhong Corporation.[46] Although the formation of such organizations, rather than the outright recovery of the rights that had been the stated aim of the establishment of the Chinese competitor, was generally regarded as a defeat for the Chinese, it did nevertheless allow the Chinese some voice in the operation of the foreign mines.

In other countries, such as Russia and post-independence India, foreign firms actively sought local collaborators because of their ability to deal with the local authorities and with the labour force.[47] This added another incentive for collaboration to that provided by government regulations and political pressures. In China, however, foreign firms preferred to employ compradores or hire agents rather than to recruit Chinese business partners as a way of dealing with the problem of adjustment to local conditions; they used the contract labour system to shield them from too much contact with the workers. For them the pressure towards collaboration was primarily political, and from a management point of view they would have preferred to run the enterprises on their own.

Foreign companies did sometimes express appreciation for the services of their Chinese managers. Gu Zhen, who joined Kailuan in 1929, provided vital links with the bureaucracy and especially with the railway administration. The British chief manager described Gu's services as of immense value. Nevertheless it was political pressure exerted through the government rather than such considerations which led to the formation of the joint company in 1912 and instigated the reorganization of 1934 that led to Gu's appointment as joint chief manager.[48]

Once the joint firms were founded, numerous accusations were made that (despite formal equality) real power lay in the hands of the foreigners. It was practically a universal opinion among the Chinese, whether in respect of the Sino-British KMA or Fu-Zhong,[49] of Sino-Japanese companies like Benxihu or Luda,[50] of the Sino-German Jingxing,[51] or even of those companies with no foreign share of equity capital but operated jointly with foreign creditors.[52]

Nor were such claims merely nationalist rhetoric. An examination of the internal organization of such mines shows that the foreigners did indeed hold the dominant position. In Kailuan up to 1934 the chief manager was British, this being practically guaranteed by the wording of the supplementary agreement for the formation of the KMA.[53] In addition four of the five collieries had Belgian staff in most of the major positions, despite the fact that two mines had originally been opened by Luanzhou; only at Majiagou did Chinese staff run the mine.[54] In this case there was not even formal equality. Not only did the Japanese remark on the real British control over the mines,[55] but even the British chief manager wrote of 'effective foreign control' over the KMA even after the 1934 reorganization.[56]

In the two major Sino-Japanese companies, the agreement at Benxihu specified equality in numbers between Chinese and foreign staff, while in Luda there was a built-in Chinese majority on the board.[57] This formal equality in fact merely proved a front. At Benxihu not even the letter of the agreement was adhered to, as only about one-third of all staff members were Chinese.[58] At Luda, seventy-one out of the eighty-nine staff members in the mining department, the key organ that actually ran the Zichuan mines, were Japanese.[59] The Japanese themselves acknowledged that they made the real decisions in the company.[60]

Thus formal specifications favourable to the Chinese were insufficient to ensure them genuine control. The real determinants of the balance of power can again be located primarily in the sphere of politics, as was shown by the reaction of the various companies to the rise of Chinese nationalism. The

British compromised; the Japanese did not. Of the two major British mines, the Peking Syndicate mines at Jiaozuo were closed by a patriotic strike in the wake of the May 30 Movement in 1925. Although they were later allowed to mine enough coal just to keep the boilers working and the pumps going, they did not properly resume operations until 1933. Then, against a background of fervent opposition by local nationalist groups, the joint sales administration with Zhongyuan was re-established, this time with the Chinese partner as the senior, holding just over 50% of the capital.[61]

Kailuan, although less severely hit, also felt the pressure of Chinese nationalism, and agreed to alter the balance of its internal organization to give an at least formally equal say to the Chinese Luanzhou company, and to appoint joint Chinese and foreign chief managers, instead of the powerless Chinese director-general and a British chief manager who held all the real authority. Moreover a systematic policy was instigated of replacing foreign with Chinese staff at the mines. This was made easier for the British by their dissatisfaction anyway with many of the Belgian middle-ranking staff but, as the British manager put it, it meant that they were 'robbing other mines in China of the best of their men'.[62]

Not only was there no question at all of shifting the balance in the Benxihu Company in Manchuria towards the Chinese side, but even in Shandong the nationalist movement proved quite unable to shake the Japanese position in Luda. It failed even to replace the Chinese directors with men who would pursue a more assertive policy with regard to the Japanese.[63] The difference can mainly be accounted for by the firmer backing given to the Japanese companies by their government, while the position of the British in China was gradually weakening; the KMA's foreign manager attributed the decline in the power and influence of the foreign staff 'partly to the weakening of the attitude of the British government and partly to their own inability to adapt themselves to the altered conditions under which they were required to work'.[64]

There were other reasons also for the stronger foreign position. Their greater financial resources put them in a strong bargaining position with their Chinese counterparts. This is shown particularly in the case of Luda where, initially at any rate, the political situation favoured China, as the European powers were pressing Japan to reduce its presence there; but the advantage was largely lost when the Chinese had to make concessions in order to get the Japanese to agree to reduce the amount of equity capital to be raised.[65] In the KMA, too, Luanzhou's directors were constrained by the conditions of raising capital in China, continually facing strident demands from their shareholders for high dividend payments, while the British shareholders were more understanding in times of difficulty. Luanzhou also often found it hard to match the British in providing working capital when Kailuan needed it.[66]

Foreign staff often possessed greater technical experience and expertise, which enabled them to exercise disproportionate influence. This is very difficult to quantify or even to document, as one must beware of taking at their face value all the strictures of foreign observers. Nevertheless, particularly in the first two decades of the century, the major Chinese-owned mines did find it necessary to hire foreign technical staff, and when Zhongxing wished to modernize in the 1930s it re-engaged a German chief engineer.[67] In 1932 the KMA's chief manager said that the Chinese staff there made 'little positive contribution' to technical operations because they had insufficient prestige.[68] Within two years, however, Kailuan began to replace foreign staff with Chinese, and with the growing numbers of trained Chinese engineers this reason for foreign predominance was probably becoming less compelling.

Foreign mines and the Chinese authorities

The relationship of the foreign mines to the Chinese authorities was a complex and changing one. They were able to win some special privileges and particularly to resist irregular imposts, but after the rise of Chinese nationalism the authorities sporadically attempted to undermine their position and even to restore ownership to Chinese hands.

Taxation was one area of special privilege. The agreements under which foreign mines operated mostly included a clause detailing the taxes to be paid. This was, however, only one avenue through which favourable rates could be obtained, and there was no great difference in the treatment of Chinese and foreign mines as far as regular taxes specified by the central government were concerned. In fact the rates for most of the early foreign mines were based on those granted to Kaiping before it fell into foreign hands. These terms, consisting of 0.1 taels per ton duty and 84 large cash per ton likin, emerged from a series of memorials and predated the establishment of a unified mine tax system.[69] In the 1900s and early 1910s not only foreign mines like Lincheng and Jingxing won similar concessions, but also Chinese mines like Zhongxing and Luanzhou.[70] The Japanese mines opened between 1905 and 1911 had slightly different terms: Fushun paid J¥50,000 per annum in lieu of likin, and also a 5% *ad valorem* tax on the value of output, which was agreed to be 1 tael per ton if output was under 3000 tons per day and J¥1 if output exceeded that figure.[71] Benxihu paid

0.1 taels per ton mine tax plus 0.06 taels in lieu of likin. It was the only case in which specific mention of a mining-area tax was made, at 0.2 taels per mou.[72]

Even after the 1914 regulations laid down standard taxes of 30¢ per mou area tax and 1.5% *ad valorem* on the value of output, foreign mines continued to enjoy special terms, even where, as with Kailuan, the amalgamation agreement specified compliance with Chinese mining regulations when promulgated.[73] Moreover, the most important foreign mining company set up after 1914, the Sino-Japanese Luda Company, was able to insist on special terms whereby it paid ¥50,000 in settlement both of mining-area tax and of mining-product tax on output up to 800,000 tons, only paying the 1.5% *ad valorem* tax over that level.[74] Yet the regular Chinese tax was relatively light and, as Chinese mines were often able to win total exemption for limited periods,[75] foreign sources even claim the tax system favoured Chinese mines over foreign ones.[76] Even if that was not so, the special provisions for foreign mines gave them little advantage.

Nevertheless that is not the whole story, because Chinese mines were much more vulnerable to the extra taxes and imposts levied by local authorities and warlords. Foreign mines were mostly able to call on diplomatic support and gain exemption from this burden. In 1910 the Belgian minister protested to the Foreign Ministry over illegal likin taxes imposed on Lincheng coal in contravention of the agreement.[77] The problem was at its most serious during the warlord period and especially in the 1920s, when the regular tax amounted to only a small proportion of the total tax burden placed on Chinese mines. Foreign companies escaped more lightly. When the military governor of Shandong tried to raise taxes on Luda coal, he was forced to back down by Japanese consular pressure.[78] When another warlord tried to levy tax on coal used by Kailuan, the company was able to refuse.[79] The tax burden on foreign companies' coal was much closer to that prescribed in the regulations than was that on Chinese mines. So, where the two coals competed, foreign mines enjoyed a definite, if limited, edge.

Backing from foreign diplomatic or even military power also enabled foreign mining companies to escape the irregular exactions that were levied on Chinese companies especially in the 1920s, as warlords demanded lump sums for military funds. Kailuan's chief manager acknowledged the value of foreign connections in this regard:

> While these civil wars were raging in the area in which we operate, the value of British protection and of the foreign staff was repeatedly demonstrated. There is no question that the existence of the British

interest in the [Kailuan Mining] Administration, and, for the first half at least of the period, the strong attitude maintained by the British government saved the Administration time and again from spoilation by the different warlords who secured successively control of the area.[80]

The KMA was pressured to advance 'loans' to militarists, and was prepared to spend money to bribe local warlords into friendship.[81] But foreign protection ensured that demands – and payments – were never as outrageous as those made on Chinese companies. Again to quote Kailuan's manager:

> All the authorities here are very hard up: they feel that the only concern in this area that has any money at all is the Administration and they would very much like to get money out of us, but do not know how to do so, and they are particularly anxious at the moment not to provoke any trouble with any British interest.[82]

Japanese companies were even less willing to compromise and, because of stronger support from their government, enjoyed even greater freedom from such problems. There can be little doubt that for a limited period the ability of foreign companies to avoid paying these extra taxes and imposts gave them a substantial advantage.

Railway freight rates and conditions were the second major area where mining companies could gain a march on their rivals. Again the formal agreements gave foreign companies little advantage, again because their Chinese competitors were able to gain similar concessions by different channels. A large variety of rates was offered to different companies by different railways, and rigorous comparison is difficult. In some cases it seems that foreign companies enjoyed a definite advantage: on the Zheng–Tai, Jingxing paid 0.614¢ per ton km for a full train load in the 1930s; of the neighbouring Chinese-owned companies, Zhengfeng paid 0.885¢ and Baochang 1.805¢.[83] On the other hand, the rates obtained by Zhongxing on the Jin–Pu were not only lower than those granted to Kailuan, but were the lowest for any company in China.[84] In general the superior location of foreign-owned mines was more important than any slight advantage they might have enjoyed in unit freight rates.

Much more important was the greater security of transport they enjoyed. The differential effect of civil-war disruption on the various railway lines was discussed in Chapter 6. Chinese-, as well as foreign-owned, mines along a particular railway benefited from its relative stability, and the mines of Boshan, for instance, were at least as able to take advantage of the opportunity afforded by the continuing operation of the Jiao–Ji as was the Sino-Japanese Luda Company.[85] Yet foreign connections still helped individual mines, making it more difficult for warlords to confiscate the rolling stock which was separately owned by major companies; Kailuan, owning its own stock, was less vulnerable than most to the general depletion of freight capacity. Again, even while transport on the Jing–Han was almost entirely at a standstill, Jingxing, although it had only 25% German participation, still had special trains running, allowing it to monopolize the market along that railway. Thus, in contrast to the series of heavy losses made by other mines, in only one year did Jingxing fail to make a profit.[86]

Foreign interests were very well aware of the importance of their control over the railways. The chief manager of the KMA wrote: 'What we want, if we can get it, is action by the Powers calculated to ensure that the railways shall not be controlled by Chinese militarists, but that their free use for civilian traffic shall be continuously possible.'[87] They were equally aware of the important advantages more reliable transport gave them over less fortunate companies,[88] advantages that were paralleled on a larger scale by the special position of the Treaty Ports in the Chinese economy.

The rise of the Nationalist government from 1928 faced the foreign companies with a new set of problems. The new government reduced, though by no means completely removed, the incidence of excessive taxation and railway disruption.[89] This made for a more-stable environment for foreign mines, but the improvement was greater for Chinese mines, which now offered increasingly serious competition.[90] The new government began with an aggressive policy of rights recovery, but increasingly its major concern became the provision of the ordered environment that would remove the justification for foreign privileges such as extraterritoriality. In this context it was keen to integrate foreign mines more completely into Chinese administrative arrangements.

Foreign companies reacted to these problems in ways in keeping with the general position of their country in China. Japanese interests, as we have seen, brooked no compromise, but the British, whose interests in China were more peripheral to their other concerns, had to and were prepared to give ground before the rise of Chinese nationalism. Both the Peking Syndicate and the KMA had to recognize Chinese claims through internal reorganization. The KMA was also faced with demands for its return to Chinese control, but the government soon reverted to more practical objectives.[91] The lack of any clear definition or mapping of the Kailuan mining area in the 1912 agreement gave the new government considerable leverage to extract concessions.[92] Therefore from mid-1934 Kailuan agreed to pay regular mining taxes, backdated to 1 July 1933, according to Chinese mining law.[93] In return in December 1935 they obtained at last a mining permit, and one for an area larger than could have been obtained from a 'strictly honest Minister of Industries'.[94] Despite its origins, by the mid-1930s the KMA fitted in well with the government's policy of cooperation with foreign capital on conditions of equality and integrated into Chinese tax and other industrial legislation.

Foreign mines in the Chinese economy

Very different interpretations can be given to the predominance of foreign or Sino-foreign mines in the industry. Some argue that it is a measure of the contribution foreign investors made to the Chinese economy, others that it shows that privileged foreign mines impeded the growth of the indigenously owned sector. To make a definitive analysis of either position would require much more data than is available, but there is sufficient information to argue that neither adequately describes the reality of the impact of foreign investment.

The first possible contribution that might be made by foreign investment is the supply of otherwise unavailable capital, and thereby the creation of new incomes and employment. Hou Chi-ming concludes:

> Foreign capital played a significant role in bringing about whatever economic modernization existed in China before 1937. The most obvious link between foreign investment and China's economic modernization was that the former not only performed the pioneering entrepreneurial function of introducing modern technology into a number of fields, but also accounted for a large share of the modern sector of the economy.[95]

Elsewhere Hou implicitly equates the share of foreign mines in the industry with the contribution of foreign capital.[96]

There are two reasons why one cannot accept such a simple equation. First, in the case of Kailuan, the second-largest foreign mine, foreign control was gained not by investing capital, but by issuing bonus shares to foreign creditors.[97] While foreign funds were certainly lent to the company, they were repaid, and it is difficult to regard Kailuan's output as a foreign 'contribution' to the industry.

Such an argument also assumes either that no Chinese funds would have been forthcoming to develop the projects that were in fact undertaken by foreign capital, or that such funds as might have been available were put to equally profitable and productive uses. In the former case one would expect to see a direct request by the Chinese for foreign funds, and in some cases this is what happened. But many of the major foreign mines originated less in a consciously felt Chinese need for capital than in foreign seizure of Chinese rights. The clearest case of this is the German mine in Shandong, the cession of the rights for which was forced from the Chinese using the pretext of a missionary incident.[98]

The cases of other mines were generally more complicated, with at least a degree of Chinese acquiescence in the original foreign investment. Nevertheless, while the Fushun mine had borrowed Russian funds, the Japanese takeover was through military and political force, and much of their later investment was financed out of profits; again it would be wrong to see Fushun output as a net foreign contribution. Similarly Jiaozuo: while the origins of the concessions lay in the request for a loan by a Chinese company, the actual working of the concessions was performed over strong Chinese protests. The Chinese themselves set up mines in the area, and it is difficult to say with certainty that these would not have expanded their output in the absence of foreign capital to a total equal to that of the Chinese and foreign mines.

These arguments should not be taken to imply that foreign capital made no contribution to the Chinese coal industry. The required rate of return on foreign capital was below that on Chinese , which led Chinese companies sometimes successfully to resort to foreign loans when domestic sources of capital proved insufficient. And while one cannot say, for instance, that Fushun would not have been developed by the Chinese, it is unlikely (but not impossible) that its expansion would have been so great and so rapid.

Moreover, the second possibility – that Chinese funds that might have been invested in the mines found other equally profitable outlets – remains, and makes any final answer to the question impossible. Even if some of the funds were diverted to consumption, and that consumption went to improve the low standard of living of the Chinese masses, that equally could have been a contribution. But it may well rather have been that the money not invested in mines went to finance not peasant consumption but luxury consumption, partly of imports, by the elite.

Foreign investment is also credited with the introduction of modern technology into developing countries. There is, of course, no question that the development of the modern Chinese coal industry required the importation of Western technology. As we have seen, before the training of a corps of Chinese engineers and the development of a machine-making industry, imported technicians and machinery were needed. While some mines and machine shops developed limited manufacturing capacity, sufficient to supply small mines with the basis for modern operations,[99] large mines were still dependent on imports for major items of equipment. Zhongxing bought most of its equipment from Germany or Switzerland even in the 1930s,[100] and the mines at Datong in Shanxi were developed in the decade before the war with the use of Japanese machinery.[101]

But the very hiring of foreign engineers and import of machinery raises the question as to what if any advantages foreign investment brought in this respect. If any advanced and patented technology is involved it can be cheaper for the imported country to use it through a foreign investor, but coal mines did not use such advanced technology, only equipment standard in Europe for two decades. There was therefore little problem in acquiring the necessary technology and little advantage in the special connections available through foreign investors.

Indeed such connections could be positively damaging if they lead to the use of equipment not suited to local factor proportions. The employment of unnecessarily capital-intensive technology is a frequently heard criticism of foreign companies operating in underdeveloped countries.[102] In China such criticisms were also made of the German engineer at Zhongxing in the early 1910s, whose connections with German capital-goods manufacturers led to his insistence on the most complete modernization.[103] But, as shown in Chapter 3, foreign managers were well aware of the advantages of using labour-intensive methods where wages were low.

A further contribution foreign firms can make to developing countries is the training of local technical and managerial personnel.[104] Kailuan set up a training school for foremen, and in 1936 it established an apprenticeship scheme for young graduates.[105] Nevertheless the foreign companies did not fulfil this role very well, and most staff remained foreign. In Japanese mines this was the case up to 1937: Japanese technical personnel ran both the Luda and the smaller Bodong mines in Shandong throughout the period.[106] The same was even more true for the Manchurian mines, as Fushun made very little contribution to the technical education of Chinese engineers.

When Kailuan decided to change the policy of using foreign staff, it recruited Chinese staff from other mines, robbing them of their best men. Since Chinese mining companies, particularly Zhongxing, had been most central to the training and early careers of many of these men, it appears that Kailuan was actually parasitic. Certainly there is little evidence of a major or concerted effort by foreign mines to train local staff except at the lowest level.

References to the 'oppression' of Chinese mines by competition from foreign mines are legion in Chinese sources both at the time and since 1949. But the whole question is something of a quagmire. It is by no means sufficient merely to quote, as Hou Chi-ming does, the evidence of a stable or even growing Chinese share in total output as indicating that there was no such oppression.[107] For it is possible – indeed likely – that in the absence of foreign investment the Chinese sector would have been larger than it actually was: that is, unless *no* Chinese funds were displaced from mining by the foreign investment. On the other hand, total output would almost certainly have been smaller, as Chinese investors would not have supplied as much capital as that imported by foreign concerns, nor would they have practised such a high rate of reinvestment.[108] How one should weight the importance of Chinese ownership against growth of total output is a political more than an economic question and cannot be answered in any rigorous way. What will briefly be examined here is how important the 'foreignness' of a foreign mine was in its competition with its Chinese rivals.

Our earlier discussions showed that, while scheduled tax and freight rates gave foreign mines at the very most a marginal advantage, their greater freedom from irregular imposts and disturbances was a major factor in the relative profitability of foreign mines during the civil wars. But in the longer term, geology and particularly location were overwhelmingly the most important determinants of a mine's success, relative and absolute, provided that even the fairly low level of political and social stability attained in China in the 1910s and 1930s was maintained. On the whole the foreign mines were well endowed in this respect, Fushun enjoying exceptionally favourable geological conditions, Kailuan a location close to sea transport. On the other hand, when a Chinese mine had similar advantages, it also enjoyed success. Zhongxing, for example, recorded very high profit figures in most years, and Kailuan's management feared it as a competitor. 'We are trying to prevent Chung Hsing [Zhongxing] from competing with us in Japan, to which country they last year started exporting their coal. As it is a superior coking coal to ours they could do us serious harm in the Japan market unless we come to some arrangement with them.'[109] Even in the 1930s when Kailuan's profits were very badly hit indeed by the depression, Zhongxing was still making ¥1.50 per ton profit, one of 25% on subscribed capital.

This is not to argue that other Chinese companies were in general as successful or as profitable as foreign companies; merely that it was the good location and geology of Kailuan and Fushun which were most important for their success, except in the late 1920s. During the civil wars foreign connections were invaluable in protecting a company against exactions and in keeping open communications. At other times the foreignness of a foreign company was not decisive.

8

CHINESE ENTREPRENEURS AND THE CHINESE STATE

Although the huge foreign mines produced most of China's coal, the majority of mining companies were still Chinese owned. While foreign enterprise dominated the coastal areas, in the interior Chinese companies produced and sold most of the coal. Even in the coastal markets, a small number of Chinese-owned mines were able to compete with the foreign giants. So output from modern mines under Chinese control grew strongly over the period, at just over 10% per annum (see Table 36).

This growth was the result of the investment of considerable amounts of capital by Chinese entrepreneurs over the period. Both the figures compiled by Yan Zhongping[1] (which are, admittedly, suspect) and the *a priori* assumption that around ¥10 investment produced one ton of annual output suggest that total investment by Chinese capitalists was, by the mid-1930s, around ¥70–80 million. In addition they invested a slightly smaller amount, around ¥40–50 million according to Yan, in Sino-foreign companies, although these investments were often in the form of mining lands rather than cash or other liquid assets.[2]

The changing nature of China's society and economy at any particular time determined the sources of this capital and the type of investors involved. In this, as in other aspects of the industry's history, whereas the overall level of activity was influenced primarily by the economic interplay of supply and demand, the pattern of that activity reflected at least as much the ephemeral political changes in China. Thus relations both with the formal state machine and with individual bureaucrats in it were often a key determining factor in the success or failure of individual mining enterprises.[3]

The social origins and environment of Chinese entrepreneurs and investors

Up to 1895 the state was the main entrepreneur in Chinese industry. First, provincial officials set up arms factories, but by the 1870s a new type of enterprise, with both state and private participation, began to engage in

Table 36. *Annual average output from large mines under Chinese control*

Period	Average annual output ('000 tons)	Percentage of total large-mine output
1902–6	325	25.8
1907–11	866	23.6
1912–16	1,116	14.6
1917–21	3,126	26.5
1922–6	4,189	26.6
1927–31	4,064	22.7
1932–6	6,702	28.1

other types of industry, often subsidiary to arms manufacture. Various formulae were used to attract private investment, but that of official supervision and merchant management (*guandu shangban*) was the most common.[4] Although some officials, such as Zhang Zhidong, continued to prefer full state control, the joint company became the predominant form by the 1890s, and even Zhang was often forced to try to attract merchant participation in his enterprises.[5]

Coal mining closely followed this pattern. Active interest among the bureaucracy in mining coal began in response to a temporary shortage of British coal in the early 1870s, after which the authorities at the Fuzhou shipyard in Fujian decided to develop the coal resources of Taiwan. In 1876 they began to open a mine at Jilong in north Taiwan, using the services of an English engineer.[6] The first coal was produced in 1877 but, despite various measures taken over the following twenty years, the mine was never a success. The deposits at Jilong have never proved capable of sustaining a very large mining industry, but the early twentieth-century history of mining there under the Japanese shows that this was not the only constraint,[7] and indeed four factors were operative which were to prove common problems for China's early coal mines: uneven quality of coal because of incomplete modernization of operations; competition from low-cost native mines exploiting shallow seams; transport difficulties which raised the price of the coal at market; and a bureaucratization of management which prevented necessary decisions from being taken along commercial lines.[8]

Similar linkages with other state enterprises – the supply of coal for the arsenals or the provision of cargo for the China Merchants' Steamship Navigation Company – ensured continuing interest on the part of the authorities in running coal mines. Some officials tried to follow the Taiwan example and do without private capital, as did Zhang Zhidong, who opened two unsuccessful mines in the 1890s to provide fuel for his Hanyang ironworks. These were completely state run,[9] but they were to be the exceptions to the increasing role of private investors in the industry. This was the result mainly of the financial difficulties of the government, and in the 1880s and 1890s funds for coal mining increasingly came from the pockets of private individuals, whether gentry, merchants or officials. The political influence of a high official and the capital and commercial expertise of the treaty port merchants was the combination that went into the most successful state-sponsored enterprises,[10] such as the Kaiping coal mine.

Kaiping was established in 1878 and was run for Li Hongzhang, the governor-general of Zhili, by Jardine's former compradore, Tang Tingshu. Li provided some initial capital from government funds, but the mine expanded in the 1880s mainly with money raised by Tang in Shanghai. Kaiping was the only fully modernized mine in China in this period, and rapidly expanded its output to cover 200,000 tons per annum by the late 1880s. It drove foreign coal out of the Tianjin and Hebei markets, and secured for itself a small but expanding stake of the Shanghai market. The importance of Tang's connections and ability was brought home by the need for his bureaucrat successor, Zhang Yanmou, to resort to foreign funds in the early 1890s, thus laying the basis for the foreign takeover in 1900.[11]

Other joint state–private enterprises were opened during the late 1870s or early 1880s in Hubei, Anhui, Guangxi, Shandong and Hebei. Most suffered from the uneven quality of product, poor communications and unimaginative management that had plagued the Jilong mine. The most successful of them, that at Yi xian in south Shandong, drew its capital initially from the local gentry rather than from treaty port merchants. Its good access to the Grand Canal enabled the mine to build up a large market in the traditional sector of the economy, and its expansion – never beyond the opening of small pits with steam-powered winches for raising coal and water – was funded mainly by bureaucrats in Li Hongzhang's entourage, a development which foreshadowed the predominant early twentieth-century pattern of investment by individual bureaucrats. The Yi xian mine remained highly profitable up to 1895, when the conservative governor, Li Bingheng, used the pretext of a serious accident to close it down.[12] But that year the situation of Chinese industry was transformed by much wider events.

A new era began for coal mining in 1895, in the aftermath of the signing of the Treaty of Shimonoseki. As an indirect result of the treaty, foreign capital and entrepreneurs flowed into the industry.[13] Particularly in the next eight years (1895–1903) and to some extent right up to 1937, this formed the context in which Chinese entrepreneurs operated, either in cooperation with or in reaction against those foreign interests.

Up to 1903 cooperation was the key note, as Chinese entrepreneurs, whether private or state, found that they had insufficient resources to develop mines on their own. So even the enterprise whose organization showed the most continuity with the previous period was developed with the aid of foreign loans. Zhang Zhidong was continuing his search for fuel for the Hanyang ironworks, which in 1896 he had changed into a *guandu shangban* enterprise under Sheng Xuanhuai, and in 1897 he decided to exploit the coal deposits at Pingxiang in Jiangxi. Financed with German loan capital, Pingxiang expanded to become the largest Chinese-owned mine in the country up to 1920. Along with Hanyang and the Daye iron mines it became part of the private Hanyeping Company in 1908.[14]

Other mine owners were in effect, if not necessarily in intention, mere front men for foreign interests, and several important foreign mines originated in this way. The mining centre of Jiaozuo in Henan, operated in the twentieth century partly by the British Peking Syndicate, originated in 1898 when the Yufeng Company acquired the rights to minerals in Huaiqing prefecture, in which Jiaozuo was situated, and immediately made them over to the Peking Syndicate in return for a loan; the managers later absconded with what money had been handed over.[15] Similarly the mine at Jingxing in Hebei was first opened in 1898 by a local landlord, but less than a year later he accepted German investment in and control over the mine.[16]

Even before 1903 some far-sighted officials tried to protect China's rights. In 1897 Li Hongzhang called for the reopening of the Yi xian mines in order to forestall German ambitions in the area. The promoters, however, failed to raise sufficient funds from Chinese sources, and after negotiations with Li Hongzhang's German adviser, Gustav Detring, the Sino-German Zhongxing Company was set up the next year, in which the Germans were to subscribe 40% of the capital. The patriotic origins of the company were evidenced in the stiff terms set for German participation, and in fact no foreign capital was ever subscribed.[17]

Between 1904 and 1911, reaction and resistance to the foreign position in mining came not only to dominate the politics of the industry but also to play a considerable role in national politics. The rights recovery movement – the attempt to regain China's rights over both railways and mines – was one of the most important forums through which the provincial gentry expressed their new-found power and influence. In many cases they succeeded, with the help of provincial and local officials and sometimes of the central government, at least in limiting the concessions granted to foreign companies or in renegotiating contracts so as to leave more control in Chinese hands. Several companies were set up either to operate a concession recovered from the foreigners or to compete with a foreign mine, but insofar as political rather than economic considerations motivated the establishment of such companies, their future was not bright. A Japanese consul in Manchuria pointed out the problems:

> With China's day of peril approaching, [it is believed that] local industry must be built up and foreign imports resisted. But no detailed research into the general socio-economic situation or the relations of supply and demand is done. No comprehensive consideration is given to projected income and expenditure. No such preparations, generally necessary for establishing industries, are made. On dangerous foundations caused by these vague and immature practices, perhaps to satisfy the demands of higher officials, perhaps to answer the clamouring of the people, with no understanding of the nature of industry, Rights Recovery combines the gullibility of officials with the ignorant views of the half-understanding gentry.[18]

While it would be wrong to imagine that carefully calculated economic rationality lies behind every successful enterprise, the fact that particular rights had to be recovered and particular areas protected meant that it was difficult to guarantee economic viability along with nationalist satisfaction.

This proposition is well illustrated by the history of the Shanxi mining rights, which had been made over to the British Peking Syndicate in 1897. In 1908 the Baojin [Protect Shanxi] Company, formed by provincial gentry and traditional bankers and backed by the provincial government, bought back the rights for 2.75 million taels (¥3.85 million).[19] It is difficult to value such an asset, but any value had certainly been reduced by the discovery that the seams were thinner than hoped, and by the success of the Chinese government in preventing the Syndicate from building a railway to take the coal direct to Pukou.[20] Most of the capital was raised through the use of tax revenues, and the nature of the motivation behind the establishment of Baojin clearly emerges from the fact that, once the actual rights had been recovered, those tax revenues were redirected back to military use.[21] So the redemption payment took up nearly all of the company's capital, and very little was left over for equipment.[22] Whether because of the excessive price paid to the British, because of the inability to modernize operations, or because of later inefficient management, Baojin was never very successful financially and only at the height of the postwar boom did it manage to make even meagre profits.[23]

In remoter areas, too, the story was similar. At Jiangbeiting in Sichuan the mining rights were redeemed for 220,000 taels in 1909, when work had not even started on the mine; the deposits were never worked by modern methods until after the beginning of the war and the Guomindang retreat to Sichuan.[24] Overall, the failure of the movement is evidenced by the fact that in 1911 only about 18% of China's modern coal output came from mines owned by Chinese.

Although the political context in which they operated changed from one of cooperation with foreigners to one of opposition to them, the pattern of entrepreneurship showed some consistent trends over the late Qing period. These were for a growing privatization of the industry, but in a context where bureaucrats still played the predominant role in establishing mining companies – although now as individuals, not in their official capacity.

While the first three new mines opened after 1895 were government enterprises, that form rapidly declined, with only five out of twenty-four mines opened between 1905 and 1911 being run by the government, and another two being government-sponsored companies. Significantly, Luanzhou, the company formed by Yuan Shikai to compete with Kaiping, was the only one of these that went on to be a major producer during the Republic.[25]

Links with the state machine were still necessary, however, and these were now being provided informally rather than formally. Most investment in coal mining was still made by men who held or had held official rank. Ten of the private mine owners of the period whose origins are known were bureaucrats, only four merchants. Again the pattern was for companies which were in the future to run the larger and more successful mines to be owned by bureaucrats. The new Zhongxing Company running the Yi xian mines was sponsored by two high officials in Beijing – Yulu and Zhang Yanmou – and the driving force was Zhang Lianfen, a long-serving middle-rank official in Shandong. He created a precedent in 1908 by resigning his official position to work full time for the company.[26] Successive governors of Shandong also paid close interest, and one appointed an expectant *daotai* to help Zhang raise the necessary funds. By 1912 the origins of the major shareholders clearly illustrate this pattern: three had been officials in Shandong; three (Xu Shichang, Zhao Ersun and Liang Shiyi) were major figures in the national bureaucracy; another was the son of a former governor of Shandong; there was only one whose origins appear to have been in the Tianjin commercial world, although little is known about him.[27]

Similarly two expectant officials established a mine in Ci xian, Hebei. An expectant *daotai* – and son of a provincial governor – opened one at Liuhegou in Henan, and two mines in Fushun county in Liaoning were both run by expectant officials.[28] Not surprisingly the private investors and officers in the semi-official Luanzhou company also came from the world of officialdom, being mostly followers of Zhou Xuexi, a bureaucrat-entrepreneur in Yuan Shikai's entourage, to whom the running of the company was entrusted.[29]

Men from a commercial background also responded to the government's encouragement and invested in coal mines. Most importantly, Wu Yue, a salt merchant from Zhejiang – an occupation locating him very much in the traditional sector of the economy – invested in the Liuhegou Company in north Henan and became general manager in 1911.[30] Again a group of merchants took out a permit for the Dayaogou mine in Liaoning in 1905, and up to 1917 the mine expanded largely on the basis of further merchant investment.[31] In Anhui the Datong mine was opened in 1911 by another merchant in collaboration with a local landlord.[32] In a slightly different category was Mi Xianchen, a Yi xian member of the gentry who had run a coal mine there until forced to close by the powerful Zhongxing Company; he moved to Ningtai xian in central Shandong, where he opened the Huafeng mine.[33] These exceptions, however, are insufficient to undermine the general picture of the industry as dominated by bureaucrats and men with bureaucratic connections.

Taking into account the changing *loci* of political power in China, much the same was true in the early Republican period up to 1927. Especially in north China, the large mines were controlled either by the warlords themselves or by their associates. Table 37 summarizes the information we have on the shareholders, directors and chief managers of Chinese coal mines between the fall of the Qing and the rise of the Guomindang government. Over 75% of the persons identified came from the civilian or military bureaucracies. Although most of the 'unknown' group would probably fall outside this category, if the overall percentage was weighted by size of mine and the importance of the personnel within each mine, then the picture of bureaucratic predominance would be strengthened.

This presents a stark contrast to developments in China's consumer industry centre, Shanghai, where Parks Coble describes the rise to power of a Shanghai capitalist class to a large extent independent of China's political rulers:

> Particularly during the decade prior to 1927, when the disintegration of the political system reached its peak, the political and economic power of the Shanghai capitalists grew rapidly. The capitalists developed their own independent organizations and, in the absence of a strong central government, gained control of banks and enterprises that originally were semi-government in nature.[34]

The pattern of entrepreneurship in Shanghai's cotton mills showed the emergence of this more-independent commercial and industrial class; only three of the fifteen cotton mills set up by Chinese entrepreneurs between

Table 37. Background of leading Chinese personnel at the major Chinese and Sino-foreign coal mines, 1912–27

Province	Mine	Approximate maximum output in period ('000 tons)	Background of leading personnel				
			Bureaucracy Civilian	Military	Banking	Industry/commerce	Unknown
Hebei	Kailuan[a]	4,500	7	2	—	—	2
	Jingxing[a]	650	4	—	—	—	7
	Zhengfeng	350	1	3	—	—	—
	Lincheng	250	3	—	—	—	1
	Yili	250	1	1	—	2	2
	Zhonghe	200	—	—	—	—	—
	Liujiang	200	1	—	—	3	—
	Changcheng	150	—	3	—	—	1
Heilongjiang	Hegang	200	4	—	—	—	1
Rehe	Beipiao	300	2	—	—	—	—
Jilin	Muleng[a]	200	2	—	—	—	—
Liaoning	Benxihu[a]	450	4	1	—	—	—
	Fuzhouwan	100	2	2	—	1	2
Shandong	Badaohao	50	—	2	—	—	1
	Zhongxing	850	11	8	1	2	3
	Luda[a]	700	5	2	1	2	1
	Huafeng	50	—	—	—	—	2
Henan	Zhongyuan	950	3	—	—	—	2
	Liuhegou	600	7	—	2	—	4
Shanxi	Baojin	400	1	—	—	1	1
Anhui	Lieshan	100	3	—	—	—	1
	Datong	50	1	—	—	—	—
Jiangsu	Jiawang	200	—	2	—	—	—
Hubei	Fuyuan	100	1	—	—	7	2
Zhejiang	Changxing	50	—	—	—	—	—
Jiangxi	Pingxiang	950	3	—	—	1	15

Notes: [a] Denotes a Sino-foreign company.
'Leading personnel' refers to general managers, directors and shareholders active in the company at any time between 1912 and 1927. A complete list of the persons involved, their positions and the category to which they have been assigned, together with a detailed list of the sources used, is available on request from the author.

1916 and 1922 were controlled by men whose backgrounds were primarily bureaucratic.[35]

The explanation for this divergence of experience lies mainly in the different effects of China's weak government and chaotic politics on the two groups of entrepreneurs. Shanghai capitalists were protected to a great extent by the foreign presence in the city, so that they were able to take advantage of the political situation to strengthen their independence. Mine owners in north China were much more directly exposed to the chaotic exercise of political and military power in the vacuum left by the weak central government; lacking foreign connections, they had to try to gain what protection and advantage they could by allying themselves to influential individuals in the state machine. The third section of this chapter describes the types of advantages that could be gained from such connections.

Other reasons were important too. Sheer geographical separation discouraged investment in coal mining by the Shanghai capitalists and commercial capital in general was much weaker in the north. Managers and shareholders in other north Chinese industries were also mostly from a bureaucratic background.[36] The warlords and their associates indeed held some of the largest accumulations of wealth in China, a part of which they were prepared to invest in coal mining.

Warlords and bureaucrats provided most of, for example, Zhongxing's capital. In the mid-1920s Li Yuanhong held ¥600,000 of the company's shares, and three other warlords, Zhang Huaizhi, Ni Sichong and Zhang Xun, each held over ¥200,000. Warlords or politicians also held many of the smaller shareholdings and, although shareholding does not necessarily imply investment, it is the best measure available. Control over the company was also in the hands of the warlords or politicians. Xu Shichang became chairman of the board in 1916, to be succeeded in 1919 by Li Yuanhong. The company's general manager between 1916 and 1928 was Zhu Qiqian, adopted son of Xu Shichang, who remained active in politics at least up to 1919, and whose wealth allegedly was made through the misuse of official funds.[37]

Smaller companies sometimes depended on a single warlord and his family. A merchant opened a mining company at Lieshan in Anhui in 1904, but development was seriously constrained by lack of capital. The local magistrate then introduced the operators to the governor of Anhui, the warlord Ni Sichong, regarded by observers as one of the most greedy and unscrupulous of the militarists. Ni had been involved in setting up the Jincheng Bank, and had a series of industrial investments in Tianjin. He invested ¥1 million in Lieshan, and his family continued to run the mine with great success up to the mid-1920s.[38] Similarly in Jingxing county, Hebei, a group of local notables set up the Zhengfeng Company to compete with the Germans in the area. They made little progress until they invited the son of Duan Qirui to be chairman, after which there was a substantial inflow of capital.[39]

Warlord management of coal companies was, their critics alleged, invariably dishonest, and had disastrous effects on the industry. They could point to several examples. Cao Rulin and Lu Zongyu, two leaders of the 'New Communications Clique', arranged in 1920 for the repayment of the Belgian loan to the Lincheng Mining Company, and so for the return of the mine to Chinese control. At the same time they used their political influence to force the company's owners to sell them most of the shares at a low price. Now in control, they sold Lincheng's coal cheaply to a trading company which they owned, thus draining any profits away from the remaining shareholders in the mine, and leaving Lincheng in a poor financial position.[40] Similarly, members of the Political Study Clique with political connections in Beijing were instrumental in bringing together three Chinese companies in the Jiaozuo area of Henan to form the Zhongyuan Company as a counterweight to the British presence in the area. Their critics, however, accused them of defrauding the shareholders of the original companies, and one of the clique members later absconded with the company's money.[41] Nevertheless even for individual companies other factors, such as location and quality of coal, were generally more influential in determining relative success.

On the fringes of the main north China coal-mining area and also in other fields of central China, some quite large mines were financed by Shanghai merchants or industrialists. The boom of the late 1910s had greatly increased the amount of capital in their hands, and the steep increase in the price of coal in Shanghai attracted some investment in mining. Investors paid particular attention to coalfields in central China, which would not incur the crippling cost of coal freight which was at the time the main factor behind the high price of north Chinese coal. So the owners of the Changxing mine in Zhejiang (two Shanghai merchants and shipping magnates) greatly expanded its operations, and other major Shanghai capitalists also invested in the mine. The merchant and industrialist, Zhu Baosan, was chief manager from 1922, and Yu Xiaqing, described by Coble as 'a leading commercial and banking figure' in the city, and who was at this time investing in a number of industrial and commercial enterprises – most notably in shipping[42] – was a major shareholder.[43] In addition Liu Hongsheng, Kailuan's sales agent in Shanghai, headed a group of coal merchants who, from around 1917, invested in the Liujiang mine, near

Qinhuangdao. They were able to take advantage of the high prices then prevailing in Shanghai to make large profits in these early years;[44] the group ran the mine until its occupation by the Japanese in 1935.[45] Other fringe mines were also run by merchants: Datong in Anhui, Fuyuan in Hubei, and Yuesheng in central Shandong were the major examples. But Liujiang and Yuesheng both benefited from the relative stability in their area, brought about by a strong foreign presence, while the other three were in central China, where merchant capital was much stronger than in the north. They did not really challenge the pattern of domination over the Chinese-owned sector of the industry by the large mines of Hebei and Henan run by bureaucrats or warlords.

A much more varied pattern of ownership and control characterized the Nanjing decade. Governments, provincial and national, played a more-direct role, and the more-stable environment offered some hope for private enterprise to flourish. Both as major sources of loan capital and as links to the new government, the Shanghai banks came to acquire managerial control over several mines, although ownership mostly remained with the old warlord families.

Changes were least in those areas still controlled by the militarists. In the north-east up to 1931, the warlord Zhang Zuolin and his son Zhang Xueliang invested heavily in mining and came to control most of the non-Japanese mines in Liaoning. Both government and private capital was invested in the North-east Mining Bureau, which ran the mines, and the manager was the younger brother of diplomat Wang Zhengting.[46] In Shanxi, too, the military governor, Yan Xishan, was interested in coal mining as part of his plan for an industrial base in the province. In 1924 he opened a mine in Datong in the north of the province, entrusting its management to his uncle. In 1928 he reorganized the enterprise and, as a political move to win over an important member of the local elite, appointed the son of that man as manager. In 1932 he turned the North Shanxi Mining Bureau into a nominally private company and set up the Datong Coal Trading Company in order to gain a monopoly in trading all the coal produced in the area.[47] He also fostered development in central Shanxi, and the mine operated by his North-west Industrial Company near Taiyuan was becoming a major producer when its development was interrupted by the Japanese invasion.[48]

In most of China, however, the new authorities were committed to eradicating the economic as well as the political power of the warlords; in neither were they entirely successful. Only the families of minor warlords, dead or long out of power, lost out; others held on to their investments, although sometimes after a struggle. The authorities in Anhui confiscated the Lieshan mine in 1929 as the property of Ni Sichong; in 1930 they returned the other shares to the original owners, but held on to Ni's shares over the protests of his family, and operated the mine as a joint venture. Internal disputes and economic depression prevented the mine recreating in the 1930s the success it had enjoyed in the 1920s.[49]

Ni Sichong's family also lost their investment in Zhongxing, which was confiscated in 1928 as a warlord enterprise, although in fact this was merely a manoeuvre to extract a further contribution to Guomindang military funds in addition to an earlier 'insurance' payment the company had made. Zhongxing's major creditors, the Shanghai banks which had lent the company ¥3 million in 1926, strongly objected, and Jiang Jieshi (Chiang Kai-shek) was forced to back down and to return the mine to its former owners, confiscating the shares only of Ni and another former warlord, Zhang Jingyao.[50]

In central Shandong, the Huabao mine was confiscated in 1929 by the provincial government after allegations of violence and murder on the part of its warlord manager, a follower of Zhang Xun, whose family was a major shareholder in the company.[51] In 1930, however, the mine was returned to its former owners, and Zhang Xun's wife increased the family investment in the mine and became chairman of the board in 1934.[52]

The previous owners were even more difficult to dislodge in the case of the Chinese partners in Sino-foreign companies; several attempts were made to replace the Chinese directors of the Sino-Japanese Luda Company in Shandong with nominees of the government, but the protection afforded them by the Japanese presence was sufficient to cause all these attempts to fail.[53] Indeed the only major mine that authorities did take over and keep was Lincheng in Hebei, which the provincial government ran from 1929. But the mine was never financially successful, nor did the authorities succeed in holding Cao Rulin to account for his dishonest dealings over the company.[54] Overall there was no wholesale dispossession of the warlords, most of whom retained their holdings.

Mines run by merchants or industrialists were still relatively small, although their number and importance increased to some extent over the decade. Although the Changxing mine in Zhejiang was taken over and run for four years, first by the provincial government and then by the Reconstruction Commission, its Shanghai merchant owners regained control in 1931.[55] In Shandong the Qingdao merchant and compradore, Ding Jingchen, greatly expanded the operations of his Yuesheng Company in Boshan, to an output of over 400,000 tons per annum in the mid-1930s,[56] and it is also possible that two major Shanghai industrialists invested in the area around that time.[57] Merchants also took over two medium-sized mines in central China. The dominant figure in the Lieshan Company after its return to private enterprise following the confiscation of the Ni family's holdings was a Shanghai trader, Tang Shaohou.[58] And a Shanghai merchant group headed by Liu Hongsheng took over the Jiawang Mining Company in north Jiangsu after the death of its former owner, a nephew of Yuan Shikai.[59]

Much more important mines came under the control, if not the ownership, of the major banks. The new influence of the banks lay partly in the close ties they enjoyed with the Nanjing government and their consequent political influence, but more in their ability and willingness to provide the funds sorely needed by mining companies almost bankrupted by the civil wars. Many companies became indebted to the banks in this way and had to accept some control over their affairs by the banks.

Both factors were at work with the Zhongxing Company. A consortium of Shanghai banks bailed out the company with loans of at least ¥8 million between 1926 and 1929, providing the funds to enable it to restart operations after the wars. Their influence in Nanjing also led to the restoration of the company to its former owners in 1928. Only the shares of two minor warlords remained in government hands, but a new board of directors and management reflected the changed situation. The banker Qian Yongming took over as chief manager, and Zhou Zuomin, manager of the Jincheng Bank, joined him on the board. In 1934 another banker, Ye Jinggui, became company chairman.[60]

Liuhegou in Henan was another company that fell into debt to the banks. Mainly because of the almost complete cessation of railway transport in 1926–7 when the company was unable to sell its coal, it lost nearly ¥3 million between 1926 and 1929 and another ¥2.5 million over the next four years. In the early 1930s it was paying around ¥700,000 per annum on loan repayments, and successive attempts to raise share capital in order to repay these debts met with only limited success.[61] As a result the real power in the company was exercised by Tan Jintao, the representative of the company's creditors, although Wang Zhengting, a Beijing diplomat and politician, was chairman of the board throughout the 1930s and his brother, Wang Zhengfu, held important positions in the company. With Tan and Wang Zhengfu, the third member of the management committee was Li Guangqi from the Sino-Japanese Exchange Bank, a major shareholder in the company, while Qian Yongming was also on the board.[62]

Liuhegou was far from alone in incurring debts in the late 1920s that cast a shadow over the whole of the 1930s. Changxing had a similar legacy and bankers were able to dictate company policy there.[63] At Jiawang in Jiangsu, the company owed substantial sums to the Jincheng and Salt Banks, although there the creditors had to take the directors to court (unsuccessfully) to try to assert their rights.[64] In the negotiations over the reorganization of the two companies at Jiaozuo after the establishment of the Zhong-Fu Mining Administration in 1933, the Anglo-Chinese Finance and Trade Corporation, which had lent the Administration ¥2.3 million, was one of the main advocates of reorganization.[65] So the major banks exercised a strong influence over the management of many mines in the 1930s.

The central government at Nanjing also itself became an entrepreneur in the industry.[66] Realizing that a mine well situated in central China would have good prospects of success in the Shanghai market, the National Reconstruction Commission decided in 1929 to open the Huainan mine in Anhui. Work started in early 1930 and by 1937 the value of the mine was estimated at ¥9 million, while production was over 600,000 tons per annum. The project was well chosen, and the government was prepared to raise funds not only to open the mine, but to build a railway to the Yangzi at Wuhu. As a result profits amounted to over ¥1 million in 1936 and showed every sign of increasing if the war had not intervened. In line with other enterprises run by the Reconstruction Commission, Huainan was made over in 1936 to the ostensibly private (but government-linked) China Development Finance Corporation, in which Song Ziwen was the most important, although not the largest, shareholder.[67]

Towards the end of the Nanjing decade the level of government activity increased. Song's China Development Finance Corporation entered into a joint project with the Shaanxi government to open a coal mine, while Jiang Jieshi's National Resources Commission confiscated several mines in the Xiangtan–Changsha area of Hunan in its programme for the industrial development of the region.[68] Nevertheless of the government mines only Huainan was of any importance up to 1937, and the state did not dominate the industry as it was to after the war. The pattern of ownership and control was clearly in flux, the old warlord families still retaining ownership of many mines, but new social groups advancing to influential positions at least in the management of several enterprises.

Central government policies towards the industry

The broad outlines of central government policy regarding the mining industry were contained in the various sets of mining regulations promulgated in 1898, 1899, 1902, 1904, 1908, 1914 and 1930. These laid down the requirements for the registration of a mine with the government, the degree to which foreign participation was permitted, and the various rates of tax to be paid on output, mining area and profits.

In terms of these formal regulations the hand of the central government lay rather lightly on the industry. The rights to minerals underground were recognized as property rights,[69] although the 1930 mining law limited the exploitation of iron ore, oil, copper and coking coal to the state or to those holding leases from the government.[70] Mineral rights were acquired by staking a claim with the relevant ministry (the title of which underwent several changes); after satisfactory maps and plans had been tendered and the relevant fees paid, the ministry could grant a permit if the claim did not infringe on other claims or on places of historical or commercial importance.

Holders of mining permits had to continue to provide the ministry with maps and plans of operations under way, to start those operations within one year, and to pay the necessary taxes; otherwise they could be deprived of their claim.[71] Where they did not also own the surface land they had to pay the landlord rent for land used and compensation for any damage to property due to mining operations.

Tax was levied both on mining area and on output. At first the rates were laid down in the regulations for each individual mine, but the 1902 regulations specified a 10% *ad valorem* tax on output; those of 1904, one of 5%.[72] In 1908 the regulations levied an 0.1 tael per ton tax on output.[73] The 1914 mining law, a more-complete set of regulations than the earlier ones, reduced the output tax to 1.5% of the pit-head price, and stipulated taxes on mining areas at 5¢ per mou if the area was only being prospected, 30¢ if it was being mined.[74] In 1930 the new mining law raised output tax to 2% of the 'average price in markets near the place of production', and set mine-area tax at 1¢ per are for land being prospected, and 2¢, rising to 5¢ after five years, if the land was mined;[75] an amendment in 1932 set output tax at between 2% and 10%, and coal was usually taxed at 5%.[76] Only in the late Qing was there a provision in the mining laws for a tax on company profits – 25% in 1902.[77]

Both the mine-area and the output taxes were central government taxes, the former accruing to the Ministry of Industry or its predecessors, the latter being collected by provincial governments on behalf of the Ministry of Finance.[78] As with other taxes the provinces were not always prompt in handing over the revenue to the centre.[79] Far more information on the price elasticity of demand would be needed to judge the impact of the taxes on the industry, but it is unlikely that taxes at these officially prescribed levels would have been a crippling burden. As will be described in the next section, however, these taxes were often only the tip of the iceberg, and a host of supplementary taxes did represent a real burden on the mining companies.

While mining law established the formal environment in which the central government wanted coal mining to operate, it was not the only way in which state policy influenced the pattern of the industry. The concerns of the late Qing government with the promotion of industry and more urgently with dealing with foreign incursion have been discussed in this and the last chapter. During the early Republic the central authorities were so weak that their policies had little effect on the industry. But the Nationalist government in Nanjing, with its pretensions to be a national government, not only (as described above) revived the role of the state as entrepreneur, but also was concerned to formulate policies to deal with the economic problems of the coal industry as a whole.

These problems centred on the poor financial situation of many, especially Chinese-owned, mining companies whose transport had been closed down during the civil wars and whose markets in the mid-1930s were also affected by the impact of the depression – first the flood of cheap imports and later the more-general industrial recession. The government considered three lines of action to aid the industry: financial subsidy, tariff protection and various forms of regulation or cartelization within coal mining. In addition industry interests persistently called for lower taxes and cheaper railway freight charges.

Concern over the state of the industry led in 1932 to the establishment of the Chinese Coal Relief Association in Shanghai, and the next year the Ministry of Industry called a conference of coal-mining interests to try to find a solution for their difficulties. From these there emerged a proposal for a ¥20 million bond issue to be supported by the government but to be repaid by the industry, and to be used chiefly to repair and replace the rolling stock on the coal-carrying railways. In the end, however, the government's difficulty in selling its own bonds meant that the Finance Minister, Song Ziwen, was unwilling to back such a loan.[80]

Tariff protection was undoubtedly the most important contribution by the central government towards easing the industry's problems. Brought in as part of Song Ziwen's anti-Japanese tariff policy in May 1933,[81] it survived Song's resignation (unlike the tariffs on many manufactured products), and led to a permanently reduced level of imports in China's major markets.

Some degree of cooperation or cartelization of coal sales was called for in the 1933 conference on the coal industry, and the intensive discussion in late 1933 among Chinese academic and government circles on 'economic control' touched on coal mining. The Shandong government also attempted in 1934 to form a coal cartel at a provincial level, but this foundered on the opposition of Japanese interests in the area. An all-Chinese scheme in Shanxi in late 1935 was more successful, while some of the major north Chinese mining companies also had limited agreements over cooperation in some markets.[82]

So the attempt made by the Ministry of Industry in mid-1936 to form a national coal cartel, aimed basically at freezing existing market shares, had precedents within the industry. Its explicit aim was to ameliorate the problem of excessive competition among Chinese mines, but it also provided an opportunity for the Nanjing government to extend and strengthen its influence in north China. The attempt foundered because the two groups of mines – those in central Shandong and those in Anhui – whose shares of the market were increasing most rapidly refused to participate. Even though Huainan, the major Anhui mine, was run by the National Reconstruction Commission, the Ministry of Industry had insufficient influence with that body to ensure the mine's adherence to the proposed arrangements. Even more adamant in their opposition were the Japanese interests in central Shandong; here again economic advantages militated against their participation, but more-general considerations of Japanese policy towards China also weighed heavily with the Japanese staff.

Although a formal decision was made to go ahead with the scheme, it was void without the agreement of the Shandong and Anhui mines. The abortive project illustrates well the limitations of central government power in an industry still dominated by foreign interests and concentrated in an area outside the full territorial control of the regime. Whether the government would have made any further attempts to extend its influence in this way is an open question, as the short-lived boom of late 1936 and 1937 lessened interest in the control of competition and the Japanese invasion in July 1937 changed the scene completely.

Chinese entrepreneurs and the Chinese state

Formal government policies towards the industry tell only a small part of the story, and the need for connections with the state machine to obtain special favours and privileges for individual enterprises was the main determinant of the pattern of entrepreneurship outlined in the first section of this chapter. While the wealth of the warlords and politicians, together with the paucity of alternative sources of capital in north China, offer an additional explanation, in a freely competitive capital market more funds from the Shanghai bourgeoisie would have been attracted into the industry by the high profits available. But the privileged position of the bureaucrats in the state machine enabled them either to force the cession of a mine into their hands, or to bring exceptional benefits to an enterprise in which they invested.

Before 1895 the support of a highly placed official was indispensable for the operation of a modern mine. This was partly due to the traditional prejudice against mining: even in the 1860s, a man who opened a mine could be called a 'treacherous merchant'.[83] More specifically, if a mining company hoped to sell coal in the growing treaty port market, it needed special tax concessions: the tax on native coal shipped between Chinese ports was 0.67 taels per ton, but the import duty on foreign coal was 0.05 taels. So Shen Baozhen requested a reduction of the tax on coal from the semi-modern mine in Taiwan to 0.10 taels per ton, and when this was granted the sponsors of other modern mines followed suit.[84] The governor-general, Li Hongzhang's success in getting the same terms for Kaiping largely determined the company's tax burden into the 1930s.[85] Li's tacit protection of the railway built for Kaiping, which was an indispensible contribution to the mine's success, again demonstrates the impossibility of a mine flourishing without official protection: even Li did not dare to report it to the court, so the building of a railway by any other company would have been out of the question.[86]

After 1895, when the formal links mines had with the bureaucracy through the *guandu shangban* and similar systems were gradually replaced by informal ones, the type of service rendered remained much the same. All mines had to be registered with the government and mining companies had to obtain a licence to operate within an agreed area. The initial acquisition of this licence was not always straightforward, and a director or manager with government connections was invaluable in easing the process. Opposition from the Sino-German Jingxing Company for a long time held up the granting of a licence to the neighbouring Zhengfeng Company but, after Duan Qirui's family was invited to take over Zhengfeng, such problems were quickly solved.[87] Another major warlord, Feng Guozhang, performed a similar service for a mine near Beijing.[88]

Disputes and litigation over mine-area boundaries allowed further opportunities for the exercise of political influence. When the Zhongxing Company in 1909 had a dispute over boundaries with an adjacent mine, the Ministry of Agriculture, Industry and Commerce sent Zhou Xuexi to make a report. Zhou's father was a major shareholder in the company, his brother a director. The issue was decided in Zhongxing's favour.[89] Such expedients were open not only to large modern mines. When the small Pole mining company in Jiangxi, whose chairman was a director of the Shanghai Chamber of Commerce, was involved in a dispute with its neighbours, it got an influential figure in Nanjing to intercede on its behalf.[90]

A related problem was that of competition from small mines using traditional technology. Able to produce coal at least as cheaply as their larger neighbours, such mines provided very unwelcome local competition to the major companies. At times, although by no means always, they were operating illegally actually within the area granted to the large company,[91] but in any case the big company was always eager to close them down and win for itself a monopoly in the local market. Unable to outcompete the small mines, it was forced back into trying to get the authorities to use administrative means to gain the same end. As early as the 1870s the authorities closed down small mines in Taiwan which were allegedly interfering with the operations of the modern mine there. In the 1900s the large companies operating at Pingxiang in Jiangxi and at Yi xian in Shandong benefited from government action to close down competitors. Even in the 1930s the Nationalist government put a ban on the transport of coal from small mines operating in the Jiaozuo area, thus effectively preventing them from competing with the Sino-British Zhong-Fu Mining Administration.[92]

Even abstracting from special and local taxes, mining taxation remained on an *ad hoc* basis up to 1914, and to some extent up to the 1930s. Rather than having to conform to any unified national regulations, modern mining companies tried, through their sponsors, to get the same terms as Kaiping; thus in 1908 Zhongxing's regulations stated that the company was to pay taxes on this basis.[93] The sponsors of the Pingxiang mine, Zhang Zhidong and Sheng Xuanhuai, were even more successful, securing, from 1896, four successive five-year periods of exemption from taxes, although this applied only to coal sent to the ironworks, coal sold elsewhere being subject to a low rate of tax.[94] The Baojin Company was also granted five years' exemption from likin in 1909, later extended for another two years, and again for ten years.[95]

In 1914 uniform mining regulations prescribed rates of taxes on mine output and mining area, but as the output tax was *ad valorem*, based on a rather vaguely defined 'market price', there remained considerable scope for negotiation over the actual tax paid. At the same time as the regulations came into force, the central government was rapidly losing control over the country and in the next ten to fifteen years a host of supplementary and local taxes sprang up to plague coal mines.[96] Many of these were levied as the coal was transported to market. In 1928, the Datong Company in Anhui had to pay 12¢ per ton in regular output tax, but local and supplementary taxes amounted to 33.6¢ per ton if the coal was sold at the pit-head, 49¢ per ton if it was sold at nearby Bengbu, and no less than ¥1.70 per ton if it was transported from Bengbu to Pukou.[97] Baojin had in the 1920s to pay twelve taxes totalling nearly ¥35 per twenty-ton wagonload of coal just to ship it as far as Shijiazhuang.[98]

Under the Nationalist government many of the irregular taxes were abolished, but there still remained much scope for haggling. With the fall in coal prices in the depression of the 1930s many companies requested a cut in the nominal prices used as the basis for the output tax. Zhong-Fu asked for a 50% reduction in 1936 on such grounds, although it was only granted one of 12%.[99] Simultaneous requests by the Mining Association for cuts in the *rate* of tax were firmly rejected by the government, which pointed out that the taxes paid were much lower than those paid before 1927.[100]

Room for negotiation also existed over the shipment and other taxes still levied on coal away from the mine; although much less of a burden than before, these still created a problem. Huainan's managers described the 24¢ per ton tax which had to be paid on Huainan coal shipped from Pukou to Shanghai as a serious problem.[101] This company, which had been allowed to put its tax on account in its early years, also negotiated in the Jiangsu and Anhui governments over the tax it had to pay at the port of shipment on the Yangzi (Pukou and later Wuhu).[102]

One-off demands for contributions to military funds had perhaps even more serious implications for company finances than did spiralling taxes on coal. Coal mines, situated away from the protection of the treaty ports, were particularly vulnerable to such demands and, as warfare intensified in the mid-1920s, many warlords looked to the highly capitalized (relative to other potential sources of revenue) and vulnerable coal mines to pay for their armies. Most mines were faced with such demands, although those with foreign connections were in a better position to resist them. The story of three mining companies in Ci xian, Hebei, illustrates well the problems encountered in this period. Throughout 1926 they were embroiled in wars between rival secret societies, and at the end of the year the local warlord, Chu Pupu, faced them with a demand for ¥2.5 million. The largest and best connected, Yili, got off with paying a few tens of thousands, but serious damage was done to the smaller Zhonghe and Fuan companies, and Fuan's manager was tied to a horse and dragged behind it for ten miles. Two years later, after Yili had been occupied by rebels for over six months, the company raised ¥18,000 to restart operations, but was immediately faced with demands from the army for ¥80,000; it was forced to hand over the ¥18,000 while the army took away nearly ¥70,000 worth of coal.[103]

In Shandong, Zhongxing – a much larger company – also faced similar demands. The company was paying around ¥500,000 per annum for the upkeep of Zhang Zongchang's forces in the mid-1920s, and in addition in 1927 it bought ¥900,000 of Guomindang bonds, hoping to insure itself against a Guomindang victory. In fact when the Guomindang forces did occupy the area in 1928, they demanded a further ¥5 million from the company. Even though this was reduced to ¥1 million after representations by the Shanghai banks, the company emerged from the 1920s with a heavy burden of debt.[104]

It is difficult to document the ways in which warlords and bureaucrats connected with a mine could protect it from such extortion, or the extent to which they were successful. In Zhongxing's case the relationship of the Shanghai banks to the Guomindang leadership was certainly important in getting the company off the hook, and it does also seem that Yili's better connections enabled it to escape more lightly than the other mines in Ci xian. In Shanxi, one source says that Yan Xishan's mine in Datong was able to escape extortion and indeed rather to practise it on others.[105] In Heilongjiang the owners of the Hegang mine tried (in the end unsuccessfully) to ward off an impending takeover by the provincial government by appointing a former provincial governor as their chairman.[106] Although concrete examples do not abound, all mining companies were eager to use such connections to seek protection. The fluidity of the situation meant, however, that one day's protection could be the next day's pretext for extortion: Zhongxing was well connected with the warlords, but fell foul of the Guomindang. Only in an area continuously controlled by one warlord would a well-connected mine really be able to escape the extortion.

The large mining companies with which the politician investors were connected also started out with considerable advantages in negotiating favourable railway freight terms. As suppliers of coal to the railway they were often able to reach a mutually beneficial agreement to sell cheap coal in return for cheap transport.[107] Small-mine owners consequently demanded, not always successfully, a share in the contract to supply the railway mainly in order to get a better bargaining position over transport.[108]

Further concessions could be won through the exercise of political influence. The cheapest rates in China were enjoyed by Zhongxing. In the 1910s that company's major shareholders included Xu Shizhang, who ran the Jin–Pu from 1917 to the early 1920s,[109] Zhu Yao, who also held an important post in the management of the Jin–Pu as well as several other economic posts,[110] and Shi Zhaoceng, the director-general of the Long–Hai;[111] its chief manager, Zhu Qiqian, served for a time as head of the northern section of the Jin–Pu.[112] In addition many of its shareholders were important warlords or politicians in Beijing. While one cannot document the connection, it is unlikely that the company's exceptionally good terms had nothing to do with its influential shareholders.

By the 1910s and 1920s the availability of railway capacity to transport their coal was to the mining companies of an importance often even greater than the rates charged. Ni Sichong not only procured for Lieshan preferential rates, but also allocated three trains to carry its coal; such was his influence that in the 1930s the manager described it as having been central to Lieshan's early success.[113] Similarly in Shanxi, Yan Xishan used his military and political power to gain control of the two local coal-carrying railways in Datong, thus enabling him to prevent other local mines effectively competing with his Jinbei mine. Moreover, when for a brief period in 1928–30 Yan's territory extended as far as Beijing, so that he controlled the whole length of the Jing–Sui line, he reserved six trains for Jinbei's special use and granted the mine exceptionally low freight rates. These concessions were cancelled when Jiang Jieshi took over Beijing in 1930, but revived after Yan's reconciliation with Jiang in 1932. His control over railway transport was one of the major levers Yan used to force other local mines to join the company he set up to control sales of Datong coal.[114]

During the 1930s economic power in urban industry was increasingly concentrated in the hands of government officials and their associates.[115] In the mining sector such a concentration had been almost complete in the 1910s, and in the Nanjing decade, by contrast, the ties between mining companies and government personnel weakened slightly. Increasingly the Mine Owners' Association prepared joint submissions containing reasoned arguments to the government over matters such as tax rates, railway charges or import tariffs.[116] But this process was only beginning and mining companies with no bureaucratic connections remained at a disadvantage even in the Nanjing decade.

9

THE WORKING AND LIVING CONDITIONS OF
THE CHINESE COAL MINER

Just as an independent bourgeoisie in China was only gradually emerging from among the traditional elite, so the transition from the old society to a modern one is again a key theme in the social and political history of the workers in Chinese coal mines. Their origins and work organization, their wages and conditions, as well as their level of consciousness and common action all indicate a society and economy in transition. Many features of work and the workforce still bore the imprint of the traditional agrarian society from which China was emerging, but both the imperatives of the operation of modern enterprises and the gradual awakening and politicization of the Chinese people as a whole were creating new forms more suitable and adequate for a modern industrial society, albeit one still at an early stage of development.

Who were the miners?
Probably between 200,000 and 300,000 miners worked in large and at least partly mechanized collieries during the 1930s, and several hundred thousands more were engaged in small mines for at least part of the year.[1] All the workers in the large mines and almost all those in small mines were male. Women worked in a few mines in south China: in Mei xian, Guangdong, female porters carried the coal on the surface, but no women worked underground.[2] In Chenxi county, Hunan, women also worked as hauliers underground, but this was a very rare phenomenon in China.[3]

Although many more children than women were employed, the technology that led to an increase in child employment in Britain[4] does not seem to have had the same effect in China. Some modern mines employed child labour, mostly boys in their early teens. In north-east Hebei most of the coal sorting on the surface at the Liujiang mine was done by child workers.[5] As many as 25% of the workers at the Zhongyuan mine in Henan were under eighteen, and in Zichuan, Shandong, 10% of the Luda Company's workers were under fifteen, 40% under twenty.[6] In the early 1910s a report stated that most of the fatal accidents in the Jingxing mines involved child labourers.[7] On the other hand, at the massive Fushun collieries only just over 100 out of 30,000 workers were under fifteen.[8] Similarly Lui Shaoqi, who went to Pingxiang as a labour organizer in 1922, reported that only a minute proportion of Pingxiang's workers were under age.[9] Most large mines did not report any under-age labour at all.

More children worked in the small native mines. The Chenxi mines mentioned above employed children alongside women, and in Tongguan xian in Shaanxi most of the coal was hauled along the underground roadways by young boys[10] – something very reminiscent of early modern England. There were reports of children being lured into mines in Shanxi and being forced to work there,[11] and in Sichuan children under ten were sold to miners to act as their helpers.[12] But even in the small mines the employment of children never reached the proportions or attracted the attention it did in England.

Legislation passed in 1925 banned the employment of males under twelve by mining companies, and limited females and males between twelve and seventeen to surface work,[13] but few of the act's other provisions were observed, and it is unlikely that it was an important factor behind the low level of female and child employment.[14] The fact that abundant supplies of adult male labour were available at low wages certainly accounted for much of the explanation, although the high proportion of women workers in India[15] suggests that cultural factors, too, may have played a part.

By far the most important of the cultural factors discouraging the use of female labour was the practice of footbinding. Whereas peasant women in south China often had normal feet, in the north even beggars had their feet bound.[16] As a result the participation of women in agriculture or other types of labour had traditionally been much less common in north than in south China.[17] Similarly when modern industry began to be established, the use of female workers was much more prevalent in central than in north China,[18] and observers cited footbinding as one of the reasons for the lower productivity of workers in Chinese than in Japanese textile mills.[19] Whereas the decline of the custom in the early twentieth century – Gamble's survey in Ding xian shows that under 20% of girls born between 1910 and 1914 had bound feet[20] – created a potential labour force which did become more widely used in the textile industry,[21] there was no trend towards the employment of more women coal miners. No doubt it was less acceptable to begin to introduce women into an industry such as coal mining than it was into textile mills, and so female labour was never of much significance in Chinese mines.

No such relatively simple explanation exists for the comparatively small number of child workers, but in England many child workers were part of a

Table 38. *Ages of workers at major Chinese coal mines*

Mine	Percentage of workers (in age groups)			
	25 or under	35 or under	45 or under	55 or under
Fushun	33	78	97	100
Liuhegou	10	49	78	96
Zhongxing:				
Directly hired workers	14	55	83	96
Contract workers	24	67	93	100

Sources: MMT, rōmuka, 1931, p. 28; China, shiyebu, laodong nianjian bianzuan weiyuanhui, 1933, 1:190–1; Liu and Shi, 1932, pp. 43–4.

family unit, coming from communities entirely dependent on mining. In China mining was often a subsidiary occupation and purely mining communities were still at an early stage of development, so that children were often used for agricultural tasks instead. In any case, the nature of the work meant that most workers were young male adults. A survey of over 50,000 miners in twelve mines in the early 1930s showed that 25% were between sixteen and twenty-five years old, 38% between twenty-six and thirty-five, and 25% between thirty-six and forty-five.[22]

Table 38 illustrates also other features of the age pattern of mining labour. Where labour was recruited from migrants from other provinces, as was the case in Manchuria, the average age was much lower than where there was a relatively stable local workforce. Moreover, as one might expect, skilled workers tended to be older than their unskilled counterparts: at Zhongxing, the directly hired workers, some (although not all) of whom were skilled, were considerably older than the unskilled contract labourers.

Other industries, too, used a mostly young workforce, and indeed the average age of miners was considerably higher than that of most factory workers, many more of whom were children or young unmarried women.[23] The very process of the emergence of an industrial society meant that as coal mining became established so its workforce gradually became older, and older workers, while more experienced, tended to have less physical strength. So companies were concerned to counteract the ageing of their workforce and in the 1930s Kailuan initiated a programme to weed out older workers in order to improve productivity.[24]

Traditionally coal mining had been very largely a subsidiary occupation engaged in by farmers in the off-season and, in this transitional period too, most miners were recruited from peasant stock, many companies relying on local farmers. Small mines, which mostly operated sporadically and seasonally, required a flexible labour force, and so from Chahar and Shanxi in the north to Mei xian in Guangdong they used local peasant labour, mainly on a part-time basis.[25] The large mines of the north China plain also recruited unskilled labour mostly from the local peasantry: 90% of the workers at Jingxing were locals, and 97% of the contract workers at Zhongxing came from Shandong, 89% of them from Yi xian, where the mine was situated.[26]

In some areas, most importantly Manchuria, there were too few local farmers to supply mining labour, and the major companies attempted to attract workers from other provinces. Of these some stayed, but many were single men who returned to their home provinces of Hebei or Shandong after serving a spell in the mines. As a result of its recruitment programme to attract workers from north China, only 12% of Fushun's workforce in 1930 came from the province of Liaoning, as against 82% from Shandong and Hebei.[27] Similarly Benxihu employed only 2255 workers from Liaoning, but 5054 from Shandong and Hebei.[28] While active recruitment in other provinces declined in the depression of the late 1920s and early 1930s, migrant labour remained important in the area.[29] Shortage of local labour also affected some mines in central China, and the Changxing Company in Zhejiang recruited labour from Anhui when the local supply failed in the late 1920s.[30] Mines in south Anhui were also mainly dependent on miners from the north of the province.[31]

The growth of a modern industrial and mining sector itself gradually created a proletariat which formed another potential recruiting base for companies seeking to augment their labour force. From the beginning of modern mining, skilled workers were recruited from other centres of industry, either from abroad in the case of a small number of top technicians, or from the shipyards and other industries of south and central China. The mechanics at Kaiping in the late nineteenth century were recruited from Guangzhou and Xianggang; even in the 1920s most of the mechanics there were Cantonese.[32] Later the small engineering works of Tianjin and other cities became a source of engineers for north Chinese mines: 30% of the workers in the machine shops in the mines at Datong in north Shanxi came from Hebei,[33] and over 30% of the directly hired workers at Zhongxing were migrants from other provinces.[34]

Existing mining centres were targets for recruitment by newer mines. While most of the migrant workers in the north-east were from peasant stock, efforts were also made to recruit experienced miners from Boshan. In 1929 local mine-owners expressed fears that they would be robbed of their labour force.[35] The large mines in north China established in the first decade of the twentieth century also came to supply labour to mines established later, often in central China. Half the miners in the mines of the Datong Company in Anhui came from Tangshan (the Kaiping mine) or Zaozhuang (the Zhongxing mine),[36] and workers at Maanshan in Hubei came mostly from the mining district of Daye in the same province.[37] So while the local peasantry remained the main source of mining labour to the end of our period, there was gradually emerging a potentially mobile mining proletariat prepared to take the best work it could find.

The organization of work

Forming a bridge – for the great majority of miners over the period – between the social life of their villages and homes and their working lives in the pit was the system of contract labour.[38] All systems of labour organization reflect both the type and number of workers in the unit and the level of development of society as a whole. So the contract system suited a situation where the work was of some scale but of a low level of mechanization, where national or regional labour markets were at an early stage of development, and where both workers and supervisors were unaccustomed to the exigencies of a modern enterprise.

While the basis of the contract system was for the workers a more or less free contract, albeit one with the contracting intermediary rather than with the mining company, other more-primitive forms of labour organization still existed in twentieth-century China. Unfree or semi-free adult labour, rather than child labour, was therefore the main target for reformers. Only in Sichuan do we read of the use of convicts,[39] who in Japan were forced to provide much of the workforce in nineteenth-century and even early twentieth-century coal mines,[40] but some cases of other forms of servile labour were found. In the early 1880s Zhu Cai reported that mine owners in Yi xian, Shandong, used to force workers down the mines, and kept them working there until death.[41] In the same period the governor of Hunan described debt servitude in his province, where people were ensnared into debt by gambling or drinking dens, and then forced to sell themselves to work down mines in Hengyang.[42] This situation persisted into the twentieth century, when such workers were forced to work in the most appalling conditions.[43] In several areas of Sichuan, coal mining was done by servile labour,[44] while in the north another scandal came to light in Shanxi in 1933, when provincial authorities raided some mines near Taiyuan and freed large numbers of slave workers. At these mines there were both free and slave workers; the latter had either been kidnapped by force to work in the mines, or had been inveigled there by false promises. Once they were in they were never let out, but forced to work on a totally inadequate diet and under constant threat of physical punishment.[45]

Horrifying though such reports are, most of the labour in Chinese mines was not organized in this way; unfree labour was unknown in the modern mines and rare even in mines in the unmodernized sector of the economy. Although the contract system did have some pre-capitalist features, and indeed was a common organizational form in pre-modern China, it centred in the main on a contractual relationship between a free worker and a contractor, as well as between the latter and the company.

The contract labour system was universal in modern Chinese coal mines up to the 1920s and remained the predominant form of labour organization up to 1937 and beyond. The central feature of the system was that workers were provided in groups to the company by contractors, and the company had no direct relations with that part of its workforce. In nearly all cases wage payments were made through the contractor, and in most the contractor provided supervision of the labour at work.

The contractors functioned as recruiters of labour for the company, which then did not have to bother to find unskilled workers. In the area in which the supply of labour posed the greatest problems, however, the companies played the greatest part in labour recruitment. The SMR set up recruitment offices in many areas of Hebei and Shandong, while Benxihu also recruited miners in Shandong. This suggests that recruitment was not the central function of the contractor; in Japan, on the other hand, recruitment had been the main job of the *naya* heads, and the rise and fall of the system there was closely connected to changes in the supply of labour.

More importantly, the contractor undertook functions of line management and supervision of labour that the lack of trained managerial personnel would otherwise have made into a serious problem for the company. The company contracted out sections of work to the contractor, thus instituting a 'self-acting' incentive to ensure that he had an interest in keeping up output. The company thus did not have to pay (directly at least) large numbers of middle-level staff whose skills were scarce in China, but had just to take over and weigh the coal on the surface.

Another important role of the contract system was that of risk sharing. It meant that the largest part of a mine's labour force was easily dispensible in times of poor sales. The workers directly hired by the company had greater job security and tended to remain on the books even as output declined, but the number of contract workers fluctuated closely with output. It is also possible that even in times of steady demand the system enabled the companies to keep down the cost of their coal. This was argued by the proponents of the system in China and elsewhere, but a *ceteris paribus* calculation is impossible, and the validity of the argument probably depended very much on the specific conditions pertaining at the time and place.

From the late 1920s certain inherent problems which had always existed in the system, combined with the political changes in the wake of the Northern Expedition, led to a gradual decline in the incidence of contract labour. The very assumption of the management function by the contractors, on the one hand of benefit in saving the company from having to provide supervisors, on the other led to the working of the deposits in the short-term interests of the contractors rather than in the longer-term interests of the mining company. This was particularly undesirable in larger and more-mechanized pits which required working to a centralized plan; as Chinese mines very gradually modernized, their managers became increasingly dissatisfied with the supervisory part of the contractors' function.

With companies becoming more concerned with building up a regular and stable workforce, moreover, complaints that the contract system held down the quality of the labour force grew more numerous. The flexibility inherent in the system, of benefit to the company in times of economic downturn, also encouraged the seasonal employment of the agricultural population rather than the cultivation of a body of full-time miners.

The most important disadvantage of the system was, however, the workers' growing opposition to it. As the Nationalist armies occupied north China, party branches encouraged the establishment of unions at many mines. While in many cases these unions were closely tied to management interests, or were even infiltrated and controlled by the contractors, they were susceptible to pressure from below, and at most mines there was a more favourable environment for the workers to express their opposition to the contract system, which they felt directly depressed their wages by the amount of the contractors' margin.

At some mines, as at Fuyuan and Fuhua in Hubei, the workers won a quick victory, obtaining the abolition of the contract system. At others, like Kailuan, although the position of the contractors was weakened, the miners had to wage a continuous struggle against the system throughout the 1930s, a struggle which formed the basis of most of the strikes and labour disputes of those years. Attempts to meet the workers' grievances elsewhere took the form only of certain modifications to the system. At Fushun the SMR changed the system of payment of wages through the contractor to one whereby the contractor merely got a commission for the labour he supplied, the wages being paid directly by the company to the workers.

Where the system was replaced, contracts were often still let out to small groups of workers acting collectively and sharing the profits among themselves. This was a form of collective piece-work, which brought to the company both the advantages (quantity) and the disadvantages (lack of quality) that the system entailed. It did not solve the contradiction between the interests of the company and those of the men charged with hewing the coal. It did, however, get round the conflict between the workers and the contractors.

The other option open to the company was to employ men individually on time or piece rates. There the one implied an incentive problem, the other difficulties with the quality of work. These problems, together with the fact that the contractors wielded considerable social power and ability to cause trouble if their services were dispensed with, meant that the trend towards the abolition of the contract system was only incipient up to 1937.

The composition of the workforce

Workers employed by mining companies or through contractors performed a wide variety of tasks apart from actually cutting coal: opening up the mine, moving the coal both underground and on the surface, maintenance and operation of equipment and machinery, and preparation of coal for the market, represent only the main tasks involved. For instance, a report on workers directly hired at the Jingxing colliery (excluding the contract workers) listed over eighty categories.[46] But the main economic distinctions lay between the hewers of the coal, other underground workers (such as hauliers) and men who worked on the surface; in addition there was a small but significant group of skilled mechanics and technicians.

Other things being equal, it was in the management's interest to keep the proportion of hewers in the total workforce as high as possible, in that way maximizing output per head, for the hewers were the direct producers. But the increasing size of a mine as deposits ever further from the pit bottom were exploited necessitated the employment of more auxiliary (oncost) workers to carry the coal to the hoists and to maintain the roadways. So hewers tended to become a declining proportion of the underground labour force. On the other hand, the sizes of the surface and underground labour forces depended on relative levels of mechanization and on the number of tasks undertaken to prepare the coal for market.

Chinese collieries seem to have employed quite a high proportion of surface workers. Whereas in Great Britain up to the 1920s, only about 20% of employees worked on the surface, and in Japan between 25% and 30%,[47] a survey of thirty-six Chinese mines in the mid-1930s showed that surface workers made up just over 35% of the total.[48] There were wide variations between mines, and a survey of Shandong mines at the same time suggested a proportion of surface workers of only 27%.[49] If, as is probable, there were rather more surface workers in China than elsewhere, this suggests that the level of surface mechanization lagged further behind overseas practice than did that underground. Descriptions of the loading of coal and other goods on to ships or trucks in China then (and indeed more recently) make this a not improbable conclusion.

A seemingly paradoxical situation emerges from the few figures for the proportion of hewers among total workers. Thus whereas in south Wales before 1914 hewers made up just under 50% of the total workforce, and the proportion was clearly declining,[50] at the Jinbei Company's collieries in north Shanxi that proportion varied from 43% at a very slack period to a probably more normal 53%,[51] and at Jingxing 58.5% of the shifts worked between 1932 and 1935 were worked by hewers.[52] If – and it is a big if, as the data are very fragmentary – this represents the general picture, the rather surprising conclusion emerges that in China there was a higher proportion of hewers but a lower proportion of underground workers than in pre-1914 Britain. If this was the case, two factors might explain it. The Chinese collieries were younger than the British, so needed fewer hauliers and other auxiliary underground workers. Almost certainly part at least of the difference was also caused by the lower level of division of labour in Chinese mines, with hewers performing some tasks that were allocated to other workers in Britain.

Numbers of skilled workers are difficult to estimate, because each category of workers in the statistics included a range of skills. According to the most thorough prewar survey, of the Zhongxing coal mine in Shandong,[53] skilled workers made up around 5% of directly hired workers in the mining section in the early 1920s, and rather over 10% if the machine and electric-power sections are also included; if, however, contract labourers are taken into account, these proportions would sink to 2% and 4% at the most. Similarly at Jingxing, the proportion of directly hired workers paid over 65¢ per day and therefore presumably to some extent skilled was under 7%.[54]

The educational level of the workforce as a whole was very low: 66% of 29,000 workers surveyed in twelve mines in the early 1930s were totally illiterate, a further 28% almost so. Less than 10% had even completed elementary schooling.[55] Nearly 80% even of the directly hired workers at Zhongxing in 1931 had had no education at all, and under 6% had had four years or more; no less than 96% of the contract labourers were illiterate.[56] While not decrying the degree of skill required for the job of an ordinary coal miner, the picture comes across of an overwhelmingly unskilled and uneducated workforce, in this of course reflecting the characteristics of the population as a whole.

Hours of work

In the early twentieth century shifts for miners varied from twenty-four hours or longer in small unmodernized or semi-modern mines down to eight hours in the more progressive large mines. The factors that gradually ameliorated conditions in other respects – that is the higher productivity of satisfied and healthy workers and the emergence of a union movement – were partly responsible for the differential between modern and old-style mines and, during the 1920s and 1930s, for the gradual reduction of hours in the modern sector.

Because the main constraint on output in most unmodernized or semi-modern mines was the raising of coal out of the pit, which had to compete with the raising of water (in leather buckets) and the letting down and pulling up of men into and out of the mine, such mines mostly operated on twenty-four-hour or longer shifts. Although Zhongxing used the twelve-hour shift in its modern mine in 1915, workers in the small pits run by the same company worked for twenty-four hours at a stretch.[57] In other areas, such as Mentougou near Beijing, the differential was less, the modern mine operating on an eight-hour shift, the small mines on a twelve-hour one.[58] The situation was as bad or worse in the remoter areas. Mines in Sichuan mostly worked twelve- or twenty-four-hour shifts,[59] but it was in Shaanxi that the solution to the bottleneck existing in the winding process was most drastic. There it was the practice for workers, once underground, to stay there for many days, working what was called a 'big shift' – although of course this period also included time for rest and sleep. In the Xincungou mine in Tongguan county, workers stayed underground for eighteen days at a time,[60] and twenty days was very common in the province.[61] At one mine the workers actually remained underground for fifty-five days.[62] Such practices were so common in Shaanxi that a reporter thought it worth special mention when the workers in one mine came up out of the pit to sleep.[63]

The existence of these conditions in unmodernized mines in the twentieth century is no proof that such was the situation in late traditional China. It is possible, for instance, that the exigencies of competition with modern mines led to a deterioration in the conditions for workers in small mines. But such an argument, while possibly valid for Shandong or Hebei, is less convincing for Shaanxi, and in general E-tu Zen Sun contends that there was little significant change in the traditional sector of the mining industry between the late Qing and the Republican period.[64] Thus the somewhat shorter hours prevailing in the modern mines might be seen as a sign of progress for the miners.

Although Kaiping operated from the start on an eight-hour shift,[65] up to the 1920s most of China's early modern mines, such as Pingxiang, Zhongxing and Lincheng, worked two twelve-hour shifts.[66] Even where an eight-hour day was theoretically in operation, as at Kailuan, the benefits to the workers were limited, since the daily wage was so low that many were forced to work double shifts.[67] From the 1920s the unionization of the workers led to the widespread adoption of eight-hour shifts,[68] a system used by most large mines in the 1930s. In 1927, under the influence of the Northern Expedition, Zhongxing, for example, reduced its working hours from twelve to eight or nine,[69] and Fushun, the largest employer of labour in the industry, cut its shifts from ten to eight hours in 1929.[70] Nevertheless some mines still lagged behind and, in a 1931 survey in Manchuria, eight out of sixteen coal mines surveyed operated the eight-hour day, two had a nine-hour day, four worked for ten hours, and one each for eleven and twelve hours.[71] Nor was worker opposition the only factor behind the fall in working hours. Mining companies recognized long hours as detrimental to efficiency, and as early as 1923 the SMR was becoming increasingly aware of the defects of long hours and planning a reduction.[72] Similarly in the early 1930s, when discussing the practice of working double shifts at Kailuan, the chief manager wrote: 'We know that it is a very common practice, and one that definitely decreases the overall efficiency underground.'[73] No doubt the aim of increasing productivity also induced the managers of other modern enterprises to agree to cuts in hours, although the history of most countries suggests that the demands of the miners were the most important consideration.

Accidents and safety

Safety conditions in Chinese mines were as bad as or worse than any in the world. No national system of accident reporting operated, and more fragmentary evidence must be used, but the picture that emerges is unambiguous. Whether the available statistics are computed in relation to output or to units of labour, even the lowest mortality rates in China were higher than those of any other country. Tables 39 and 40 indicate that death rates in Japan were very high by international standards, both in terms of deaths per million tons of output and in terms of deaths per worker employed.[74] Nevertheless in China only the series for the Jingxing mine 1922–33 yields a rate close to the Japanese, and even that is clearly above. The carnage that went on in the mines is shown by rates from twice to five or more times as high as the Japanese. The figures for 1932 and 1933 in thirteen small mines in Henan suggest that even more miners were dying in the semi-modernized and unmodernized sectors than in modern mines, and it is quite possible that the bias of the information in these tables to the larger, more modern, mines actually understates the horror of what was happening in China.

Other, less systematic, evidence backs up the overall picture. In the Duijinwan mine in Lu xian, Sichuan, the *Mining Weekly* reported that one or two miners used to die every day, in a mine where the total workforce was

Table 39. *Fatalities per million tons of output*

(i) International

Country	Period	Fatalities per million tons output
United States	1910–21	4.80
India	1917–37	9.98
Japan	1899–1930	21.18

(ii) China

Mine	Period	Fatalities per million tons output
Jingxing	1922–33	25.70
Zhaogezhuang	1927	31.67
'18 large mines'	1925–8	33.30[a]
Fushun	1927–36	36.00
Fushun	1907–19	69.21
Luda	1932–4	42.44
Baojin	1918–22	89.82
13 small mines in Henan	1932–3	103.11
Benxihu	1913–23	212.14

Note: [a] Calculated as per million tons of modern mine output, and therefore an underestimate.
Sources: Shurick, 1924, p. 359; Seth, 1940, pp. 282–3; Kōzan konwakai, 1932, vol. 2, Table 38; Yu, 1926c, pp. 214–16; MMT, 1938, p. 1727; Yu, 1926d, pp. 64–5; Zhang Huiruo, 1936, pp. 195–6; Xie, 1926, pp. 71–2; China, shiyebu, Zhongguo jingji nianjian bianzuan weiyuanhui, 1935, K56–70; KYZB 380 (28 April 1936): 1182–3; MMT, shomubu chōsaka, 1929, p. 96: China, guojia tongji ju, 1958, p. 84.

only around 1700; it did, however, add that the situation had improved by the time of the report (1935).[75] In north Shanxi, one mine was said to have a death rate of several tens per year out of a total workforce of about 600, and that was the *best* record in the district.[76] The frequency of reports from all periods of the closure of mines because of flooding also suggests that many miners must have lost their lives in these accidents.

Major disasters rocked the industry with some frequency. As shown in Table 41, at least twelve disasters occurred over the forty-two years of this study, in each of which 100 or more miners perished. The worst of all took place in the evening of 11 January 1917, when an explosion of coal dust at the Ōyama pit in the Fushun complex shook the town, cut the electricity, damaged the ventilation system, and filled most of the mine with dense black smoke. Only about 170 miners were saved, and 900 Chinese miners perished, together with seventeen Japanese staff.[77] While this was the worst disaster in East Asia up to the war, there were four other disasters in China with a death toll of over 400.

Table 40. *Fatality rates per worker and per shift*

(i) International

Country	Period	Fatalities per 1,000 workers	Fatalities per million shifts
France	1922–34	0.99	—
Belgium	1922–35	1.12	—
Germany	1922–35	1.14	--
India	1917–37	1.26	—
Great Britain	1880–1913	1.35	—
Great Britain	1922–34	—	4.27
Japan	1899–1930	3.17	13.19
United States	1910–21	3.26	14.64

(ii) China

Mine	Period	Fatalities per 1,000 workers	Fatalities per million shifts
Jingxing	1922–33	—	17.00
Fushun	1907–19	5.35	21.93
Fushun	1927–30	8.30	27.57
Yuesheng	1934–5	—	30.66
Baojin	1918–22	12.01	38.07
13 small mines in Henan	1932–3	16.72	54.15

Sources: Shurick, 1924, p. 359; Kōzan konwakai, 1932, vol. 2, Table 38; Seth, 1940, pp. 282–4; MMT, 1938, p. 1727; Yu, 1926c, pp. 214–16; Yu, 1926d, pp. 64–5; Zhang Huiruo, 1936, p. 388; KYZB 380 (28 April 1936): 1182–3; China, shiyebu, Zhongguo jingji nianjian bianzuan weiyuanhui, 1935, K56–70; Griffin, 1975, p. 275.

The immediate causes of these largest disasters were usually either floods or explosions. Explosions caused the disasters at Fangzi in 1907, Kailuan in 1920 and Shuidong in 1928, as well as that already described at Fushun in 1917. In addition the irruption of water into modern pits from the abandoned workings of their predecessors remained a problem for Chinese mines as it did for British mines. The disasters at Zhongxing in 1895 and 1915 and at Zichuan in 1935 resulted from just such a cause. The other major cause of disaster was fire, which struck at Fushun in 1916 and three years later at Benxihu. As was the experience in most countries, however, most lesser accidents were caused by roof-falls. Table 42 indicates that in this respect, Chinese experience was much like that of other countries, even though the level of accidents was higher.

This appalling record may have improved slightly over the period, although the evidence is somewhat ambiguous. There was a very clear trend at Jingxing between 1922 and 1933 towards fewer fatalities per unit of work

Table 41. *Major disasters in Chinese coal mines, 1895–1936*

Date	Mine	Cause	Number of fatalities
1895	Zhongxing	Flood	300 +
1907	Fangzi	Explosion	112
1915	Zhongxing	Explosion and flood	432
1916	Fushun	Fire	151
1917	Fushun	Explosion	917
1919	Benxihu	Fire	217
1920	Kailuan	Explosion	451
1927	Zichuan	Flood	151
1928	Fushun	Flood	482
	Shuidong	Explosion	148
1935	Zichuan	Flood	536
1936	Baojin (Datong)	Flood	100

Note: Only those disasters in which 100 or more workers were killed are included.
Sources: MMT, chōsabu, 1937a, p. 12; IMC, *Returns and Reports, 1907*, part II, vol. 1, p. 123; Gu, 1916, 8:58–64; Yu, 1926a, pp. 115–17, and 1926c, p. 212; Kōzan konwakai, 1932, vol. 2, pp. 628–30; Zhongguo geming bowuguan, 1981, pp. 111–12 (this source quotes an official report that 451 died in the 1920 Kailuan explosion, although earlier reports, such as those in NCH, 30 October 1920, quoted a figure of 422); China, shiyebu, Zhongguo jingji nianjian bianzuan weihuanhui, 1934, 0347–8; KYZB 1 (21 April 1928): 10–11; KYZB 2 (28 April 1928): 34; KYZB 131 (21 February 1931): 20; KYZB 335 (21 May 1935): 353; KYZB 336 (28 May 1935): 375; KYZB 394 (14 August 1936): 146; Hou Defeng, 1929, p. 252.

Table 42. *Causes of mine accidents*

Percentage of accidents caused by	Benxihu deaths and injuries 1918–20	Luda deaths and injuries 1932–4	Jingxing fatalities 1922–33	India fatalities 1937–8	United States fatalities 1916–21
Roof-falls	60	64	63	58	48
Coal wagons	16	21	8	17	18
Explosions	10	3	15	3	15
Other	14	12	14	22	19

Sources: Yu, 1926a, pp. 123–5; Zhang Huiruo, 1936, pp. 212–14; KYZB 380 (28 April 1936): 1182–4; Seth, 1940, p. 285; Shurick, 1924, p. 360.

and per unit of output. Fushun's overall safety record improved in terms of fatalities per unit of output between the periods 1907–19 and 1927–36, but fatalities per unit of work increased between 1907–19 and 1927–30.[78] Moreover, if one excludes the two major disasters that took place in 1917 and 1928, leaving a 'normal' or 'regular' accident rate, the record by both measures got substantially worse over these years. In the only other case where a reasonable judgment is possible, the record at Benxihu, although very bad throughout, did improve somewhat over the years for which records are available.

The limitation of this discussion, mainly to fatalities and to a lesser extent to injuries, is a reflection of the sources and of the concerns of the time. It is surely certain that occupational diseases would have been at least as common as in the West, but such was the seriousness of other aspects of the miners' plight that there is virtually no mention of the ravages of pneumoconiosis, nystagmus and other such diseases, and certainly no systematic study of their incidence. That management paid little attention to health underground is indicated by the fact that it took substantial pressure from the medical profession before even lavatory facilities were installed underground for workers at Fushun.[79]

It is difficult at this distance in time to make any judgment on the causes of China's high accident rate. As usual the companies tried to blame it on the workers. The SMR blamed it on the ignorance and stupidity of their workforce,[80] and the KMA attributed accidents such as the Tangshan disaster of 1920 and the fire at Majiagou in 1932 to the carelessness of the miners.[81] Such claims are made by employers all over the world, but it is generally found that most of the responsibility rests with the management, and in China (not necessarily unbiased) outside observers generally attributed to management the main blame for mining disasters.

Thus Chinese observers blamed the 1917 explosion at Fushun on the ineffectiveness of the humidifiers and the consequent excess of coal dust,[82] and the official Chinese government report on the 1920 Tangshan explosion claimed that antiquated equipment and the engineers' disregard for the workers' lives were responsible for the disaster.[83] Similarly in 1932 the *Mining Weekly* attributed the Majiagou fire to poor equipment, which had led to a series of accidents.[84] The chief manager himself admitted that the magnitude of a disaster at Kailuan's Tangjiazhuang colliery in 1934 was due to poor coordination between senior and subordinate staff.[85] According to the *Mining Weekly* the flood at Luda in 1935 was caused by the company's cutting back on materials and timber to save money, and the workers there had suffered from a high accident rate for many years because of the robbing of pillars.[86] In fact the profusion of old workings in which water and gas accumulated created difficult conditions for mining, but dealing with them was the responsibility of the management, and failure to do so resulted either from incompetence or, probably more often, from a desire to cut costs.

The low value put on the lives of their workers by the mine managers is also clearly demonstrated by the terms of compensation offered in case of accident. In the late nineteenth century, Kaiping paid a mere ¥30 compensation for a life lost[87] and, up to 1925, ¥50 plus a free coffin was a common standard adopted by many companies.[88] A very understandable point often made by the workers was that the cost to the company was less if a worker was killed underground than if they lost a mule.[89]

In common with other aspects of conditions of work, in the late 1920s there was some uneven improvement in arrangements for workers' compensation. At Zhongxing union pressure succeeded in achieving a substantial improvement in quite a short time. At the time of the 1915 disaster, the company paid around ¥70 to bereaved families, and from then up to 1927 the regulations laid down a payment of ¥78. In 1927, after the formation of a union at the time, this was raised to ¥100, and later to ¥150–200 depending on the type of worker involved. By 1932 the families of contract workers killed got ¥50 funeral expenses plus ¥150 compensation, and those of directly hired workers between one and two years' wages (depending on length of service).[90]

Progress was uneven, however, and a wide range of compensation terms was in operation during the 1930s, although in general the larger and more modern the mine, the larger the payments tended to be. Many small and medium companies still only paid something close to the old ¥50 plus a coffin: the Tianyuan Company in Zhangqiu, Shandong, paid only ¥45; a small mine near Pingxiang, ¥42.[91] The small modern mine at Jiawang paid ¥40 plus a coffin,[92] but most large modern mines were paying several hundred yuan to the families of dead miners. The government mine at Huainan paid ¥150, but this was near the bottom of the scale. In 1935 Kailuan paid ¥350, and in the same year the Shandong government intervened to negotiate a ¥330 per man compensation after the disaster at Zichuan.[93] Even the smaller mines in the north-east, where labour was scarcer, paid large sums: ¥300 at Huoshilingzi in Jilin.[94]

The pattern was not simple or uniform by any means, and could be affected by many local or temporary conditions. At Mentougou, the largest mine, Zhongying, paid only ¥60 while the small native pits paid ¥200. This was because Zhongying mainly employed migrants from Henan, while workers in the small mines were local, so that their families could cause more trouble.[95]

While these reforms no doubt slightly ameliorated the plight of those whose breadwinner was killed in the mines during the 1930s, they can only just have begun to change the thinking of managers to take greater account of safety measures in the operation of the pits. As with so many other things, the war interrupted any long-term trend in this case, as the exigencies of increasing production under the Japanese led to a sharp fall in safety standards: in just two massive explosions at Jingxing in 1940 and Benxihu in 1943, over 3000 workers were killed.[96]

The standard of living

Matching the dreadful conditions at work was the poverty-striken and miserable standard of living at which Chinese miners had to subsist away from work. Chapter 2 discussed, as far as possible, the overall structure and behaviour of wages, and concluded that the generally adequate supply of labour meant that only during the political upheaval of the late 1920s was there any general and sustained rise in wages, although there were numerous local and temporal variations. Whether before or after that rise, wages were barely sufficient to support the miner, let alone a family.

Any comparison of miners' wages with the cost of living illustrates the tightrope the miners had to walk between starvation and survival. While the average wage at Kailuan in the late 1920s was under 50¢ per shift, the cost of living for a family of four was over ¥1 per day.[97] Even worse seems to have been the situation at Jiawang, where the average wage for an unskilled worker bought less than two catties of rice.[98] Many workers, therefore, had to work more than the one shift per day to support themselves, and especially to support a family. Even then a family man at Fushun in the late 1920s had to spend over 60% of his budget on food (a sure sign of a low and precarious standard of living) and in any case ended the month with a slight deficit of income in relation to expenditure.[99]

The diet on which miners and their families survived was a poor one, barely providing enough nutrition to support life. Kailuan workers ate bread made from maize flour while walking on their way to the face.[100] At Zhongxing the workers' diet consisted mainly of sorghum and wheat pancakes, with just a little salted vegetable or green onion. In exceptionally good times they liked to eat rye bread rolls, and only at festivals might they treat themselves to a little meat. In general their families ate even more poorly than did the workers themselves.[101] At Fushun a worker's daily diet consisted of 260 grams of millet, 30 grams of soybeans, 540 grams of maize and 20 grams of salt.[102]

Most Chinese, of course, lived in what seems, to a modern Westerner at least, miserable poverty, and it is not easy to put miners' living standards in perspective. Leonard Ting compiled a table comparing coal-mining wages with industrial wages in Shanghai, which put mining wages close to the bottom of the scale of unadjusted money wages.[103] That is, however, probably misleading, for two reasons. Two of the three industries ranking below coal were cotton spinning and silk reeling, by far the largest employers of labour, although of course much of that labour was female. Also, fuel and possibly food and housing were cheaper in mining areas than in Shanghai, so that a simple comparison understates the relative position of mining labour.

How well miners lived in comparison with their rural cousins is a difficult question, made more so by the very different forms of income accruing to the peasant household. Evidence from Yi xian in 1929 suggests that average wages for unskilled miners were ¥10.82 per month, for agricultural labourers ¥7.21.[104] Similarly in Manchuria in the 1930s coal miners' wages averaged 64¢ per day, those of agricultural labourers about 30¢.[105] While large regional differentials in prices and wages make generalization difficult, it seems that the standard of living of miners exceeded that of agricultural labourers, and probably, as suggested in a survey by the SMR at Fushun, approximated that of middle peasants.[106]

Insofar as poor conditions affected productivity and the formation of a stable workforce, mining companies were sometimes prepared to take direct measures to improve conditions, such as by the selling of cheap food, or the provision of housing, medical care, education or recreational facilities. Some of these services had earlier been provided by the contractors, but the benefits were widely seen to accrue to the contractors far more than to the workers, or even to be at the expense of the workers. Yet again, political pressure combined with economic imperatives gradually to bring about greater direct involvement by mining companies in these fields, a process that began to accelerate in the 1920s.

Arrangements whereby contractors set up shops to sell food to workers, which might or might not deteriorate into the truck system, were common at Chinese mines. The import of food to the mining areas of Kailuan was mostly in the hands of companies controlled by the contractors, and the workers complained that the prices charged were as great as or greater than market prices.[107] At Mentougou collusion between contractors and grain merchants meant that grain prices went up at the time wages were paid.[108] Fushun's contractors were so powerful that their shops were able to outcompete those of the company, and they used them to exploit the workers still further. The SMR, which had set up shops in the wake of the inflation of the 1910s to provide cheap food for the workers, eventually bought out the contractors in the 1930s and set up a network of shops, one at each mine, which did in all J¥1.6 million of business in 1935; as workers spent between J¥7 and J¥8 per month on food (for a single man), this suggests that the company shops were supplying something under half the food for their more than 40,000 workforce, or perhaps a little less taking into account the fact that some workers were family men.[109] At Jingxing, too, the company operated shops to sell food to the workers at under market prices, selling some ¥60,000 of food per annum, which would have supplied probably only 15–20% of the workforce.[110] Even such an arrangement was, however, unusual, and most companies took little direct part in the supply of food to their workers.

Provision of housing was a central function of labour contractors in Japanese coal mines, and indeed of those in the Shanghai textile industry,[111] but our sources have rather few references to contractors providing housing in Chinese collieries, although some did – for example, those at Zichuan and, in the early years of the century, at Pingxiang.[112] Where companies used local labour, no provision of housing was necessary; dormitories built by Liujiang for its workers remained largely unused because most were locals.[113] Most small mines also relied on labour from the immediate vicinity but, in the few cases where such mines did employ migrant labour, they sometimes provided accommodation.[114] The larger mines, unable to rely solely on labour recruited from within commuting distance, had greater call to build housing, and mostly offered accommodation to their staff, sometimes to their workers.

When Kaiping brought skilled workers from south China in the late nineteenth century, the company provided housing for them,[115] and by the 1920s and probably earlier, they erected large dormitories at each of their collieries, catering for both single and family men, and accommodating in all around 10,000 workers. Single workers slept five or six to a room, and paid around 12.5¢ per month in rent.[116] Similarly at Fushun the SMR set aside an area for workers' and staff housing, again providing housing for both single and family men, with a total capacity by 1935 of 21,548 persons.[117] Benxihu also offered five grades of accommodation, the lowest for its Chinese workers.[118]

Although at least seventeen mines outside the north-east, including even such minor mines as the Minsheng Company in Shan xian, Henan, provided dormitories for their workers,[119] none did so on the scale of Kailuan or Fushun, and the situation at Zhongxing was probably more typical. There the most the company did for its workers, at least up to the 1930s, was to allow the most favoured of them to build hovels within the mine precincts as a protection from bandits.[120]

Hospital treatment was a more specifically 'modern' service offered by many mining companies to their workers; as the service tied most closely into the production process, dealing with injuries received at work, it was one often offered. The pattern was similar to that in other welfare facilities: the very largest mines, Kailuan and Fushun, offered such services more or less from their establishment, while at other mines, progress was more gradual, accelerating from the 1920s. Kaiping's clinic was open at least as early as 1884,[121] and the SMR replaced the earlier army clinic with a hospital in 1908. The company's hospitals treated 88,825 inpatients and 270,093 outpatients in 1919; not surprisingly, the most common complaints were external injuries, ear, nose and throat, respiratory and skin diseases.[122] On the other hand, Zhongxing opened a clinic only in 1919, a hospital in 1923, both of which offered free treatment to the whole neighbourhood.[123] A dozen or more mines outside Manchuria had such clinics or hospitals in the 1930s but, whereas that at Kailuan treated almost 300,000 patients, the second largest, at Jiaozuo, treated only 7000.[124] This no doubt partly reflects the degree to which the hospitals were open to others than workers, but it also illuminates the general low level of availability of health care outside the very largest mines.

Schools and educational facilities, apart from job training, had little direct connection to the production process, and so were seldom provided by companies. Educational provision was rare before the 1920s: the Liujiang and Baojin companies, for example, did nothing more than pay small subsidies to local schools.[125] Generally the first step was a school for the children of staff, which, often under union pressure, was also opened to the children of workers. Thus Zhongxing set up a primary school for the children of staff in 1923, but only in 1928, after demands from the union, was it opened to those of workers.[126] Even where schools were provided, it was often difficult to get workers to send their children to them.[127] In addition some mines also ran classes expressly aimed at upgrading the training of their workers, rather than of their children; but these, too, tended to cater mostly for those who already had some skills – at Zhongxing, for example, no contract labourers at all attended.[128]

Where companies provided recreational facilities for workers, the story was much the same, as the kinds of activities offered seemed of little relevance to most workers.[129] One popular form of entertainment was traditional Chinese opera, and in the early 1920s Kailuan opened theatres at its Zhaogezhuang and Linxi collieries; audiences at the latter were so large that the original system of free entry had to be changed to one where a fee was charged.[130] Zhongxing also sometimes staged performances of Chinese operas for its workers, but most miners – especially the single men – mainly spent their leisure time in the brothels and gambling dens organized by the contractors.[131] Li Dazhao wrote in 1919 how the miners at Tangshan tried to finish two weeks' work in one week and spent the other week in wild sprees of eating, drinking, whoring and gambling.[132] No doubt there was an element of cliché in such descriptions, just as there was in the stereotype of the English miner in the nineteenth century, but the number of single men in the workforce and the migrant nature of many of the mining communities lend substantial plausibility to the picture.

Such pleasure sprees apart, Chinese miners mostly lived a miserable and poverty-stricken life, which the welfare measures of the companies did only a little to alleviate. The history of such measures does, however, back up that of wages in suggesting that the brief upsurge in union activity during and after the Northern Expedition did result in some permanent, although limited, gains, in terms of better health care and educational opportunities as well as slightly higher wages. Like the rest of the Chinese population, however, the miners were still far from having a secure and decent living in this period.

10

THE LABOUR MOVEMENT

Kerr and Siegel have put forward the hypothesis that the isolation of miners from the community makes them a particularly cohesive group and one prone to aggressive industrial action.[1] In most countries coal miners have stood at the forefront of the labour movement and have been among those who most frequently go on strike.[2] But in China the formation of distinct and separate mining communities still lay in the future and, particularly in the early part of our period, miners kept close links with the agricultural society, links which broke down this cohesion and aggressive consciousness in several ways. Socially, the pseudo-kinship ties within the contract groups through which they were recruited, and the divisions among the workers fostered by that system, acted to hinder the emergence of class solidarity. Ideologically, many miners before the First World War looked to the secret societies as a focus of protest, which diverted their attention from issues of class conflict. Economically, many miners still only partly depended on mining for their livelihood, and so had less incentive to struggle for higher wages in what remained a subsidiary occupation.

The history of the labour movement in Chinese mines is the story of the gradual change in these conditions: the uneven emergence in some places of a permanent mining community, the slow change in consciousness under the impact of radical education and propaganda, and the consequently increasing solidarity among the workers and against the contractors. It is also the story of the changes that took place among the ranks of the 'opposition' – management and the authorities – whose divisions and uncertainties allowed brief periods of success for the workers. But all of these changes remained very incomplete up to 1937, and unions and labour organizations lived a very precarious existence, the workers for all but the briefest periods coming off worse in their struggle with their opponents.

As had been the case in the early days of Indian coal mining,[3] most disputes in China up to the 1920s (and some afterwards) were sporadic, often violent, outbursts over an immediate grievance such as maltreatment of a worker by a foreman or manager. The first strike at the Pingxiang colliery in 1905 was later described by a participant as 'beating the foreign devils'; it had been triggered by a foreign manager beating up a Chinese worker, although there was also a dispute about the company falling behind with the payment of wages. Despite initial concessions by the company, the arrest and execution of the strike leaders led to increased exploitation of the workers in the longer term;[4] indeed there was another (unsuccessful) strike in 1906 over the reintroduction of a twelve-hour shift.[5]

In 1915 the miners again went on strike in protest over collusion between a German engineer and exploitative contractors.[6] A shadowy presence in all these strikes, and one which links them very much to pre-modern rather than modern forms of organization, was the Gelao Hui (Elder Brother Society).[7] That there was some connection between the 1905 and 1906 strikes and the Ping–Liu–Li uprising is plausible, although incompletely documented.[8] The ambiguity of these early strikes is illustrated by the involvement of the Gelao Hui in 1915, when the strike was in part in opposition to the contractors, whereas the society also had close ties with the same contractors, joining them, for instance, in running gambling dens and brothels in the town.

Miners and their disputes also got caught up in the complex local politics of bandits, police and militia. A strike in 1915 in Qiancheng xian, Hunan, against an increase in hours led to police arresting the leaders. The workers then rioted and broke into the police station, while the local militia came out in support of the miners. After the rebellious miners followed the classic bandit strategy of retreating over the provincial border into Sichuan, the company then hired a new workforce.[9]

Sectional disputes among the workforce were a major problem for Kaiping in its early years. Resentment by the local labourers at the better wages and conditions of the skilled Cantonese mechanics led to a strike as early as 1882 over equal treatment between the two groups, and trouble erupted also in 1883 and 1891. Both the structure of the labour force and the consequent sectional divisions remained similar up to the 1920s, when they were major factors impeding the formation of a union.[10]

By the 1920s modern labour organizations and dispute methods were beginning to emerge. The basis on which this happened was, of course, the great growth in Chinese industrial production, and hence in the size and stability of the proletariat, which took place in the late 1910s. Between 1914 and 1923 coal output from large mines doubled, doubtless necessitating a similar increase in the size of the workforce. Great concentrations of labour emerged, with Fushun and Kailuan employing around 30,000 or more workers each, and smaller centres such as Pingxiang and Jiaozuo around 10,000.

Moreover, as the history of the mines grew longer – Kaiping's forty years, Pingxiang's twenty – the workers were more likely to be full-time miners, while their ties to rural society grew weaker. This process was only beginning, and even in 1937 was very far from complete; indeed the emergent nature of the working class goes some way to account for its relative weakness throughout the period. Nevertheless it was certainly no coincidence that the earliest and most important manifestations of organized labour took place in the two oldest mines – Kaiping and Pingxiang.

At the same time, members of the elite were, really for the first time, becoming concerned with the plight of workers, and political cadres were going among them to spread new ideas and methods of organization. The Chinese Communist Party probably played the leading role in this process, both in coal mines and elsewhere. Even before the party had been founded, members of the Marxist Study Group in Beijing were active among the workers of north China. Because of the distance of the Kailuan mines from Beijing, their activities there began relatively late, but they eventually set up contacts with the miners through students at Tangshan's Communications University.[11] A prime target of the student activists in the mines was the contract system, which was a major impediment to labour organization, both by creating vertical divisions among the workers and by more direct methods of control: the chief manager at Kailuan spoke of the 'rigid control' over labour exercised by the contractors.[12] When Liu Shaoqi went to Pingxiang in 1922, some of the earliest lessons he tried to teach the workers attempted to break down the link between workers and contractors, and to point out the common interests of the workers in the face both of contractors and of capital.[13]

Finally, together with the gradual increase in the size and consciousness of the working class, the attitude of the authorities even more gradually changed from one of unvarying hostility to one where workers and radical movements could be a potential ally. In the late Qing the government still retained vestiges of the traditional distrust of large concentrations of miners.[14] The part played by secret societies in early labour organization and the possibility that disturbances could turn anti-dynastic made their distrust stronger, and the participation of the Gelao Hui in the Pingxiang strikes of 1906 and 1915 contributed to the government's decision to send in troops to put down the strikes.[15] The warlords continued in the main to show bitter hostility to manifestations of worker unrest, but by the early 1920s the configuration of political forces in China was such that a warlord might want to look to the workers and the Chinese Communist Party as allies. Wu Peifu's brief alliance with Sun Yat-sen, the Communist Party and the workers of north China during 1922 is the most important example.[16] Similarly in Hunan certain sections of the elite were prepared to ally themselves with the labour movement in the cause of nationalism, thus giving it room to develop and flourish.[17]

It was in this context in 1922 that there was a national upsurge in workers' activity, with two of the most important strikes taking place at mining centres. At Pingxiang, following a visit by a group of communists in late 1921, Li Lisan arrived in January 1922 to set up a school. In May that year Li and his colleagues established the Anyuan Rail and Mine Workers' Club, which by September had so alarmed the management that they asked for local troops to close it down. The soldiers were slow and hesitant to act, and on 12 September, after the arrival of another Communist Party organizer, Liu Shaoqi, the club led the workers out on strike in protest at the non-payment of wages. Again, local troops proved unwilling to act against the workers, and five days later management granted thirteen union demands, making this one of the greatest victories of the Chinese workers' movement to date.[18]

In the next month, October 1922, the Kailuan workers, influenced by a successful strike of railway workers at Tangshan and Shanhaiguan, put forward demands for improved wages and conditions. After the management's refusal to meet these demands, they additionally demanded the recognition of their workers' club as a negotiating body, and on 23 October the workers at the Tangshan, Zhaogezhuang, Linxi and Tangjiazhung collieries went on strike, to be followed three days later by those at Majiagou. But the alliance between Wu Peifu and the radicals was beginning to become strained, and in perhaps the first sign of its imminent collapse,[19] Wu sent troops under one of his lieutenants to crush the strike. Fifty workers were killed or injured by the troops on 25 October, and the strike leadership was scattered to the villages, from which some absconded with the strike funds. So after twenty days the strike ended on terms which represented a small concession by the company and a much larger one, in terms of their demands, by the workers.[20]

The most important factor accounting for the different fate of the two strikes was probably the renewed firmness of warlord hostility to labour in north China, contrasted with a still vacillating attitude in Hunan. In addition more preparation and organization had gone into the Pingxiang strike, with Communist Party cadres working there for almost a year. At Kailuan, on the other hand, the strike was as far as we know a more short-term reaction to successes elsewhere, so that organization, leadership and funding were all inadequate for success.

Wu Peifu's murder of railway workers in February 1923 marked the final

Table 43. *Strikes and disputes in Chinese coal mines*

Year(s)	Strikes	Other disputes	Total	Quadrennial totals
1915–21	8	—	8	—
1922	2	—	2	—
1923	—	—	—	—
1924	—	—	—	—
1925	7	—	7	
1926	3	—	3	
1927	1	—	1	14
1928	3	—	3	
1929	6	7	13	
1930	5	3	8	
1931	8	5	13	45
1932	8	3	11	
1933	4	1	5	
1934	8	—	8	
1935	8	2	10	27
1936	3	1	4	

Note: This table is compiled from various issues of KYZB and other sources; it includes only those strikes and disputes which are dateable and placeable; that is, it does not include the listing of 'no. of strikes, etc. in mines' in the *China Year Book*.

breakdown of the Wu–Sun–Communist Party axis, and Table 43 indicates that there were no major strikes or disputes in 1923–4. Some activities continued, however, and Liu Shaoqi's cautious line at Pingxiang kept the union operating and won a 5% wage rise for some of the workers. Liu attributed these successes to the unity, determination and perceptiveness of the workers.[21] The May 30 Movement of 1925 precipitated the next national upsurge, but only one of the seven strikes which took place in coal mines in 1925 was directly related to the Movement: in early July about 2300 workers walked out in protest against British imperialism at the Peking Syndicate mines at Jiaozuo, forcing the closure of the mines for eight years.[22] Although the Japanese at Fushun succeeded in forestalling a strike, several skilled workers resigned from those mines as a gesture against imperialism.[23]

Overall the balance of forces was still very much against the workers, especially where foreign interests joined with local warlords and capitalists in opposition to the workers. In Hunan the military governor was becoming firmly identified with anti-revolutionary forces, and his troops scattered a union meeting at Pingxiang in 1924.[24] In 1925 his soldiers killed eighteen miners in suppressing a strike at the small mine of Tanshanwan,[25] and at Pingxiang several months of activity by the workers, both in protest against the non-payment of wages and in solidarity with other nationalist causes, ended in September with the forces of three warlords moving in to crush the Workers' Club and execute its leaders.[26] Behind the scenes Japanese insistence on weeding out anti-Japanese elements had been vital in putting together the anti-worker coalition. Likewise at Kailuan, the British were able to have the army commander at Tianjin disperse a strike over union recognition, occupy the mines and force a return to work.[27]

Whereas the miners of Kailuan and especially of Pingxiang had been among the leaders of the workers' movement in 1922 and to a much lesser extent in 1925, they lost any such conspicuous role in the great wave of strikes in 1926 and early 1927, when the lead was taken first by the workers of Xianggang and Guangzhou and later by those of Shanghai. The miners of Anyuan (Pingxiang), known as 'Little Moscow', continued to give support to the revolution, taking part in several battles in the Northern Expedition, but the focus of struggle had shifted away from the mine itself.[28] North China was relatively quiet, and only a strike at Tangshan against closure of the mines during a period of transport disruption hit the headlines.[29]

Somewhat special circumstances also led to a peak of strike activity in the north-east, lasting from around 1925 to 1928. Only partly tied in to the political turmoil in the rest of China, these strikes were also a response to the collapse of the Chinese currency in the area and the consequent deterioration in living standards.[30] Table 44 shows that the incidence of strikes more than trebled between 1924 and 1927, before gradually tailing off to the very low level of the 1930s. Whereas mining only accounted for a small proportion of the disputes, the sector was much more important in terms of numbers of workers involved, of whom over 40% were miners in both 1926 and 1927.[31] Both Fushun and Benxihu were the scene of major strikes over wages in 1926–7,[32] but the movement has been little studied, overshadowed as it was by what was happening in Shanghai.

In China's cities the Nationalist government, from April 1927, crushed or emasculated existing active unions, but in the mines the situation was more ambiguous. The arrival of Nationalist troops and cadres in the wake of the Northern Expedition changed the previous situation in two ways. First, it introduced modern ideas of political and union organization to mines previously isolated from wider political currents. Previously, only in mines such as Pingxiang, in the political hot-bed of Hunan, and Kailuan, the largest and oldest concentration of miners, had such ideas been influential. The effect now was to raise the expectations of workers and concentrate their opposition to such institutions as the contract labour system.

Second, particularly in the early years of Nationalist rule, when some revolutionary spirit was still alive, the local party branches offered concrete

Table 44. *Strikes in Manchuria, 1916–34*

Year	Total number of strikes	Total number of workers involved	Number of strikes in mining enterprises
1916	5	1,290	n.a.
1917	5	1,019	n.a.
1918	20	5,975	n.a.
1919	55	11,336	n.a.
1920	18	3,694	n.a.
1921	7	959	n.a.
1922	25	4,021	n.a.
1923	27	4,177	n.a.
1924	29	5,256	n.a.
1925	59	8,889	n.a.
1926	67	12,642	8
1927	94	23,539	13
1928	79	17,606	6
1929	41	6,507	5
1930	35	2,785	10
1931	20	3,031	2
1932	8	1,134	—
1933	29	6,345	1
1934	11	863	—

Sources: MMT, keizai chōsakai, 1936a, p. 133; Nishimura, 1972, p. 50.

organizational support and backup for the unions, furnishing them with a connection with local government which mitigated the hostility previously shown towards the workers by the authorities. The year 1929 thus represented a high point of union formation, and unions were set up at Changcheng (north-east Hebei), Daye (Hubei), Jiawang, Lincheng, Liuhegou, Liujiang and Zhengfeng;[33] at Fuhua and Jingxing unions were set up in 1927 and 1928 as a direct result of the arrival of the Northern Expedition.[34]

From the start, however, the Nationalist attitude towards the mining unions showed all the ambiguity of the party's aims, with revolutionary ideals gradually being submerged by the needs of the state to manipulate the populace. Many unions were disbanded and reorganized several times before their activities and personnel received official approval.

The union at Zhongxing went through vicissitudes similar to many. After some early activity in 1925, a union was formed in the wake of the Northern Expedition, but the early leaders were very radical, and many disputes arose. In mid-1928 a centrally appointed official reorganized the union, but several months later the provincial party committee sent another man to run affairs. He turned out to be too radical, and in December 1929 the central government ordered his replacement. His two successors also proved in turn too radical, and it was only in December 1930, after many changes of personnel, that the central government was sufficiently satisfied to allow the final establishment and registration of the union. Union activities were, however, now concentrated on workers' education, health and other welfare issues.[35] The company nevertheless continued to try to undermine the union, bribing union officers to sow discord amongst the workers.[36] By the time the great strike of 1932 took place, the union played only a secondary role,[37] and there is no further mention of the Zhongxing union in the pages of the *Mining Weekly*.

This manipulative tendency was pushed further in the mid-1930s, as the balance of class forces swung further against the workers. The government now saw the role of the unions mainly as one of controlling workers and keeping out communist influence, and was prepared to dispense with them when they were no longer seen as helpful.[38] In July 1933 the Kailuan union, which had been among the most active in the furthering of the workers' interests, was closed down.[39] This closure cannot be directly attributed to the actions of the Nanjing government, which by this time had little control over north-east Hebei, but it was by direct order of Jiang Jeshi that the union at Jiaozuo was disbanded as part of the Zhong-Fu reorganization in 1935.[40] The functions unions were expected to undertake are shown by the organization by the local party of a coal miners' guild in Mizhi xian in Shaanxi in 1936 in order to raise output, cut prices and reduce the influence of the Communist Party among the workers.[41] Similarly a plan to form a union at Lieshan in 1936 was explicitly aimed at avoiding disputes.[42]

Unions of whatever sort had only a tenuous hold on the workforce. A survey of mining unions in the 1933 *Labour Yearbook* lists eighteen coal-mining unions with just over 25,000 members.[43] This represented only about 10–15% of the total workforce, too low a proportion to enable a successful labour movement to flourish. Union membership tended to be concentrated among the skilled workers directly hired by the company. The hold of the contractors over the unskilled workers, although weakening, was still strong enough to inhibit the growth of unions among them: thus of 202 union members at Lincheng only thirty-two were contract labourers,[44] at Liuhegou contract labourers did not dare to join the union,[45] and at Zhengfeng all union members were workers directly hired by the company.[46]

A further factor contributing to the weakness of the unions was their penetration in many cases by the contractors themselves. The union at Liujiang was used by the contractors from 1929 to work for the reintroduction of the recently abolished contract system, and the fact that, after the collapse of the Kailuan union in the mid-1930s, many of its leaders got jobs under contractors suggests that the situation was similar there.[47] Finally, many unions were financially dependent on contributions from the employers, which could be reduced or stopped almost at will.[48]

Despite these many weaknesses in the union movement among coal miners, the overall atmosphere of the Nanjing decade did not generally permit the brutal and bloody suppression of strikes which had been the hallmark of the warlord era. Many disputes arose over the period, especially in the first four or five years of the regime, and even in the mid-1930s the level of disputes was still higher than it had been before 1928. Unlike earlier years where strikes can often be seen in the context of wider political events, during the Nanjing decade the causes of disputes and the objects of demands were mostly local and economic. As with strikes everywhere, however, causation was complex, with the workers reacting against a number of grievances and putting forward varying demands.

Earlier chapters have already connected the widespread increase in wage rates in the late 1920s to the political climate among the workers. But this link was due more to the general demoralization and defensive attitude of management at the time than to the specific demands put forward in strikes. Some strikes, it is true, did centre around a demand for higher wages, as for instance at Kailuan in 1929 and Mentougou and Jiaozuo in 1933.[49] Nevertheless these made up only a small proportion of strikes. Indeed the successes of the workers in achieving higher rates contributed to the inability of the mining companies to pay the wage bill, which in turn was one of the major causes of disputes in the 1930s.

Defensive aims lay behind most strikes, as workers attempted to ward off a reduction in their standard of living rather than to achieve an improvement. Reflecting the generally weak position of the working class this proposition was true for most of the period. Even strikes ostensibly aimed at achieving wage rises were sometimes mere responses to the fall in living standards caused by inflation: in 1917 some workers at Fushun struck for higher wages in order to restore their real income at a time of rising prices. At other times strikes took the form of resistance to explicit wage cuts, as it did at Zhalainuoer in 1925, at Jiawang in 1931 and at Liuhegou in 1932.[50]

More often strikers were protesting against a company's falling behind – sometimes for many months – with the payment of wages. The difficulties of the coal industry, first in the civil wars and later through the world depression, added possibly to the rise in wages, made this a frequent phenomenon during the Nanjing decade. As early as 1928 workers at Jiawang went on strike for this reason, and the dispute dragged on for two years.[51] In 1930 Liuhegou fell no less than fifteen months behind with the payment of wages, and in 1932 there was a strike at Zhengfeng over the same issue.[52]

The third type of defensive action was against the retrenchments several companies enforced in the course of the depression of the mid-1930s. The main example is Kailuan where workers at Majiagou, always a troublesome pit for Kailuan's management, struck in 1934 against cuts in hours; the pit was not reopened after the New Year's holiday of 1936.[53]

Opposition to the conditions under which the miners worked, notably to the contract labour system, was another common cause of strikes and disputes. As the nexus between workers and contractors broke down under the impact of radical education and propaganda, the workers increasingly came to see the difference between the price per ton paid by the company to the contractor and the wages paid by the latter to his workers as a deduction from their income; although this neglects the various contributions made by the contractors to the process of production, it held enough truth to be a powerful motive for disputes. Added to that was resentment at the often brutal treatment handed out to the workers by the contractors.[54]

Strikers, such as those at Kailuan in 1922 and 1931, and at Jiaozuo in 1933, often demanded the abolition of the system,[55] and as many as 80% of the labour disputes at Kailuan in the early 1930s were caused in some way by relations between the workers and the contractors. The problem there was exacerbated by the large size of the contract groups and the several tiers of contractors therefore placed over the workers; so a strike in 1934 was attributed to exploitation by second- or even third-grade contractors.[56] All this activity, together with more purely managerial considerations, contributed to the gradual decline of the system.

Some strikes were explicitly called for nationalistic reasons, thus by nature being demonstrations rather than disputes. While the strike against the Peking Syndicate at Jiaozuo was the most important example, Japanese mines suffered too, even in Manchuria. In Shandong, production in the Sino-Japanese Luda Company's mines was interrupted in 1928 and 1931 by stoppages which were at least in part patriotic in motivation.[57]

Finally, in one or two strikes the issue of union recognition was central, as in Kailuan and Pingxiang in 1925. But the generally marginal role of unions in the workers' lives meant that this was a demand seldom at the forefront of workers' minds.

The overall success of these strikes in the attainment of their ends was not great. They did, it is true, even when crushed, generally elicit at least some formal concessions from the management. Even at the Kailuan strike of 1922, crushed by the army and characterized by Deng Zhongxia as a failure, the company granted wage rises to the lowest paid workers and other improvements in conditions.[58] Similarly the arrest of the strike leaders at Zhongxing in 1932 still left the company having to meet the workers' demands to pay bonuses to contract as well as to directly hired workers.[59] Any gains made were, however, mostly peripheral, and the poor financial situation of the companies often left them unable to pay increased wages or to carry out promises to pay back wages owed to the workers. Strikes over the organization of work certainly contributed to the gradual long-term decline of the contract system, but elicited only small immediate concessions. Patriotic strikes were by their very nature aimed less at gaining proximate ends than at demonstrating a point.

Despite the growth in size and activity of the working class, and the mining proletariat in particular, since the First World War, it remained weak in relation to the forces ranged against it. No union or workers' movement is likely to be successful where there is a plentiful supply of surplus labour, unless it can control the entry of new workers and new companies to the industry. So in China where the workers did show signs of organization and solidarity, the company always had the option of replacing them with more docile members of the reserve army of peasant labour. Moreover, the financial difficulties of many companies in the 1930s, caused by factors beyond their control, meant they were often unable, even if willing, to grant the workers' demands. In a general situation of overproduction, the strike weapon was not likely to be effective, nor the workers' position strong.

In this situation of general weakness of the workers' movement, the immediate cause of failure was mostly the superior resources and power that the management could call on. Right up to 1937 it was very much the exception for the authorities to look favourably on the labour side of a dispute. This was not unknown, the few examples being mainly from the early years of the Nanjing regime. In 1929 the local government supported workers' demands for higher wages at the Changcheng mine in north-east Hebei,[60] and in Shandong listened favourably to similar demands by Boshan workers.[61] At Kailuan local authorities played a mediating role in disputes in 1920 and 1929, no doubt in order to avoid trouble and its diplomatic consequences.[62] Finally, in 1930 mediation, not suppression, was used at a strike at Yuesheng over an unjust dismissal.[63]

While such mediation might well have often taken place when small disputes were involved, in major disputes the local authorities mostly intervened firmly on the side of management. The brutal methods of the warlords were still used in Manchuria by the Japanese: eighty-six workers were killed by Japanese mine police at Fushun during a labour dispute in 1935,[64] and such actions no doubt went far to account for the very small number of strikes in that area in the 1930s. Nanjing tended to be less ruthless, but still the authorities often used to arrest the leaders to force strikers back on shift. During the 1932 strike at Zhongxing, police arrested fifty workers on suspicion of communist connections, and thus removed those elements least willing to accept the company's offer.[65] Most mines had a contingent of police stationed there, control over whom was a matter of dispute between the company and the local government; the police chief at Jiaozuo was attacked as a traitor for the support his men gave to the Peking Syndicate during a strike in 1933.[66] At Kailuan in 1932 the police chief appointed by Zhang Xueliang showed himself favourable to the union, so the company exerted itself to get rid of him;[67] later, in 1935, when the Japanese were in control of that area, General Umezu made it quite clear that they were not prepared to brook any labour unrest at all.[68]

Police suppression itself sometimes provoked worse trouble than that it was supposed to solve; faced with a united workforce, Kailuan's manager described the police as 'impotent'.[69] Workers at Lieshan struck in 1931 over the arrest of some of their number in the course of a dispute,[70] and another strike occurred at the same mine in 1934 after a clash with police.[71] Nevertheless police intervention mostly resulted in a weakening of the workers' movement and often in an enforced return to work.

This crucial role of state power in the handling of labour disputes meant that in a situation where the working class was numerically small and socially weak, the development of the movement depended more on the broader configuration of political forces in the country than on the solidarity and organization among the miners themselves. Miners were totally unable to ward off the steep deterioration in conditions of work and standards of living under the Japanese occupation, and it was only with the advent of a completely new regime in 1949 that their situation improved, and then only very unevenly.

11

CONCLUSION: THE COAL INDUSTRY IN CHINA'S MODERN HISTORY

The role of the coal industry and indeed of industry in general in modern China was conditioned first of all by the still small weight of the modern sector in the total economy. Because of this, even the considerable growth rates that were achieved could be subsumed in an overall picture of stagnation and failure, and the growth of demand was held back, in the final analysis, by the vicissitudes and difficulties of the peasant economy. Similarly the weakness of the capitalist class – as evidenced by the domination of the industry by bureaucrats and warlords, and in the lack of influence exercised by industrial capitalists in national politics – had its basis in their small weight in the economy. So also did the fragile strength of the working class, a tiny fraction of the Chinese population vulnerable to oppression by warlord armies or to replacement from the massive pool of underemployed peasant labour.

The phenomenon of growth

The material presented in this study supports John Key Chang's conclusion that substantial industrial growth took place in pre-revolutionary China, especially up to 1937. Although there is still room for disagreement over details, it is unlikely that future studies will suggest a radically different rate of growth for total industrial output, nor does this study attempt to do so. Thus the history of China's modern coal mines up to 1937 was one of success rather than, in any real sense, of failure. They grew, albeit on the basis of a non-mechanized sector of substantial size, from virtual non-existence in 1895 to equality with many medium-sized industrial powers like France, Belgium, or Japan, in the 1930s. The industry's rate of growth compared not unfavourably with that of mining in other countries, and it was able to displace imports from their strong position in the coastal market; by the early 1920s, the share of imports was rapidly falling, and although the process was temporarily halted by the civil wars of the late 1920s which stopped coal being shipped from the interior to the ports, by the mid-1930s foreign coal was of negligible importance. Chinese mines now supplied not only demand within the country (Manchurian mines within Manchuria) but had begun to play a decisive part in the international market of East Asia.

While growth continued much more widely and rapidly in the 1950s, the imprint of the prewar period can still be seen in the fact that only two of the eight mining bureaux which in the 1970s produced over 10 million tons per year were in areas essentially undeveloped before 1937; the same is true for only four out of the nine mines producing 5 to 9 million tons and seven out of the fourteen mines whose output lay between 2 and 4 million tons.[1] The giant complexes of Fushun and Kailuan, which dominated prewar coal production, are still among the four largest producers.

After a discussion of the growth of Chinese cotton mills in which he points to similar achievements, Kraus nevertheless concludes: 'The industry was a failure. It was a failure from a business point of view because during the mid Thirties virtually all mills were either shut down or selling yarn at a loss.'[2] This study, on the other hand, shows that while many coal-mining companies did face economic difficulties, some remained highly profitable, and that the industry as a whole was returning to a more prosperous situation on the eve of the war.

Several factors indicate that, once the railways had been restored to operation, the supply of coal to the Chinese market was adequate: the strong growth of output historically, the virtual disappearance of imported coal from the market, a substantial and rising volume of exports, and depressed prices in Chinese cities for most of the 1930s. Theories that place emphasis on supply factors such as shortage of capital or entrepreneurial inefficiency thus fail to give a convincing explanation of the history of the industry.

Demand was, potentially by the 1920s and actually by the 1930s, the main constraint on growth; this conclusion parallels that reached by Kraus in his study of cotton mills.[3] Here the small size of the modern sector, which, whether in the form of manufacturing or transport industries or of urban households, provided the main market for coal, again becomes a crucial explanatory variable. For the coal industry had inevitably to remain small until either the size of the modern sector was drastically increased or coal consumption was widely extended into the non-modernized sector. A thorough study of the ultimate determinants in the trends in demand would have to work with a macro-economic picture of the economy, but there is little doubt that the failure of the agrarian sector decisively to increase its rate of growth or to enlarge its contribution to constructive investment in the modern sector was the background constraint on the development of coal mining as of the rest of the economy.

Chinese versus foreigners

On the whole the Chinese-owned sector of the industry tended to grow slightly faster than the foreign-owned sector. While it would be putting too much weight on this fact to argue from it that foreign firms did not 'oppress' or hamper the growth of Chinese ones, it does suggest that the reality was less one-sided and more complex than sometimes suggested.

Historically, foreigners managed during a fairly short period to get possession, often by underhand or forcible means, of some of the best sites for coal mining in China. As a result they were able to build up a predominant position in prewar mining. But they did not hold *all* the best sites and, once this short period was over, Chinese mines were able to develop on some sites, laying the basis for a strong and relatively prosperous sector. They were not strong enough to shake the foreign position, but nor did they find themselves helpless before the foreign onslaught.

As suggested in the last paragraph, the crucial factors in inter-firm competition in the industry were geology and location. This led to a more complicated pattern than, for instance, in the cotton industry, where there was often a fairly simple dichotomy between profitable foreign mills and unprofitable Chinese ones.[4] While foreign interests abandoned or failed to develop any unprofitable sites they acquired, the record for Chinese entrepreneurs was more mixed, and those with the best sites enjoyed in normal times a record as good as any.

Relations between foreign companies and the Chinese authorities were likewise complex. The state, forced to grant favoured treatment to the foreign firms as a legacy of the past and of China's continuing weakness, nevertheless retained formal sovereignty and attempted, with varying success, to restrict and hamper the intruders. They were least successful in Manchuria, where even before 1931 the Japanese, in full control of the vital railway, brooked little or no interference with their enterprises. From 1931 Manchuria was of course occupied by Japan and separated politically from China. Within 'China proper', too, the Japanese were the most intransigent and stood firm against the rise of Chinese nationalism in the 1920s and 1930s. They were, however, unable substantially to increase their stake once their takeover of German interests in Shandong had been completed.

The British, whose interests were less centrally involved, were much more inclined to compromise, and a balance which had been heavily in favour of foreign interests up to the 1920s began to be less one-sided following the rise of the Nationalists. The Peking Syndicate resumed operations at Jiaozuo in 1933 with a now minority participation in the joint sales administration with its Chinese neighbour. Even Kailuan, a more important and less vulnerable enterprise, came to a *modus vivendi* with Chinese nationalism, which involved its integration for the first time into the Chinese tax system, and the granting of a much greater say to the Chinese partners within the company.

Not only were the Chinese more resourceful in their efforts to control foreign penetration than is often supposed, but there are reasons for believing that, had not war intervened, the foreign share outside Manchuria would have been of decreasing importance. The foreign position was based almost exclusively on limited rights gained during the period 1895–1903. Although these did include many of the best sites in China, there was potentially a limit to their development. No new mining rights were being granted to non-Chinese companies, and so, as the industry expanded, it is reasonable to expect that the weight of those older mines would decrease. Kailuan's difficulties in the 1930s and its consequent attempt to ally itself with the Chinese government in the formation of a coal cartel presaged a growing degree of Chinese control over their own economy and production. Such control was still in the future, as the success of the Japanese in sabotaging the cartel showed, but the trend was definitely in that direction.

Capitalists versus workers

All classes were weak in early twentieth-century China,[5] and the capitalist bourgeoisie and the proletariat were not exceptions. The recruitment of managers and shareholders primarily from the bureaucracy or those closely associated with it, was a reflection of the weakness of industrial capitalists. In Shanghai, relatively immune from oppression by other groups in society, capitalism flourished in the 1910s and 1920s, and there emerged a bourgeoisie with a distinct economic and even political identity.[6] In the coal mines of north China, on the other hand, enterprises were more vulnerable than almost anywhere else to the exercise of arbitrary power by social forces outside the industry. Thus in that region some connections with those social forces – the bureaucracy and warlord groups – was a *sine qua non* for success, and no capitalist class was able to establish an independent identity.

China's social and political scene changed with the advent of the Nationalist government but, because of their different starting points, Shanghai and the coalfields of north China experienced the change in very different ways. The Shanghai capitalists were brought to heel by a government eager to exert its authority in China's cities and ports.[7] But in north China there never had been such an independent group, and indeed the restoration of stability actually reduced the need for entrepreneurs to cultivate the alien state power, even though that process was merely incipient, and mine owners had little recourse against the exercise of government power if they were exposed to it.

At that point in the early 1920s when the balance between other classes and social forces was at its most unstable, China's proletariat, newly swelled and strengthened by the wartime industrial boom, was able to flex its muscles. Workers' organizations mushroomed and for a brief moment workers were a major force in national politics. But they remained a minute segment of China's population, and could only exercise any power in alliance with sections of the elite. So when the Nationalists restored a degree of stability among the elite, they turned on the workers and removed them from the political scene for the rest of the pre-communist period.

Coal miners shared in this history, but again their experience differed in some ways from that of urban workers. The earlier blooming occurred only in a few places, and most miners remained mute and down-trodden under the warlords, to such an extent that the arrival of the Nationalists brought a degree of liberation – workers' organizations sprung up, and some improvement of conditions was won. But the essential class calculus still remained the same, and the tiny mining proletariat was always vulnerable both to the use of outright force by the organs of political power and to the undermining of its position by the actual or potential recourse to the vast army of peasant labour.

So for both capitalists and workers, the small size of the modern sector was crucial in leaving them weak and exposed in the face of other social groups and forces. Both classes bore all the marks of a transitional period, as they emerged slowly from other classes, only partially and hesitantly claiming a separate identity. But the capitalists had far more to offer the holders of political power and, while weak in the face of the state or the military, were able to join with them to keep the workers in control. For those workers, as for most Chinese, existence was hazardous and miserable throughout the period.

Appendix A

Output figures for Chinese coal mines

The series normally used for Chinese coal output is that compiled by Yan Zhongping (1955, pp. 102–3, etc.) mainly from the reports of the Geological Survey of China. This series, however, does not cover the pre-1912 period, while there are no explicit criteria for including the output of a given mine in the aggregate series of modern mine output. For the purpose of this work, therefore, I have compiled a new series for large-mine output, 1896–1936, using mainly data on the output of individual mines from the Survey, but supplementing these with materials from other sources where they are more reliable or where the Survey provides no coverage. The criteria used for including mines in this series are as follows: any mine whose output was over 100,000 tons in the given year is included, as is any whose output was over 50,000 tons in the given year and that following; the output of such mines is then included for all following years up to the first of a series of five years when output fell below 50,000 tons; finally, where a mine was clearly opened from the start as a modern mine (as was mostly the case with the foreign mines) its output is included from the first year even if it was under 50,000 tons. A detailed breakdown of the figures and sources used is available from the author. Although some problems remain, for instance in differentiating between company and calender years and in reconciling very different reports of the output of an individual company, this series is both more complete and more consistent than the existing one.

For non-modernized and small mines, the Survey began by estimating a flat 6 million tons, while later estimates are often inconsistent both with the earlier Survey figures and with material from other sources. Unfortunately we have insufficient information thoroughly to revise the Survey figures for small mines; in their present form they are not reliable enough to support analysis, and local and descriptive data has to be used in the text instead. For the same reason, Table 1 reproduces, for information, only the unadjusted Survey series for total output (i.e. including output from small mines).

Appendix B

Reference table of major Chinese coal-mining companies

Name of company	Area of operation	Railway(s) mainly used	Year of establishment	Nationality of ownership	Maximum output ('000 tons) (year achieved)
Baojin	East and North Shanxi	Zheng-Tai/Jing-Sui	1908	Chinese	522 (1932)
Beipiao	South-east Rehe	Bei-Ning	1921	Chinese[a]	578 (1931)
Benxihu	South Liaoning	An-Feng	1910	Sino-Japanese	740 (1936)
Bodong	Central Shandong	Jiao-Ji	1923	Sino-Japanese	168 (1935)
Changcheng	North-east Hebei	Bei-Ning	1916	Chinese	160 (1931)
Changxing	North Zhejiang	None	1918	Chinese	198 (1933)
Datong	Central Anhui	Jin-Pu/Huainan-Wuhu	1911	Chinese	270 (1936)
Fuhua[b]	South Hubei	(Yangzi River)	1916	Chinese	130 (1934)
Fushun	South Liaoning	SMR	1903	Sino-Russian, 1903–1905/ Japanese, 1905–	9,593 (1936)
Fuyuan[b]	South Hubei	(Yangzi River)	1912	Chinese	144 (1934)
Fuzhouwan	South Liaoning	SMR	1919	Chinese[a]	220 (1931)
Hegang	East Heilongjiang		1917	Chinese[a]	365 (1936)
Huafeng	West Shandong	Jin-Pu	1919	Chinese	100 (1936)
Huainan	Central Anhui	Jin-Pu/Huainan-Wuhu	1929	Chinese government	585 (1936)
Jiawang	North Jiangsu	Jin-Pu	1898	Chinese	347 (1936)
Jinbei	North Shanxi	Jing-Sui	1924	Chinese	302 (1935)
Jingxing	South Hebei	Zheng-Tai/Jing-Han	1902	Sino-German	882 (1936)
Kailuan (KMA)[c]	North-east Hebei	Bei-Ning	1912	Sino-British	5,356 (1931)
Kaiping[c]	North-east Hebei	Bei-Ning	1880	Chinese, 1880–1900/ British 1901–12	1,434 (1911)
Lecheng	Central Shandong	Jiao-Ji	1918	Chinese	139 (1934)
Lieshan	North Anhui	Jin-Pu	1914	Chinese	126 (1933)
Lincheng	South Hebei	Jing-Han	1902	Sino-Belgian, 1902–21/ Chinese, 1921–	290 (1914)
Liuhegou	North Henan	Jing-Han	1903	Sino-Belgian, 1903–19/ Chinese, 1919–	598 (1936)

Company	Location	Railway	Date	Ownership	Output (year)
Liujiang	North-east Hebei	Bei-Ning	1914	Chinese	255 (1931)
Luanzhou[c]	North-east Hebei	Bei-Ning	1908	Chinese	733 (1936)
Luda (Zichuan)	Central Shandong	Jiao-Ji	1902	German, 1902–14/ Japanese, 1914–22/ Sino-Japanese, 1923–	
Mentougou	North Hebei	Jing-Sui	1918	Sino-British	438 (1934)
Muleng	East Jilin	CER	1924	Sino-Russian[a]	338 (1931)
Naizishan	Central Jilin	Ji-Dun	1916	Chinese[a]	228 (1936)
Peking Syndicate[d]	North Henan	Dao-Qing/Jing-Han	1905	British	694 (1923)
Pingxiang	North-west Jiangxi	Zhu-Ping/Yue-Han	1898	Chinese	950 (1916)
Xi'an	East Liaoning	Shen-Hai	1926	Chinese[a]	728 (1936)
Yantai	South Liaoning	SMR	1899	Sino-Russian, 1899–1905/Japanese, 1905–	349 (1936)
Yili	South Hebei	Jing-Han	1908	Chinese	517 (1936)
Yuanhua[b]	South Hubei	(Yangzi river)	1935	Chinese	282 (1936)
Yuesheng	Central Shandong	Jiao-Ji	1918	Sino-Russian	425 (1936)
Zhalainuoer	West Heilongjiang	CER	1901	Chinese	306 (1920)
Zhengfeng	South Hebei	Zheng–Tai/Jing-Han	1912	Chinese	436 (1936)
Zhong-Fu[d]	North Henan	Dao-Qing/Jing-Han	1933	Sino-British	1,310 (1936)
Zhonghe	South Hebei	Jing-Han	1913	Chinese	179 (1936)
Zhongxing	South Shandong	Jin-Pu	1898	Chinese	1,736 (1936)
Zhongyuan[d]	North Henan	Dao-Qing/Jing-Han	1915	Chinese	949 (1924)

Notes: [a] The Japanese took over all Chinese-owned mines in the north-east after 1931.
[b] In 1935 Fuhua and Fuyuan merged to form the Yuanhua Company.
[c] In 1912 Kaiping and Luanzhou merged to form the Kailuan Mining Administration.
[d] In 1933 the Peking Syndicate and Zhongyuan Companies formed the Zhong-Fu Mining Administration.
The dates of establishment are only approximate in some cases, and generally refer to the acquisition of a mining permit by the company in question rather than to the beginning of mining in the area. In some cases the acquisition of the permit was a long and complicated process.

NOTES

Chapter 1

1 Chang, 1969. For a critique of one of the component series see Wright, unpublished paper.
2 Hou Chi-ming, 1965.
3 Feuerwerker 1958 and 1967; Quan, 1972a.
4 For instance, see the publications by these three scholars in *Nankai Social and Economic Quarterly*.
5 Yan Zhongping, 1963.
6 Chao, 1977; Kraus, 1980; Cochran, 1980.
7 Fogel and Engerman, 1971, p. 148.
8 Liu and Yeh, 1965, pp. 69, 143, 569, 575.
9 Notably, Elvin, 1972, ch. 17.
10 Riskin, 1975.
11 Mandel, 1968, pp. 446–7.
12 Moulder, 1977.
13 Fogel and Engerman, 1971, pp. 98–162.
14 Buchanan, 1934, p. 255.
15 Read, 1939–40; Wang Zhongluo, 1956, p. 24. For this last as well as several other references I am indebted to Professor Wang Ling who generously shared the results of his research with me.
16 Hartwell, 1962 and 1967.
17 Barrow, 1806, pp. 594–5.
18 Reid, 1901–2, p. 32.
19 Richthofen, 1872, p. 6.
20 Richthofen, 1882, p. 204.
21 See Quan, 1972b, pp. 673–9.
22 Richthofen, 1872, pp. 26, 33; 1882, p. 211, and 1907, vol. 1, pp. 482, 502; Drake, 1902–3, p. 821; Moller, 1902–3, p. 142.
23 Ashton and Sykes, 1964, p. 10.
24 Caldwell, 1911–12, p. 366; Richthofen, 1907, vol. 1, p. 297.
25 Williamson, 1870, vol. 2, p. 434.
26 Ibid., vol. 1, p. 117, describing mines at Wei xian in Shandong.
27 IUP, 1971, vol. 8, p. 648.
28 IUP, 1971, vol. 10, p. 512.
29 Reid, 1901–2, p. 32.
30 Fleming, 1863, p. 564, though this mine was in fact a very steep slope mine; see also Richthofen, 1872, p. 89.
31 Hommel, 1937, pp. 2–3, 119.
32 Williamson, 1870, vol. 1, p. 117; Richthofen, 1872, pp. 26, 89, and 1907, vol. 1, p. 482.

33 Caldwell, 1911–12, p. 366.
34 Sung, 1966, pp. 204–5.
35 IUP, 1971, vol. 10, p. 512.
36 Reid, 1901–2, p. 32.
37 Fleming, 1863, p. 563.
38 Wang Zhongluo, 1956, p. 24.
39 Hartwell, 1967, p. 119.
40 Ibid., p. 122; see also Yang Kuan, 1956, p. 73.
41 Professor Hans Bielenstein made this point to me.
42 Sung, 1966, p. 189; Yang Kuan, 1956, p. 74.
43 Richthofen, 1872, pp. 31, 33; for the Kaiping area see also Guo, 1980, p. 47.
44 Grosier, 1818–20, vol. 2, p. 220.
45 MMT, chōsabu, 1937e, p. 160.
46 Jiangxi sheng, 1959, p. 40; for Kaiping, see Guo, 1980, p. 47.
47 Wang Zhongluo, 1956, p. 24.
48 Hartwell, 1967, pp. 140–1.
49 Ibid., p. 141.
50 Polo, 1958, p. 156; Cathay referred to north China.
51 Hartwell, 1962, p. 160. Guo, 1980, p. 46, states (without discussion or evidence) that coal use in China expanded during the Ming and Qing.
52 Tang Mingsui, et al., 1958, p. 54.
53 Grosier, 1818–20, vol. 2, p. 220.
54 Williamson, 1870, vol. 1, p. 154.
55 Wei and Lu, 1980, p. 34; Ho, 1959, pp. 149–53; Adshead, 1974, pp. 20–8.
56 Richthofen, 1872, pp. 6, 11–12.
57 For instance Fangshan coal taken to Tianjin, see ibid., p. 35. This might, however, have been after the emergence of a new market in the form of steamships.
58 Ibid., p. 26.
59 Nef, 1932, vol. 1, pp. 19–20.
60 Chang, 1969, p. 76.
61 Perkins, 1975, p. 117.

Chapter 2
1 For an earlier and briefer version of Chapters 2–4, see Wright, 1981b.
2 Wang Kung-ping, 1977, p. 43; Wu Yuan-li, 1963, p. 35.
3 US Bureau of Mines, 1976, p. 160.
4 Wang, Kung-ping, 1947, pp. 36–40.
5 Howe, 1978, pp. 107, 116; Hsia, 1971, p. 124.
6 Hou Defeng, 1932, p. 3.
7 Griffin, 1977, p. 20. In the eighteenth century royalties varied widely, but in some areas reached levels even higher than 20%, see Ashton and Sykes, 1964, p. 189.
8 KYZB 236 (28 April 1933): 1107; KYZB 355 (21 October 1935): 676–7.
9 Tanaka, 1920, pp. 292–4.
10 Gong, 1933, pp. 112, 209.
11 Xu, 1947, p. 33.
12 Zheng, 1931, p. 378; Tan, 1922, p. 38; KYZB 56 (28 July 1929): 118.
13 China, shiyebu, guoji maoyi ju, 1935, 6:98.
14 Feuerwerker, 1958, pp. 177–8, for the China Merchants' Steamship Navigation Company; and Chu, 1965, p. 29, for Zhang Jian's enterprises.
15 Wei, 1954, p. 111.
16 Gan, 1910, 18:17.
17 KYZB 55 (21 July 1929): 105, KYZB 317 (7 January 1935): 67–8.
18 Mishina, 1942, p. 72.

19 Gu, 1916, 8:59.
20 KYZB 288 (28 May 1934): 754: Xu, 1947, pp. 186–9.
21 Chao, 1977, pp. 142–6.
22 Elvin, 1972, ch. 17.
23 Baran, 1973, pp. 375–6; Riskin, 1975, pp. 49–84 – the quotations are from pp. 80–1; Lippit, 1978; Elvin, 1978; Riskin, 1978.
24 For Luda see SKJ 57 (November 1922): 116.
25 Griffin, 1977, p. 63; Morris and Williams, 1958, pp. 137–48.
26 Rawski, 1980, p. 22.
27 Morris and Williams, 1958, p. 138.
28 Zhang Huiruo, 1936, p. 233; Hou Defeng, 1929, p. 95.
29 KYZB 177 (7 February 1932): 129–31.
30 Coble, 1980, p. 72.
31 Wright, 1980b, pp. 716–17.
32 Yan Zhongping, 1955, pp. 132–3.
33 NP, Young to Nathan, 10 August 1931; Nathan to Young, 11 August 1931.
34 KYZB 288 (28 May 1934): 754.
35 Royal Commission, 1931, p. 21: 'Throughout the greater part of its history, organised industry in India has experienced a shortage of labour.'
36 Feuerwerker, 1977, pp. 10–11.
37 MMT, 1919, p. 495.
38 MMT, 1928, pp. 564–8; Wang Qingbin, 1928, 1:279.
39 MMT, 1928, p. 586; Yu, 1926a, pp. 97–8 and 1926c, pp. 176–8; the Benxihu figure is slightly adjusted as Yu's figures cover only eleven months of the year.
40 MMT, 1938, p. 1723; these figures are not completely comparable to the earlier ones, but this does not affect the overall trend.
41 Wang Qingbin, 1928, 1:373; MMT, rōmuka, 1931, pp. 56–7.
42 Wang Qingbin, 1928, 1:367.
43 Carlson, 1971, p. 45.
44 NP, MacFeat to Nathan, 12 February 1931; Nathan to Turner, 22 January 1936.
45 KYZB 355 (21 October 1935): 669.
46 MMT, chōsabu, 1937c, p. 172; *Zhongwai jingji zhoukan* 125 (15 August 1925): 5.
47 Hu Jixian, 1931, pp. 96, 120–1.
48 *Zhongwai jingji zhoukan* 125 (15 August 1925): 5.
49 Mauldon, 1929, p. 50.
50 Yu, 1926d, pp. 70–4.
51 Yu, 1926e, pp. 48–9.
52 See various issues of KYZB.
53 See Zhang Huiruo, 1936, pp. 239–40; there is an unexplained and very abrupt drop in output in September 1934 and 1935. While this may be harvest-related, it is puzzling that there is no trace of such a drop in the previous five years.
54 See various issues of KYZB.
55 See KYZB 187 (21 April 1932): 293–4; and also KYZB 247 (21 July 1933): 98, but these patterns are rather weak.
56 For this latter point see Howe, 1973, p. 3.
57 Hou Defeng, 1929, p. 83.
58 Hou Defeng, 1932, p. 80.
59 Hu Jixian, 1931, p. 311; KYZB 149 (7 July 1931): 840–1.
60 KYZB 163 (21 October 1931): 1057.
61 Kōzan konwakai, 1932, vol. 2, pp. 611–12.
62 KYZB 11 (14 August 1928): 180; KYZB 200 (29 July 1932): 499. The latter source records a 67% rise in mining wages as against a 6% rise in wholesale prices in north China. (See Nankai daxue, 1958, p. 11).

63 See Chapter 9 and Wright 1981a.
64 Carlson, 1971, p. 47.
65 KYZB 150 (14 July 1931): 862–4.
66 KYZB 186 (14 April 1932): 286–7.
67 KYZB 40 (28 March 1929): 646.
68 Howe, 1973, p. 19.
69 MMT, keizai chōsakai, 1936a, p. 39.
70 Howe, 1973, p. 21.
71 Brown and Wright, 1981, p. 69; Fairbank, 1975, letters 115, 119.
72 Carlson, 1971, p. 19.
73 Shaffer, 1982, pp. 73, 80; Gu, 1916, 3:53, 6:13, 8:61–62; MMT, chōsabu, 1937d, p. 242.
74 Gu, 1916, 6:13.
75 Ibid., 7:58, 65.
76 KYZB 30 (14 January 1929): 488.

Chapter 3
1 See especially Tezuka, 1943, pp. 117–76.
2 China, shiyebu, guoji maoyi ju, 1935, 6:95; Zhang Xiaomei, 1939, Q47–8; Bai, 1945, p. 51.
3 KYZB 335 (21 May 1935): 357.
4 Zhang Huiruo, 1936, pp. 118–20.
5 MMT, Tenshin jimusho, 1936, pp. 229–30; Hou Defeng, 1929, Table 1.
6 MMT, chōsabu, 1937b, pp. 146–7; Xie 1926, Table 2.
7 MMT, chōsabu, 1937c, pp. 207–12.
8 Ibid., pp. 29–31.
9 Zheng, 1931, pp. 256–8, 327–8.
10 KYZB 60 (28 August 1929): 179–80; KYZB 67 (21 October 1929): 289–90.
11 KYZB 367 (21 January 1936): 869; KYZB 381 (7 May 1936): 1194; KYZB 391 (21 July 1936): 97.
12 MMT, chōsabu, 1937e, pp. 149–56, 201–11, 318–19; Zhang Huiruo, 1936, pp. 306, 313, 316, 328, 346, 351, 357, 368–9; see also Hou Defeng, 1932, pp. 324–36.
13 MCG 14.4 (April 1934): 229.
14 See the discussion in Tezuka, 1943, pp. 163–9.
15 For this interpretation, see Chao, 1975, pp. 179–80.
16 KYZB 190 (14 May 1932): 343.
17 MMT, chōsabu, 1937c, pp. 29–31.
18 Twenty-five out of thirty-five Boshan mines surveyed in ZGJJNJ 1936, K71–8, worked at least 250 days a year in at least one of the years 1932–4.
19 Zhang Huiruo, 1936, pp. 132–4, 212, 316, 326; MMT chōsabu, 1937e, p. 146.
20 Hou Chi-ming, 1965, p. 181.
21 CEJ 6.5 (May 1930): 511–19; but Tang Tingshu in the 1880s reported daily output per worker in the traditional mines at Kaiping at around 200–250 kg. See Guo, 1980, p. 47, and Tezuka, 1943, p. 169.
22 ZGJJNJ, 1936, K71–8.
23 KYZB 302 (14 September 1934): 977–8.
24 MMT, chōsabu, 1937c, pp. 29–31.
25 Buxton, 1978, p. 113; Griffin, 1977, p. 105. Note that the same cannot be said about the next stage of mining mechanization, that of face work and loading, which has since the Second World War led to a great increase in output per worker in the United Kingdom; see Buxton, 1978, p. 238.
26 For technological advances in Britain, see Griffin, 1971; also Griffin, 1977, ch. 4.
27 For Chinese coal mining before 1895, see Brown and Wright, 1981.

28 NCH, 30 December 1904.
29 IMC, *Reports, 1878*, part 2, p. 218; IMC, *Reports, 1879*, part 2, pp. 281–3.
30 Carlson, 1971, ch. 1 and 2.
31 Manshikai, 1964–5, vol. 2, p. 109; MMT, sōsaishitsu, 1937, pp. 368–9.
32 MMT, shomubu chōsaka, 1929, p. 109; Kailan Mining Administration, 1920, p. 10.
33 MMT, shomubu chōsaka, 1929, p. 109; KYZB 247 (21 July 1933): 98.
34 Zhang Huiruo, 1936, p. 120.
35 Manshikai, 1964–5, vol. 2, p. 66; NKGB 20 (January 1930): 209; KYZB 109 (7 September 1930): 196.
36 Manshikai, 1964–5, vol. 2, p. 92–104, 198; MMT, Tenshin jimusho, 1936, p. 31; KYZB 239 (21 May 1933): 1146–7.
37 The mining companies were Benxihu, Fushun (which also operated opencast and drift mines), Huainan, Jingxing, Kailuan, Liuhegou, Luda, Pingxiang, Zhongxing and Zhong-Fu. The information is taken mainly from Hou and Cao, 1948.
38 Ibid. The fifteen companies were Baojin, Beipiao, Bodong, Changxing, Datong, Jiawang, Jinbei, Lieshan, Lincheng, Liujiang, Mentougou, Muleng, Yili, Yuesheng and Zhengfeng. All these were companies producing over 200,000 tons per year at least some time in their history. The list omits many smaller collieries which were still considered modern by Chinese standards.
39 International Labour Organization, 1951, pp. 33–4.
40 MMT, Tenshin jimusho, 1936, p. 71.
41 Griffin, 1977, pp. 108–9; Buxton, 1978, p. 70; Shurick, 1924, pp. 62–9.
42 Kōzan konwakai, 1932, vol. 2, pp. 622–3; Hou and Cao, 1948, p. 15.
43 Zheng, 1931, p. 147.
44 Ikonnikov, 1977, p. 109.
45 Kōzan konwakai, 1932, vol. 2, p. 361.
46 Hu Rongquan, 1935, pp. 183–208.
47 Zheng, 1931, p. 362.
48 Tezuka, 1944, p. 315.
49 Ibid., p. 315; MMT, sōsaishitsu, 1937, pp. 390–1.
50 Kōzan konwakai, 1932, vol. 2, p. 602.
51 Hu Rongquan, 1935, pp. 274, 296; KYZB 40 (28 March 1929): 645 (for Datong).
52 Tezuka, 1944, p. 316.
53 MMT, sōsaishitsu, 1937, p. 387.
54 Tezuka, 1944, p. 316.
55 See McCloskey, 1971, p. 291. Geological conditions were also important here, but while Chinese conditions were less difficult than British, they were more difficult than American.
56 See *Contemporary Manchuria* 2.5 (September 1938): 39–40; MMT, sōsaishitsu, 1937, pp. 384–6.
57 MMT, chōsabu, 1937a, pp. 59, 128.
58 KYZB 244 (28 June 1933): 56–8.
59 Buxton, 1978, p. 179.
60 MMT, sōsaishitsu, 1937, p. 387.
61 Tezuka, 1944, p. 313.
62 NP, Dengis to Nathan, 30 March 1948.
63 MMT, shomubu chōsaka, 1929, p. 90; Hou and Cao, 1948, p. 7; Kailan Mining Administration, 1920, p. 14.
64 MMT, chōsabu, 1937d, p. 66; KYZB 228 (28 February 1933): 974; KYZB 378 (14 April 1936): 1152.
65 Gu, 1916, 3:21.
66 Hou and Cao, 1948, p. 10; MMT, sōsaishitsu, 1937, p. 387.

67 MMT, chōsabu, 1937e, p. 23.
68 Griffin, 1971, p. 61; Tezuka, 1944, p. 314; Kōzan konwakai, 1932, vol. 2, pp. 325–7.
69 For instance in Liujiang, see Yu, 1926e, p. 40.
70 Kailan Mining Administration, 1920, p. 33.
71 Buxton, 1978, pp. 108–9.
72 See MMT, chōsabu, 1937e, pp. 214–25; no mine producing over 16 tons a day is listed as using manual methods.
73 KYZB 300 (28 August 1934): 946.
74 Bai, 1945, pp. 675–6.
75 For the Tongxing Company, see Zhang Huiruo, 1936, p. 304, and MMT, chōsabu, 1937e, p. 148.
76 KYZB 140 (28 April 1931): 700.
77 Zhang Huiruo, 1936, p. 304.
78 Kōzan konwakai, 1932, vol. 2, p. 338.
79 Bai, 1945, p. 691.
80 Hou and Cao, 1948, p. 10; MMT, shomubu chōsaka, 1928, p. 127.
81 Kōzan konwakai, 1932, vol. 2, p. 338.
82 MMT, chōsabu, 1937a, pp. 59–61.
83 MMT, shomubu chōsaka, 1929, p. 90.
84 Kailan Mining Administration, 1920, p. 13; NP, Turner to Nathan, 16 May 1933.
85 Hou and Cao, 1948, pp. 9–10.
86 MMT, sōsaishitsu, 1937, p. 397.
87 Manshikai, 1964–5, vol. 2, pp. 94–5, 101–2; MMT, sōsaishitsu, 1937, pp. 383–6; *Contemporary Manchuria* 1.4 (November 1937): 64.
88 Nef, 1932, vol. 1, pp. 28–9; Langton, 1979, p. 16 *et passim*.
89 Feuerwerker, 1977, p. 68; Arnold, 1926, pp. 533, 744.
90 Feuerwerker, 1977, p. 68; Kingsmill, 1898, pp. 76, 136.
91 Richthofen, 1872, p. 26.
92 Langton, 1979, p. 45.
93 Carlson, 1971, pp. 19–22.
94 Gu, 1916, 4:11, 5:26, 6:25, 9:53; Tōa dōbunkai, 1917–20, vol. 15, p. 908.
95 Yan Zhongping, 1955, pp. 172, 178.
96 MMT, chōsabu, 1937b, p. 153; NSGB, 5.7 (February 1919): *zhuyi* 1.
97 MMT, chōsabu, 1937b, p. 198.
98 KYZB 20 (28 October 1928): 328.
99 Quoted in Buck, 1978, p. 45.
100 IUP, 1971, vol. 14, p. 316.
101 *London and China Express*, 22 December 1915.
102 Buck, 1978, pp. 45, 49–50; Oka, 1919, pp. 21–2; *Tsūshō kōho* 467 (8 November 1917): 489–91.
103 IMC, *Reports and Reports, 1905*, part II, vol. 1, p. 79.
104 Zhongguo kexue yuan, 1958, pp. 255–6.
105 Rising demand within Japan also contributed to a declining share of Japanese coal in the China market.

Chapter 4

1 Morris and Williams, 1958, p. 18.
2 Lü, 1962, p. 2.
3 According to the figures compiled by the Chinese customs. While this of course excludes the large number of Chinese junks using the ports, it is still a high proportion even of ships engaged in foreign trade, when compared with other trade routes.

4 *Potential* demand is estimated as the demand that would have existed had market conditions been the same as in 1934, taking into account only changes in the amount of shipping and in the efficiency of fuel consumption. Thus $D_t = D_0 \cdot S_t/S_0 \cdot C^{0-t}$ where D is demand in a given year, S the amount of coal using shipping and C the rate of technical progress, that is, the percentage 'increase' in the amount of coal needed to generate a unit of power in year t as compared with year $(t + 1)$. Demand in 1934 (year 0) was about 1.963 million tons.

5 IUP, 1971, vol. 7, p. 366.

6 Liu Kwang-ching, 1962, pp. 93, 130.

7 *Chinese Repository*, 18.7 (July 1849): 392.

8 Liu Kwang-ching, 1962, p. 93.

9 IUP, 1971, vol. 9, pp. 15, 247; also IMC, *Reports, Hankow 1864*, p. 7.

10 IUP, 1971, vol. 6, p. 172.

11 Klein, 1968, ch. 5, p. 117.

12 Huang Jiamo, 1961, p. 28.

13 IMC, *Returns and Reports, 1884*, p. 260; also Brown and Wright, 1981, p. 68.

14 Sun Yutang, 1957, pp. 1090, 1096; NCH, 24 March 1886.

15 NCH, various issues; Brown and Wright, 1981, p. 73; Zhongguo shixue hui, 1961, vol. 7, pp. 113–18.

16 Thus in 1867 in Shanghai Japanese coal averaged around 6.50 taels per ton as against about 5.50 for Taiwan coal, 13–14 for British coal and 9–10 for Australian; see IUP, 1971, vol. 8, p. 319. By 1874 Japan coal at 5.60 taels was slightly cheaper than Taiwan coal at 5.90. See IPU, 1971, vol. 11, p. 435. Later, in the 1890s, Kaiping coal was in general only slightly cheaper than equivalent Japanese coals, see NCH.

17 IUP, 1971, vol. 8, p. 318.

18 Sumiya, 1968, pp. 20–1, 96–7, 185; Sugiyama, 1979, pp. 199–218.

19 IMC, *Returns and Reports, 1884*, p. 260.

20 Brown and Wright, 1981, p. 63.

21 IMC, *Reports, 1865*, p. 39.

22 IUP, 1971, vol. 9, p. 15 and vol. 12, p. 654; IMC, *Reports, 1873*, p. 30.

23 Sumiya, 1968, p. 349; Endacott, 1964, p. 133

24 This figure is estimated from the difference between gross and net imports of coal into Shanghai in the IMC Reports, given that the amounts for coal imported into other ports from the China coastal ports were rather small.

25 Tōa dōbunkai, 1919–20, vol. 15, p. 903.

26 MMT, 1928, p. 717.

27 Manshikai, 1964–5, vol. 2, p. 67.

28 For a discussion of these figures see Wright, 1976, pp. 325–9.

29 Yasuba, 1978, p. 33.

30 Sturmey, 1962, p. 84.

31 Horiuchi, 1967, pp. 738–9.

32 Kurgan-van Hentenryk, 1965, pp. 73–4.

33 The methodology used in Table 12 for estimating figures for lines which did not submit returns is outlined in Wright, 1976, pp. 303–14, although there are some slight changes to the final figures because of information acquired since those estimates were made.

34 MMT, 1919, pp. 284–5; MMT, 1928, pp. 276–7; MMT, 1938, pp. 332–3.

35 Feuerwerker, 1977, pp. 71–2; Ping-Han tielu, 1932, pp. 573–4; *Tiedao gongbao*, 1935–6.

36 Kennedy, 1978, pp. 175–6.

37 Liu Ao, 1958, pp. 43–4.

38 Quan, 1972a, p. 47.

39 Kennedy, 1978, p. 118.
40 Brown and Wright, 1981, p. 68.
41 Li Hongzhang, 1905–8, *zougao* 47:10–11.
42 Zhu, 1908, 8:14b.
43 For a list see Sun Yutang, 1955, pp. 73–91.
44 IUP, 1971, vol. 14, p. 519; Brown and Wright, 1981, p. 62.
45 Brown, 1979, p. 560, and 1981, p. 456.
46 Chang, 1969, p. 71; the index includes coal mining, but to attempt to correct it would be to suggest a greater accuracy than it in fact possesses.
47 MCG 15.8 (August 1935): 105–6; Chang, 1969, pp. 119, 122–3; Wright, 1976, pp. 319–20.
48 Buxton, 1978, pp. 56–7.
49 Ibid., pp. 86–7.
50 For the switch from vegetable to mineral fuel in Europe see Landes, 1972, pp. 174–8.
51 Milward and Saul, 1979, pp. 185, 331, 405, and 1977, p. 30.
52 Ikonnikov, 1977, pp. 92, 163; US, Central Intelligence Agency, 1976, pp. 5, 15.
53 Kōzan konwakai, 1932, vol. 2, p. 190.
54 See Quan, 1972a, pp. 47–50, 78–82.
55 Yu, 1926d, pp. 97–8.
56 NP, Nathan to Young, 11 August 1931; Quan, 1972a, p. 5.
57 Rawski, 1980, p. 22.
58 Quan, 1972a, pp. 284.
59 Manshikai, 1964–5, vol. 2, p. 461.
60 Gu, 1916, 9:89.
61 Rawski, 1980, p. 23.
62 Sun and Huenemann, 1969, p. 71.
63 Sheba, 1937, p. 831.
64 MCG 15.5 (May 1935): 16–17.
65 For the assumptions used in calculating the amounts of coal consumed by the cotton and (in the following paragraph) the silk industries, see the author's detailed notes to Table 21.
66 Ting, 1936, p. 437.
67 Lieu, 1941, pp. 113–16.
68 See the reports on the Shanghai market in NCH and in KYZB.
69 MCG 15.5 (May 1935): 16–17.
70 See Wright, unpublished paper.
71 MMT, sōsaishitsu, 1937, p. 398.
72 NP, Nathan to Turner, 27 May 1937.
73 Orchard, 1936, p. 26.
74 China, zhuji chu, 1940, p. 84.
75 Ibid.
76 MMT, chōsabu, 1937e, p. 634; *Guoji maoyi daobao*, 6.4 (10 April 1934): 257; see also Chapters 6 and 8.
77 NCH, 5 August 1936.
78 Klein, 1968, ch. 5.
79 Longfield, 1947, p. 21.
80 ILO, 1938b, vol. 1, p. 98.
81 Ibid., p. 96.
82 Ibid., pp. 99–100.
83 NCH, 8 February 1933; Luo, 1932, p. 66.
84 China, Ministry of Industry, Bureau of Mines, 1938, p. 345.
85 MCG 15.8 (August 1935): 106; unlike the other series, information is only

available for Onoda for the first and last years of the period.
86 Read, 1943, pp. 42–55; Kikuta, 1943, pp. 84–100.
87 NSGB 1.2 (September 1914): *baogao* 5.
88 Jiao-Ji tielu, 1934, Boshan xian, 14b.
89 SKJ 46 (April 1919): 1–35.
90 Tezuka, 1944, pp. 284, 295.
91 Jiao-Ji tielu, 1934, Boshan xian, 13a–b, Zichuan xian, 11.
92 China, shiyebu, Zhongguo jingji nianjian bianzuan weiyuanhui, 1934, K536: KYZB 383 (21 June 1936): 1238.
93 Jiangxi sheng, 1959, p. 40.
94 NSGB 5.2 (September 1918): *xuanzai* 5–7.
95 Jiao-Ji tielu, 1934, Boshan xian, 13b.
96 Zhang Xiaomei, 1939, R129; Wang Mingxin et al, 1930, 10:9a–b.
97 E.g. Guangxi, see Hou Defeng, 1932, p. 391; also Jiao-Ji tielu, 1934, Yidu xian, 8 for Shandong.
98 China, shiyebu, guoji maoyi ju, 1935, 7:491–7.
99 Hu Jixian, 1931, p. 102; KYZB 355 (21 October 1935): 667: Zhang Shiwen, 1936, p. 282.
100 Sumiya, 1968, p. 95.
101 Adshead, 1974, p. 26.
102 Kanda, 1936, p. 597.
103 For example, China, shiyebu, guoji maoyi ju, 1935, 4:176.
104 Cochran, 1980, p. 141.
105 KYZB 339 (21 June 1935): 417; KYZB 381 (7 May 1936): 1206–7; KYZB 396 (28 August 1936): 178.
106 *Kuangye lianhehui jikan* 3 (September 1923): *diaocha* 16–21.
107 KYZB 205 (7 September 1932): 581–7; for the antimony industry, see McDonald, 1978, pp. 69–76.
108 Jiao-Ji tielu, 1934, Boshan xian, *passim*; China, shiyebu, guoji maoyi ju, 1934, 8:504, 511, 523.
109 Buck, 1930, p. 402; Gamble, 1954, p. 114.
110 For instance in Tangyin xian in Henan, the locals worked coal mines because firewood was so scarce; see KYZB 345 (7 August 1935): 515.
111 Buck, 1930, pp. 398–9.
112 MCG 15.5 (May 1935): 31–2.
113 NSGB 8.10 (May 1922): *baogao* 5.
114 *Zhongwai jingji zhoukan* 125 (15 August 1925): 30.
115 Clark and Sowerby, 1912, pp. 17, 20.
116. Nichi-Man shōji, 1937, p. 143.
117 Buck, 1930, p. 398.
118 Gamble, 1954, p. 114.
119 Zhang Shiwen, 1936, p. 297.
120 Perkins, 1969, p. 212.
121 Myers, 1970, ch. 2, pp. 293–4; Eastman, 1974, pp. 183–94.
122 Adshead, 1974, *passim*.
123 KYZB 266 (14 December 1933): 408.
124 KYZB 133 (7 March 1931): 583.
125 *Kuangye lianhehui jikan* 3 (September 1923): *diaocha* 20; NSGB 9.9 (April 1923): *xuanzai* 31.
126 IMC, 1932, *Decennial Reports*, p. 606.
127 SKJ 21 (August 1913): 69.
128 CEJ 2.5 (May 1928): 388.
129 CEB, 10 January 1931; *Shiye tongji* 1.2 (April 1933): 3.

130 Buck, 1930, p. 403.
131 As early as 1908 an observer attributed Wuhan's estimated 200,000 tons household consumption of coal to the lack of wood in the vicinity and the expense of shipping firewood from Yichang or Sichuan, see *Shangwu guanbao*, 1908. 30 (8 December 1908): 18. In Nanjing a foraging service collected fuel from an area as much as 50 km around the city, see CEB, 5 December 1925.
132 Assuming that half of total rural consumption was used by households, i.e. around 4.5 million tons in 1933, and that rural population was around 450 million.
133 Gamble, 1933, p. 333.
134 *International Labour Review* 32.2 (August 1935): 239; see also KYZB 391 (21 July 1936): 108.
135 Gamble, 1933, pp. 333–4.
136 MCG 15.5 (May 1935): 33–4.
137 Perkins, 1969, pp. 292–5; Huang and Pang, 1966, p. 218; *Nankai Weekly Statistical Service*, 9 February 1931; these are the Customs Service figures, which cover only inadequately the number of Japanese in the north-east.
138 Kōzan konwakai, 1932, vol. 2, p. 165.
139 By the late 1920s most hewers in Japan got over J¥2 per day, those at Fushun only a quarter of that; see Kōzan konwakai, 1932, vol. 2. pp. 213–14; Hou Defeng, 1932, p. 227.
140 Wu Bannong, 1932, p. 484.
141 *Naigai chōsa shiryō* 4.3 (March 1932): 208–17.
142 *Tōa* 5.9 (September 1932): 135 *et passim*.
143 Manshikai, 1964–5, vol. 2, p. 67.
144 MMT, 1938, p. 2004.
145 Buxton, 1978, pp. 94, 98, 160–1; Jevons, 1915, pp. 113–15.
146 MMT, shomubu chōsaka, 1929, p. 179; Kuboyama, 1940, p. 440.
147 Wright, 1980b, p. 715.
148 KYZB 297 (7 August 1934): 904.
149 Nichi-Man shōji, 1937, p. 151.
150 ILO, 1938b, vol. 1, p. 48.
151 Wu Yuan-li, 1963, p. 96.
152 ZGJJNJ 1936, K70–1.
153 KYZB 380 (28 April 1936): 1187–8.
154 MMT, shomubu chōsaka, 1929, pp. 159, 178; MMT, 1938, p. 1986.
155 ZGJJNJ 1936, K70–1.
156 ILO, 1938b, vol. 1, p. 49.

Chapter 5

1 See China, guojia tongji ju, 1958, pp. 40–1 for electric power and pp. 148–50 for textiles.
2 For a more sophisticated theoretical framework than can be used in this chapter, see Langton, 1979, ch. 1.
3 r^2 is only 0.002. The correlation would be even weaker if the substantial reserves of Xinjiang and the far west were included.
4 See Chapter 4 and, for the post-1949 period, Howe, 1978, p. 107.
5 MMT, chōsabu, 1937a, pp. 10–11.
6 For a brief description of the Fushun reserves, see Sakatani, 1980, p. 124.
7 The calorific value of much Shanxi coal was equal to, or in many cases higher than, that of coal in Hebei, Shandong or Liaoning, see Tezuka, 1944, pp. 19–20. The development of, for instance, the Datong deposits since 1949 indicates also that geological conditions there were not so unfavourable as to inhibit development.

8 See Chapter 2.
9 Nichi-Man shōji, 1937, p. 155.
10 KYZB 391 (21 July 1936): 105–10; KYZB 393 (7 August 1936): 136–42; KYZB 394 (14 August 1936): 150–2.
11 KYZB 78 (14 January 1930): 475; NCH, 10 November 1917.
12 KYZB 60 (28 August 1929): 183.
13 For the structure of costs in Shanghai, Tianjin and Beijing, see MMT, sangyōbu, 1938, pp. 313–19.
14 For oil see Hardy, 1978, p. 17.
15 *Zhongwai jingji zhoukan* 125 (15 August 1925): 29.
16 Zheng, 1931, p. 398.
17 KYZB 105 (7 August 1930): 141–3; KYZB 190 (14 May 1932): 343; KYZB 301 (7 September 1934): 961.
18 Carlson, 1971, p. 20.
19 KYZB 249 (7 August 1933): 129; Hou Defeng, 1932, p. 65.
20 KYZB 62 (14 September 1929): 210.
21 KYZB 8 (24 July 1928): 125; KYZB 62 (14 September 1929): 212.
22 KYZB 363 (21 December 1935): 816; ZGJJNJ 1936, K99.
23 Schrecker, 1971, p. 16.
24 Nef, 1932, vol. 1, p. 78.
25 Richthofen, 1872, *passim*.
26 Tezuka, 1940, pp. 219–25.
27 KYZB 400 (28 September 1936): 245–53.
28 Tezuka, 1944, pp. 343–4; KYZB 397 (7 September 1936): 200–1.
29 MMT, chōsabu, 1937a, pp. 3–5, 97. The special rate for Zhongxing coal carried to Pukou was ¥2.20 per ton. The freight charge to Lianyungang only ¥0.96.
30 KYZB 386 (14 June 1936): 22–4.
31 China, jaiotong tiedao bu, 1935, *zonggang*, p. 2100.
32 Ibid., *zonggang*, p. 2101.
33 Ibid., *zonggang*, pp. 2133–6; *Kuangye lianhehui jikan* 4 (December 1923): *diaocha* 2.
34 *Quanmin bao*, 19 March 1931, see Hatano, March 1931, pp. 255–7; also *Beiping chenbao*, 24 May 1931, ibid., May 1931, pp. 335–7; and *Huabei ribao*, 3 November 1931, ibid., November 1931, pp. 63–7.
35 KYZB 270 (14 January 1934): 471–8.
36 KYZB 396 (28 August 1936): 184–91; ZGJJNJ 1936, K28–30.
37 Sun Jingzhi, 1957, pp. 94–5.
38 NSGB 4.9 (April 1918): *xuanzai* 5.
39 Gillin, 1967, p. 88.
40 Yu, 1926d, pp. 79–82.
41 NCH, 10 October 1934.
42 Gillin, 1967, pp. 186–9.
43 Kuboyama, 1944, pp. 150–2.
44 Kuboyama, 1940, p. 229 for Xuangang.
45 Quan 1972c, p. 765.
46 Tezuka, 1944, p. 60.
47 MCG 14.4 (April 1934): 231.
48 Zhonggong, 1962, p. 32.
49 MMT, chōsabu, 1937c, p. 156; MCG 14.4 (April 1934): 229.
50 Zhonggong, 1962, p. 33.
51 Sun Jingzhi, 1957, p. 94.
52 See Chapter 7.
53 KYZB 270 (14 January 1934): 478.
54 KYZB 396 (28 August 1936): 186.

55 KYZB 28 (28 December 1929): 571; KYZB 269 (7 January 1934): 452.
56 China, tiedaobu, 1933, p. 298.
57 Yu, 1926d, p. 90; Gillin, 1967, pp. 88–90, 180–1.
58 China, quanguo jingji weiyuanhui, 1936, p. 43; China, shiyebu, guoji maoyi ju, 1937, 5:19.
59 KYZB 272 (28 January 1934): 509; KYZB 273 (7 February 1934): 528.
60 Gillin, 1967, pp. 182–4.
61 For the inclusion of Rehe, see Eckstein, Chao and Chang, 1974, p. 252.
62 Eckstein, Chao and Chang, 1974, *passim*; MCG 15.5 (May 1935): 6, 10–11.
63 SMR, 1936, p. 70.
64 McCormack, 1977, ch. 5 *et passim*.

Chapter 6
1 This method is used instead of a simple link index in order to overcome the problem of a year of recovery after an exceptionally bad year seeming to register a high growth rate even though its output was in fact below that of previous years.
2 Zhou Xiuluan, 1958, pp. 14–19; Feuerwerker, 1977, p. 17.
3 Buck, 1978, pp. 130–1.
4 Cochran, 1980, pp. 123–4.
5 Zhou Xiuluan, 1958, pp. 17–18.
6 This subject is dealt with in Chapter 3.
7 Murphey, 1953, pp. 20–1.
8 Luo, 1932, p. 71.
9 Ohkawa, 1967, pp. 192–3.
10 The export price index for coal rose by well over three times between 1914 and 1920, see ibid., p. 222.
11 Takimoto and Mukai, 1926–7, vol. 4, p. 920.
12 Yang and Hou, 1931, p. 151; the value of the tael rose from J¥1.34 to J¥2.72 between 1914 and 1919.
13 NCH, 8 January 1916, 28 September 1918.
14 NCH, 28 April 1917.
15 NSGB, 5.7 (February 1919): *xuanzai* 22.
16 NCH, 10 November 1917.
17 See Huang Yifeng, 1980, pp. 57–69; also Ma Bohuang, 1980, pp. 49–66. For profits made by other coal traders see *Yinhang zhoubao* 3.4 (18 February 1919): 33–4.
18 NCH, 10 November 1917.
19 NCH, 4 May 1918; NSGB 5.3 (October 1918): *xuanzai* 23.
20 Sun and Huenemann, 1969, p. 102.
21 NCH, 21 December 1918; MMT, 1928, pp. 564–8.
22 MMT, 1928, p. 719.
23 Ibid., p. 707.
24 Nakamura Yoshihito, 1929, p. 36.
25 MMT, shomubu chōsaka, 1929, p. 274.
26 See Matsumoto, 1967, section on mining.
27 NSGB 7.12 (July 1921): *xuanzai* 23.
28 IMC, *Returns and Reports*, 1918–21.
29 MMT, shomubu chōsaka, 1929, p. 286.
30 Ibid., p. 297.
31 Kuboyama, 1940, p. 436.
32 Xie, 1926, p. 38.
33 Chang, 1969, p. 60.
34 Bergère, 1980, *passim*.

35 Allen, 1962, p. 100; Ohkawa, 1967, p. 193.
36 *Jingji banyuekan* 2.4 (15 February 1928): 3–5; MMT, 1928, p. 708.
37 Tokunaga, 1930, p. 116.
38 Nakamura Yoshihito, 1929, p. 36; MMT, 1928, pp. 719–20.
39 MMT, 1928, p. 708.
40 MMT, 1928, p. 723; MMT, shomubu chōsaka, 1929, pp. 297, 307.
41 Zhongguo kexue yuan, 1958, p. 126; this was also in part the result of falling freight rates.
42 Manshikai, 1964–5, vol. 1, p. 299, vol. 2, p. 67; MMT, 1928, pp. 708, 723.
43 Kuboyama, 1940, p. 436.
44 MMT, shomubu chōsaka, 1929, pp. 304–15.
45 Xu, 1947, pp. 184–5.
46 Carlson, 1971, pp. 57–63; Xu, 1947, p. 48; Schrecker, 1971, p. 132.
47 Quan, 1972a, p. 153.
48 For cotton spinning, see Bergère, 1980, pp. 12–13.
49 MMT, shomubu chōsaka, 1929, pp. 295–345.
50 Xu, 1947, p. 186.
51 Great Britain, *Report, 1923*, p. 12, *1924*, p. 9; see also *Shehui ribao*, 4 October 1924 and 27 November 1924 in Hatano, October 1924, pp. 61–2, November 1924, p. 368.
52 Great Britain, *Report, 1925*, p. 15.
53 *Shehui ribao*, 23 May 1925, in Hatano, May 1925, pp. 317–18.
54 *Yinhang yuekan* 8.8. (August 1928): 86.
55 Xu, 1947, p. 186.
56 KYZB 52 (28 June 1929): 51–2.
57 Nankai daxue, 1958, pp. 81–2.
58 KYZB 362 (14 December 1935): 792.
59 KYZB 335 (21 May 1935): 357.
60 *People's Tribune*, 3 November 1926; KYZB 17 (7 October 1928): 282; KYZB 20 (28 October 1928): 328.
61 KYZB 113 (7 October 1930): 266.
62 *North China Daily News*, 11 January 1934.
63 KYZB 201 (7 August 1932): 521–2; Zhang Huiruo, 1936, p. 266.
64 Kuboyama, 1940, p. 436; NP, E. J. Nathan, 'Memorandum on the History and Prospects of the Kailan Mining Administration' (1938).
65 KYZB 10 (7 August 1928): 157; KYZB 340 (28 June 1935): 425; Xu, 1947, pp. 46–7.
66 *Yinhang yuekan* 8.8 (August 1928): 86; Yan Zhongping, 1955, p. 155.
67 Xu, 1947, pp. 184–5.
68 MMT, Tenshin jimusho, 1936, p. 37.
69 Hou Defeng, 1929, p. 32 and 1932, p. 315.
70 Manshikai, 1964–5, vol. 1, p. 301.
71 MMT, 1938, p. 2002.
72 MMT, keizai chōsakai, 1936b, p. 8; MMT, 1938, p. 2013.
73 For Beipiao, see KYZB 116 (28 October 1930): 307; for Muleng (which was Sino-Russian), see KYZB 227 (21 February 1933): 956–7.
74 MMT, 1938, p. 1901.
75 Ibid., pp. 1981–2.
76 Tōa kenkyūjo, 1942–3, vol. 2, p. 305.
77 Chang, 1969, p. 61.
78 Young, 1971, ch. 8; Eastman, 1974, p. 186.
79 Young, 1971, pp. 476–8.
80 Chang, 1969, p. 79.

81 Tōa dobunkai, 1942–3, vol. 2, p. 305; NCH, 9 September, 4 November 1936, 6 January 1937.
82 See its 1936 report in Zhongguo yinhang, 1937, V11–12.
83 Wu Bannong, 1932, pp. 529–30.
84 For the dumping controversy, see Wu Bannong, 1932, *Duli pinglun* 25 (6 November 1932): 19–20, and the 1932 issues of KYZB.
85 MMT, 1938, p. 1980.
86 KYZB 207 (21 September 1932): 609; Wu Bannong, 1932, p. 491.
87 *Tōyō keizai shimpō* 1774 (21 August 1937): 678–9.
88 Wu Bannong, 1932, pp. 527–8; Tezuka, 1944, pp. 159–61.
89 Xu, 1947, pp. 46–7; MMT, Tenshin jimusho, 1936, p. 37.
90 NP, Nathan to Turner, 27 June 1932.
91 KYZB 259 (21 October 1933): 292.
92 MMT, chōsabu, 1937e, p. 17; KYZB 306 (14 October 1934): 4.
93 Liu Jie, 1936, p. 231; annual reports of Jinbei company, 1933 and 1934, in MMT, chōsabu, 1937c, p. 156.
94 KYZB 381 (7 May 1936): 1204, referring to Yu xian in Henan.
95 China, shiyebu, guoji maoyi ju, 1937, 5:21.
96 Although some of the increase in 1935 over 1934 (especially of the large increase in the Geological Survey series) was due to improved coverage of output in outlying provinces.
97 NP, Nathan to Turner, 22 October 1932.
98 NP, Nathan to Turner, 31 December 1935; NCH, 7 August 1935, 15 January 1936; KYZB 345 (7 August 1935): 514–15; KYZB 366 (14 January 1936): 854–5.
99 Nathan, 'Memorandum'; average net profit was about ¥1.86 million, see the company reports in *The Times*, 1929–37.
100 Zhang Huiruo, 1936, pp. 266–7.
101 NP, Nathan to Turner, 26 June 1936, 9 July 1936, 30 January 1937; *The Times*, 18 December 1937.
102 Kula, 1976, p. 107.

Chapter 7

1 It did, however, fall to 67–9% in individual years, only 1906–7 and 1931–2.
2 McKay, 1970, pp. 285, 385.
3 Biggerstaff, 1950, p. 132.
4 Huang Jiamo, 1961, pp. 79–80; Lefevour, 1968, pp. 79–80.
5 MacMurray, 1921, vol. 1, p. 21.
6 Li Enhan, 1963, ch. 1.
7 For an analysis of foreign investment in Tsarist Russia which provides many illuminating contrasts with the Chinese situation, see McKay, 1970.
8 See Mi, 1980, pp. 401–5.
9 MacMurray, 1921, vol. 1. pp. 658–62.
10 Xu, 1947, pp. 243–4; NKGB 22 (March 1930): 197–8.
11 Japan, gaimushō, 1961, part II, pp. 210–22.
12 MMT, 1919, pp. 469–70, 932.
13 Japan, gaimushō, jōyakukyoku, 1936, vol. 1, pp. 788–9.
14 Des Forges, 1973, pp. 145, 168; Xu, 1947, pp. 217–22.
15 MacMurray, 1921, vol. 1, pp. 115–16; Schrecker, 1971, ch. 1, pp. 179, 191.
16 MacMurray, 1921, vol. 1, pp. 131–4, 700; for the acquisition of the Henan rights, see also Yang Bingyan, 1974a.
17 Des Forges, 1973, pp. 32–4; Tezuka, 1944, pp. 465–6; for the campaign against local sales of coal, see especially Yang Bingyan, 1974b.

18 MacMurray, 1921, vol. 1, pp. 183–8; Collins, 1918, ch. 4; *Dongfang zazhi* 7.10 (26 November 1910): *zazuan* 87–91.
19 MacMurray, 1921, vol. 1, pp. 31–2, 909–11.
20 Carlson, 1971, ch. 4–6; Wei, 1954, pp. 7–97; Wang Xi, 1962, pp. 40–62; 175–7; MMT, shomubu chōsaka, 1929, p. 109.
21 Gu, 1916, 6:4–5; MacMurray, 1921, vol. 1, pp. 724–7.
22 Xu, 1947, pp. 33–4, 37–8; MacMurray, 1921, vol. 1, pp. 493–8.
23 MMT, kōgyōbu kōmuka, 1914, p. 125; Wang Jingyu, 1957, p. 768; *Dongfang zazhi*, 7.6 (31 July 1910): *Zhongguo shishi huilu* 143; Gu, 1916, 8:59; Quan, 1972a, p. 81.
24 Gu, 1916, 4.4; Xu, 1947, pp. 173–7; Xie, 1926, p. 39.
25 NKGB 20 (January 1930): 181–99; KYZB 60 (28 August 1929): 188–9; KYZB 73 (7 December 1929): 396; KYZB 97 (7 June 1930): 3; KYZB 227 (21 February 1933): 956–7.
26 Xu, 1947, pp. 183–4; KYZB 47 (21 May 1929): 765.
27 For this see Wright, 1980b, pp. 716–19.
28 Xu, 1947, pp. 66–7.
29 Saitō, 1938, pp. 171–8; Inoue, 1921, p. 2 *et passim*.
30 KYZB 178 (14 February 1932): 146–7.
31 KYZB 304 (28 September 1934): 1018; KYZB 78 (14 March 1934): 594.
32 KYZB 229 (7 March 1933): 981; KYZB 317 (7 January 1935): 69.
33 KYZB 297 (7 August 1934): 904; KYZB 317 (7 January 1935): 69.
34 KYZB 334 (14 May 1935): 338; KYZB 341 (7 July 1935): 449; KYZB 342 (14 July 1935): 465; KYZB 349 (7 September 1935): 578–80; Nichi-Man shōji, 1937, p. 16.
35 According to Tōa kenkyūjo, 1942–3, vol. 2, p. 156, the SMR owned 49,000 shares in Kaiping, and Mitsui Bussan owned about 600. See also NP, Shirosaki to Nathan, 15 August 1933; Pryor to Turner, 1 June 1935; KYZB 315 (21 December 1934): 33; KYZB 318 (14 January 1935); 81.
36 NP, Nathan to Turner, 27 April 1934; Pryor to Turner, 29 June 1935: KYZB 282 (14 April 1934): 657–62.
37 NP, Pryor to Turner, 19 September 1935.
38 NP, Nathan to Turner, 5 April 1936.
39 KYZB 381 (7 May 1936): 1193–4; KYZB 390 (14 July 1936): 81.
40 MMT, keizai chōsakai, 1936b, *passim*.
41 KYZB 317 (7 January 1935): 65; Nichi-Man shōji, 1937, p. 66.
42 KYZB 186 (14 April 1932): 274–5; MMT, chōsabu, 1937d, pp. 198–9.
43 Hou Chi-ming, 1965, pp. 109–11.
44 MacMurray, 1921, vol. 1, p. 184.
45 Ibid., p. 912.
46 Xu, 1947, pp. 96–9.
47 McKay, 1970, pp. 182–200; Kidron, 1965, pp. 263–72.
48 NP, Nathan to Young, 11 July 1929; Nathan to Turner, 22 September 1934; KYZB 304 (29 September 1934): 1013.
49 Xu, 1947, p. 16; KYZB 12 (21 August 1928): 207; KYZB 59 (21 August 1929): 161; KYZB 274 (14 February 1934): 535–6.
50 Xu, 1947, pp. 199, 225–6; KYZB 11 (14 August 1928): 169; KYZB 85 (7 March 1930): 581.
51 Gu, 1916, 6:4.
52 Ibid., 4:4, 5:18.
53 MacMurray, 1921, vol. 2, p. 967.
54 MMT, shomubu chōsaka, 1929, p. 60.
55 Ibid., p. 52.
56 NP, Nathan to Turner, 22 September 1934.

57 Wang and Li, 1960, vol. 6, p. 3907; Japan, gaimushō, jōyakukyoku, 1936, vol. 1, p. 1052; MacMurray, 1921, vol. 1, p. 794.
58 Gu, 1916, 9:28; Xu, 1947, p. 225.
59 MMT, chōsabu, 1937e, pp. 43–4.
60 Japan, gaimushō, Ajiakyoku, 1929, vol. 2, part II, p. 155.
61 Xu, 1947, pp. 123–40; KYZB 152 (28 July 1931): 883–4; KYZB 209 (7 October 1932): 641.
62 NP, Nathan to Turner, 22 September 1934, 6 February 1935; Pryor to Turner, 18 March 1937; KYZB 304 (28 September 1934): 1013; KYZB 309 (7 November 1934): 1089–90; KYZB 331 (21 April 1934): 290–1.
63 See Wright, 1980b, p. 722.
64 NP, Nathan, 'Memorandum' (1938).
65 Wright, 1980b, pp. 716–18.
66 NP, Nathan to Turner, 13 December 1931, 10 February 1934, 28 December 1934.
67 Gu, 1916, 3:52–3, 8:20; KYZB 30 (14 January 1929): 488.
68 NP, Nathan to Turner, 18 April 1932.
69 Wang Xi, 1962, p. 117.
70 Wang Xi, 1962, p. 116–17; Gu, 1916, 8:53; MacMurray, 1921, vol. 1, pp. 497, 728.
71 MacMurray, 1921, vol. 1, p. 792.
72 Ibid., vol. 1, p. 794.
73 Ibid., vol. 2, p. 966; China, caizhengbu, 1935, p. 1148.
74 Wright, 1980b, p. 719.
75 Collins, 1918, pp. 231–2.
76 Ibid., p. 190.
77 Wang and Li, 1960, vol. 1, p. 524.
78 Xu, 1947, pp. 204–5.
79 NP, Nathan to Young, 5 November 1927, 8 August 1930.
80 NP, Nathan 'Memorandum' (1938).
81 NP, Young to Nathan, 27 June 1929.
82 NP, Nathan to Turner, 13 June 1932.
83 KYZB 270 (14 January 1934): 478.
84 China, jiaotong tiedao bu, 1935, *zonggang*, pp. 2101, 2133.
85 Japan, gaimushō, Ajiakyoku, 1930, vol. 2, p. 316.
86 KYZB 340 (28 June 1935): 435.
87 NP, Young to Nathan, 5 March 1925.
88 NP, Nathan to Turner, 5 August 1933.
89 The freight figures show the recovery of the railways. For taxes, see for instance Hu Rongquan, 1935, p. 241 on Shandong, and KYZB 364 (28 December 1935): 821 on Hebei.
90 NP, Nathan to Turner, 5 August 1933.
91 Wang Xi, 1962, pp. 151–7; Wei, 1954, pp. 179–98.
92 NP, Nathan to Turner, 10 February 1934.
93 China, caizhengbu, 1935, p. 1148; NP, Nathan to Turner, 30 June 1934.
94 NP, Nathan to Turner, 31 December 1935.
95 Hou Chi-ming, 1965, p. 216.
96 Ibid., pp. 127–9.
97 Carlson, 1971, ch. 4.
98 Schrecker, 1971, pp. 33–42.
99 KYZB 399 (21 June 1935): 417.
100 MMT, chōsabu, 1937a, p. 61: Tezuka, 1944, pp. 312–14.
101 Zhonggong, 1962, p. 33.
102 Sutcliffe, 1971, pp. 159–60.
103 Gu, 1916, 8:65–71.

104 Such a provision was sometimes written into the original agreement; for the Peking Syndicate, Yang Bingyan, 1974a, p. 393.
105 Nakamura Takatoshi, 1944, p. 11; KYZB 395 (21 August 1936): 162.
106 Zhang Huiruo, 1936, p. 299.
107 Hou Chi-ming, 1965, pp. 138–41.
108 For the pressure on Chinese firms for the distribution of profits, see NP, Nathan to Turner, 10 February 1934.
109 NP, Nathan to Turner, 6 March 1935.

Chapter 8

1 Yan Zhongping, 1955, pp. 132–3.
2 This was the case, for instance, at Muleng in Jilin, see NKGB 20 (January 1930): 183–4.
3 For a more-detailed treatment of some of these points, see Wright, 1980a.
4 Feuerwerker, 1958, ch. 1.
5 Chan, 1977, pp. 99–102.
6 Huang Jiamo, 1961, pp. 119–22.
7 Zhou Xianwen, 1957.
8 Brown and Wright, 1981, pp. 70–2.
9 Quan, 1972a, pp. 47–9.
10 Feuerwerker, 1958, pp. 11–12.
11 Carlson, 1971, ch. 1–3.
12 Wang Zhenlu, 1905, 7:8–14; Zhu, 1908, 8:11–15; Wright, 1976, ch. 2.
13 See Chapter 7.
14 Quan, 1972a, pp. 78–82, 279.
15 Xu, 1947, pp. 79–80; Des Forges, 1973, pp. 32–3.
16 Xu, 1947, p. 48.
17 Wang Zhenlu, 1905, 7:11b; MMT, chōsabu, 1937a, p. 80; Wang Jingyu, 1957, p. 768; *Dongfang zazhi* 7.6 (31 July 1910): *Zhongguo shishi huilu* 143.
18 Quoted in Esherick, 1976, p. 80.
19 Li Enhan, 1963, pp. 260–1.
20 Quan, 1972c, pp. 759–61.
21 NSGB 1.2 (September 1914): *baogao* 3.
22 Gillin, 1967, p. 87.
23 Kuboyama, 1944, pp. 115–19; Yu, 1926d, pp. 79–82.
24 *Dongfang zazhi* 7.10 (26 November 1910): *zazuan* 87–91.
25 Wang Jingyu, 1957, pp. 922–3.
26 Ding, 1923, p. 10.
27 MMT, chōsabu, 1937a, p. 83; an 'expectant' official was one who had been given an appointment at a certain rank in a certain province, but who had not yet been assigned a substantive post to fill.
28 Yan Zhongping, 1955, pp. 96–7.
29 Chan, 1977, pp. 113–14.
30 Gu, 1916, 4:3–4.
31 Yu, 1926b, p. 6.
32 KYZB 40 (28 March 1929); 641.
33 KYZB 387 (21 June 1936): 43; Chen, 1957, p. 695.
34 Coble, 1980, ch. 1, quotation from p. 20.
35 Yan Zhongping, 1963, p. 175.
36 Ibid.; Mishina, 1942, pp. 46–7.
37 Zhang Huiruo, 1936, pp. 230–1; Fei, 1926, p. 166.
38 KYZB 12 (21 August 1928): 190–1; Ji Hua, 1978, pp. 156–62.
39 KYZB 43 (21 April 1929): 690; MMT, chōsabu, 1937d, p. 81.

40 Chi, 1975, pp. 685–6.
41 *Henan Zhongyuan meikuang gongsi huikan* 1 (February 1931): 47–54; KYZB 57 (7 August 1929): 134–5.
42 Coble, 1980, p. 18; Ding and Du, 1981, p. 149.
43 KYZB 13 (28 August 1928): 211; KYZB 78 (14 January 1930): 475; NCH, 10 November 1917; Chen, 1957, p. 633.
44 KYZB 22 (14 November 1928): 352; Yu, 1926e, p. 8; NSGB 7.10 (May 1921): *xuanzai* 17.
45 KYZB 334 (13 May 1935): 378; KYZB 341 (7 July 1935): 449.
46 Dongbei wenhua she, 1931, p. 1121; Ji Di, 1978, pp. 166, 168–9; the three main mines were Badaohao, Fuzhouwan and Xi'an.
47 Zhonggong, 1962, pp. 30, 34.
48 KYZB 370 (14 February 1936): 923; Gillin, 1967, p. 192; Bai, 1945, p. 688.
49 KYZB 3 (5 May 1928): 54; KYZB 106 (14 August 1930): 146; KYZB 227 (21 February 1933): 951; KYZB 233 (7 April 1933): 1047; KYZB 299 (21 August 1934): 932.
50 *Yinhang yuekan* 8.8 (August 1928): 85–99; KYZB 42 (14 April 1929): 677.
51 *Shandong nongkuang gongbao* 3 (31 December 1928): 59–77.
52 Kuboyama, 1944, p. 76.
53 Wright, 1980b, pp. 721–2.
54 KYZB 29 (7 January 1929): 472; KYZB 47 (21 May 1929): 765; KYZB 368 (21 January 1936): 890.
55 KYZB 211 (21 October 1932): 678.
56 Zhang Huiruo, 1936, pp. 383–4; MMT, Hoku-Shi keizai chōsajo, 1941, p. 189.
57 MMT, Hoku-shi keizai chōsajo, 1941, p. 140; Zhang Huiruo, 1936, p. 352; the identification of the investors in Boshan with major central Chinese industrialists is in both cases tentative.
58 KYZB 296 (28 July 1934): 883.
59 KYZB 39 (21 March 1929): 626; KYZB 140 (28 April 1931): 695; KYZB 382 (14 May 1936): 1210–11.
60 KYZB 406 (14 November 1936): 346.
61 Xu, 1947, pp. 185–94.
62 Negishi, 1934, p. 1177; KYZB 268 (28 December 1933): 440; *Gongshang banyuekan* 7.3 (1 February 1933): 107–8.
63 KYZB 280 (28 March 1934): 626.
64 KYZB 382 (14 May 1936): 1210–11; KYZB 393 (7 August 1936): 130–1.
65 Xu, 1947, p. 143.
66 For a wider exposition of Nanjing's role in industry, see Coble, 1980, ch. 8.
67 Chen, 1962, pp. 782–6. Formal transfer of the enterprises to the China Development Finance Corporation took place in 1937, but actual transfer of management was made in July 1936; see Coble, 1980, pp. 218–24.
68 Coble, 1980, pp. 222, 237.
69 Woodhead, *China Year Book, 1921–1922*, p. 183.
70 China, lifayuan, 1934, 8:244. The impact of this clause was limited by the fact that the law recognized rights acquired under the 1914 regulations.
71 Woodhead, *China Year Book, 1921–1922*, pp. 181–2.
72 Zhang Shouyong, 1902, *waibian* 24:65a–b; Wang and Li, 1960, vol. 1, pp. 108–9.
73 Shangwu yinshu guan, 1909, 10:102b.
74 Woodhead, *China Year Book, 1921–1922*, pp. 189–90; the prospecting area tax is given in this source as 0.5¢, but the correct figure is 5¢, see Shangwu yinshu guan, bianyi suo, 1919, 10:66.
75 China, lifa yuan, 1934, 8:253; as one *mou* approximately equalled six areas, the area tax remained roughly the same.

76 Shangwu yinshu guan, 1933, p. 734; China, caizhengbu, 1935, pp. 1149–51.
77 Zhang Shouyong, 1902, 24:67.
78 China, caizhengbu, 1935, p. 1147.
79 KYZB 395 (21 August 1936): 161.
80 Guomindang zhongyang dangbu, 1937, 2:64; KYZB 241 (7 June 1933): 9–11.
81 Coble, 1980, p. 125.
82 For a more-detailed discussion of 'economic control' and the coal cartel, and their background, see Wright, forthcoming. See also KYZB 241 (7 June 1933): 9; KYZB 256 (28 September 1933): 243–4; KYZB 257 (7 October 1933): 257.
83 Zhongguo shixue hui, 1961, vol. 7, p. 413.
84 Shen Baozhen, 1880, 5:17.
85 Li Hongzhang, 1905–8, *zougao*, 40: 41–3.
86 Kinder, 1890–1, p. 288.
87 MMT, chōsabu, 1937d, p. 81.
88 MMT, chōsabu, 1937b, p. 202.
89 Wang Jingyu, 1957, p. 1112, NCH, 30 December 1904.
90 KYZB 219 (21 December 1932): 816; Japan, gaimushō, jōhōbu, 1928, p. 679.
91 For Luda, see KYZB 36 (28 February 1929): 591; for Majiagou (Kailuan), see KYZB 381 (7 May 1936): 1194; KYZB 391 (21 July 1936): 97.
92 Liu Ao, 1958, pp. 44–6; Chen, 1962, p. 453.
93 Gan, 1910, 18:17.
94 Chen, 1962, p. 453; Collins, 1918, pp. 231, 234.
95 Collins, 1918, p. 234; NSGB 12.2 (September 1925): *jinwen* 25–6.
96 For a discussion of this see Jia, 1917, pp. 145–9.
97 KYZB 40 (28 March 1919): 648.
98 Hu Rongquan, 1935, p. 195.
99 KYZB 371 (21 February 1936): 943.
100 KYZB 373 (7 March 1936): 965.
101 *Jianshe weiyuanhui gongbao* 29 (May–June 1933): 91.
102 *Jianshe weiyuanhui gongbao*, various issues.
103 KYZB 326 (14 March 1935): 219–21.
104 *Yinhang yuekan* 8.7 (July 1928): 50–1; *Yinhang yuekan* 8.8 (August 1928): 86, 96–9; KYZB 17 (7 October 1928): 284.
105 Zhonggong, 1962, p. 30.
106 Chen, 1962, p. 1168.
107 *Jianshe weiyuanhui gongbao* 40 (April 1934): 96.
108 KYZB 113 (7 October 1930): 264.
109 MMT, chōsabu, 1937a, p. 36; Japan, gaimushō, jōhōbu, 1932, p. 168.
110 MMT, chōsabu, 1937a, p. 37; Japan, gaimushō, jōhōbu, 1937, p. 213.
111 SKJ 37 (January 1917): 67; Japan, gaimushō, jōhōbu, 1932, pp. 144–5.
112 Japan, gaimushō, jōhōbu, 1932, pp. 148–9.
113 KYZB 12 (21 August 1928): 190; KYZB 324 (28 February 1935): 179.
114 Zhonggong, 1962, pp. 32–3.
115 Coble, 1980, pp. 252–3.
116 See for example, KYZB 368 (28 January 1936): 885–7; KYZB 380 (28 April 1936): 1177.

Chapter 9
1 See Chapter 2.
2 Hu Jixian, 1931, p. 311.
3 KYZB 382 (14 May 1936): 1213.
4 Buxton, 1978, p. 27.
5 Yu, 1926e, p. 40.

6 Xu, 1947, p. 78; Zheng, 1931, p. 151.
7 NSGB 1.1 (August 1914): *baogao* 16.
8 MMT, rōmuka, 1931, p. 28.
9 Zhongguo shekui kexue yuan, 1981, p. 3.
10 KYZB 279 (21 April 1936): 1164.
11 KYZB 268 (28 December 1933): 435–6.
12 KYZB 281 (7 April 1934): 646.
13 Shangwu yinshu guan, 1933, p. 748.
14 Children were, for instance, employed in Shandong in direct contradiction to the law; see KYZB 297 (7 August 1934): 909.
15 Srivastava, 1970, pp. 61–2; ILO, 1938a, pp. 52–3.
16 Levy, 1966, p. 54.
17 Okabe, 1942, part I, p. 147, part II, p. 169.
18 Ibid., part I, pp. 159–60.
19 Chao, 1977, p. 159.
20 Gamble, 1954, p. 48.
21 Okabe, 1942, part I, p. 162.
22 China, shiyebu, laodong nianjian bianzuan weiyuanhui, 1934, 1:279–80.
23 Chesneaux, 1968, p. 65.
24 KYZB 395 (21 August 1936): 162.
25 KYZB 102 (14 July 1930): 109; Hu Jixian, 1931, p. 311.
26 Liu and Shi, 1932, pp. 45–6; Hou Defeng, 1929, p. 17.
27 MMT, 1928, p. 565; MMT, rōmuka, 1931, p. 30.
28 MMT, rōmuka, 1931, pp. 30–1; Yu, 1926a, p. 77.
29 SMR, 1936, pp. 121–2.
30 KYZB 67 (21 October 1929): 294.
31 KYZB 27 (21 December 1928): 438.
32 Carlson, 1971, p. 45; KYZB 44 (28 April 1929): 711.
33 KYZB 171 (21 December 1933): 40.
34 Liu and Shi, 1932, p. 45.
35 KYZB 52 (28 June 1929): 55.
36 KYZB 40 (28 March 1929): 646.
37 KYZB 230 (14 March 1933): 997; Daye also supplied miners to Pingxiang, see Shaffer, 1982, p. 76.
38 I have dealt with the contract labour system in detail in Wright, 1981a, and will here only summarize the main conclusion of that discussion. For useful information made available since that article was published, see Yan Guanghua, 1981.
39 Kanda, 1936, p. 605.
40 See, for example, Hatakayama, 1976, p. 95.
41 Zhu, 1908, 8:11.
42 Lin and Mei, 1965, p. 66.
43 *Xin qingnian* 9.3 (July 1921): 1–3.
44 Kanda, 1936, pp. 598, 605; KYZB 281 (7 April 1934): 646.
45 KYZB 268 (28 December 1933): 435–6; KYZB 270 (14 January 1934): 466–7.
46 KYZB 150 (14 July 1931): 862–4.
47 Gibson, 1922, p. 11; Kōzan konwakai, 1932, vol. 2, Table 35 (pp. 212–13).
48 Chen, 1961, pp. 927–9.
49 Zhang Huiruo, 1936, pp. 132–5.
50 Walters, 1977, p. 200.
51 KYZB 358 (14 November 1935): 734.
52 KYZB 378 (14 April 1936): 1156.
53 Liu and Shi, 1932, p. 41; see ibid., pp. 57–8 for a discussion of the difficulties of classification.

54 KYZB 150 (14 July 1931): 862–4; the figure is in fact the proportion of those groups whose average wage was over 65¢ in the total directly hired workforce.
55 China, shiyebu, laodong nianjian bianzuan weiyuanhui, 1934, 1:280–1.
56 Liu and Shi, 1932, pp. 51–2.
57 Gu, 1916, 8:50.
58 KYZB 190 (14 May 1932): 343.
59 KYZB 288 (28 May 1934): 754–5; KYZB 359 (21 November 1935): 745.
60 KYZB 205 (7 September 1932): 584.
61 KYZB 205 (7 September 1932): 585; KYZB 208 (28 September 1932): 625.
62 KYZB 379 (21 April 1936): 1165.
63 KYZB 208 (28 September 1932): 631–2.
64 E-tu Zen Sun, 1967, p. 62.
65 Carlson, 1971, p. 47.
66 Gu, 1916, 5:28, 8:50; NSGB 8.8 (March 1922): *xuanzai* 19.
67 KYZB 378 (14 April 1936): 1148.
68 Tezuka, 1944, p. 352.
69 Liu and Shi, 1932, p. 54.
70 MMT, rōmuka, 1931, p. 84.
71 MMT, keizai chōsakai, 1936a, p. 50.
72 MCG 3.1 (January 1923): 49–50.
73 NP, Nathan to Turner, 8 May 1932; see also KYZB 275 (21 February 1934): 546.
74 The seemingly paradoxical position of the United States in these two tables was due to the extremely high output per man achieved there, far higher than anywhere else in the world.
75 KYZB 359 (21 November 1935): 745.
76 KYZB 392 (28 July 1936): 114.
77 Yu, 1926c, p. 212.
78 1927–30 because data on shifts are available to me only for those years.
79 Yu, 1926c, p. 181.
80 MMT, 1938, p. 1726.
81 NCH, 30 October 1920: KYZB 209 (7 October 1932): 641–2.
82 NSGB 3.7 (February 1917): *baogao* 23–4.
83 Zhongguo geming bowuguan, 1981, p. 112; see also *China Weekly Review*, 30 October 1920 quoted in Chesneaux, 1968, p. 77.
84 KYZB 209 (7 October 1932): 641–2.
85 NP, Nathan to Turner, 20 July 1934.
86 KYZB 335 (21 May 1935): 353.
87 Carlson, 1971, p. 47.
88 Ting, 1937, part II, p. 260.
89 See, for instance, Deng, 1953, p. 80. Zhang Guotao made the same point, see Zhongguo geming bowuguan, 1981, p. 223. This complaint became something of a cliché, but does seem to have been largely true up to the 1920s.
90 Liu and Shi, 1932, p. 87.
91 KYZB 248 (28 July 1933): 122; ZGJJNJ 1936, Q71.
92 China, shiyebu, laodong nianjian bianzuan weiyuanhui, 1933, 1:198.
93 KYZB 315 (21 December 1934): 33; KYZB 339 (21 June 1935): 419.
94 NKGB 21 (February 1930): 158.
95 KYZB 190 (14 May 1932): 343.
96 Ikonnikov, 1977, p. 100; China, guojia tongji ju, 1958, p. 84.
97 KYZB 44 (28 April 1929): 710–11.
98 KYZB 39 (21 March 1929): 630.
99 MMT, rōmuka, 1931, p. 147.
100 KYZB 275 (21 February 1934): 546.

101 Liu and Shi, 1932, p. 90.
102 Yu, 1926c, p. 182.
103 Ting, 1937, part II, p. 254.
104 Liu and Shi, 1932, p. 63. Buck, 1937, vol. 3, p. 328. But note that this was a period of rapid rises in money wages in the mines, and that among the areas surveyed by Buck monthly wages for agricultural workers ranged from ¥4.5 in Ningyang to ¥13.92 in Fushan.
105 MMT, keizai chōsakai, 1936a, pp. 37, 80–1.
106 MCG 3.1 (January 1923): 59.
107 KYZB 140 (28 April 1931): 691; KYZB 169 (7 December 1931): 1–2.
108 Beijing shifan daxue, 1958, p. 16.
109 MCG 3.1 (January 1923): 59; MMT, sōsaishitsu, 1937, p. 379; MMT, rōmuka, 1931, p. 147.
110 KYZB 379 (21 April 1936): 1176.
111 See, for instance, Ōyama, 1964, p. 32; Chesneaux, 1968, p. 57.
112 Wang Qingbin, 1928, 3:13; Womack, 1969, p. 176.
113 Yu, 1926e, p. 40.
114 As at Ba xian in Sichuan and Shan xian in Henan, see KYZB 225 (7 February 1933): 920; KYZB 388 (28 June 1936): 63.
115 Carlson, 1971, p. 47.
116 Wang Qingbin, 1928, 3:7–8; KYZB 275 (21 February 1934): 546.
117 MMT, sōsaishitsu, 1937, p. 379.
118 Yu, 1926a, p. 100.
119 China, shiyebu, laodong nianjian bianzuan weiyuanhui, 1934, 3:278; KYZB 225 (7 February 1933): 920.
120 Liu and Shi, 1932, pp. 89–90.
121 Carlson, 1971, p. 47.
122 Yu, 1926c, pp. 221–8, referring to the company year April 1919 to March 1920.
123 Liu and Shi, 1932, pp. 82–3.
124 China, shiyebu, laodong nianjian bianzuan weiyuanhui, 1934, 3:275.
125 Yu, 1926d, p. 92, and 1926e, p. 56.
126 Liu and Shi, 1932, pp. 84–5.
127 KYZB 275 (21 February 1934): 547.
128 Liu and Shi, 1932, p. 84; KYZB 379 (21 April 1936): 1172.
129 Liu and Shi, 1932, p. 86.
130 NSGB 10.3 (October 1923): *jinwen* 26–7.
131 For Kailuan see KYZB 275 (21 February 1934): 547; for Zhongxing see Liu and Shi, 1932, p. 91; for Boshan see *Xiangdao zhoubao* 77 (6 August 1924): 618.
132 See Zhongguo geming bowuguan, 1981, p. 97.

Chapter 10

1 Kerr and Siegel, 1977, pp. 235–7.
2 Ibid., p. 234.
3 Similarly in India, see Karnik, 1967, p. 409.
4 Zhonggong, 1959, pp. 74–6.
5 Womack, 1969, pp. 176–7; Esherick, 1976, pp. 59–60.
6 Deng, 1953, p. 4.
7 The Gelao Hui was a secret society which became prominent from the mid nineteenth century; see Lewis, 1972, pp. 97–112.
8 Esherick, 1976, pp. 60–1; Shaffer, 1982, p. 81.
9 NSGB 1.9 (April 1915): *xuanzai* 11.
10 Carlson, 1971, p. 45; Zhongguo geming bowuguan, 1981, pp. 226–7.
11 Zhongguo geming bowuguan, 1981, p. 224.

12 NP, Nathan to Turner, 27 April 1934.
13 Womack, 1969, pp. 188–9.
14 Sun, 1967, p. 47.
15 Womack, 1969, pp. 177–8.
16 Wou, 1978, pp. 205–29.
17 McDonald, 1978, p. 195.
18 Shaffer, 1982, pp. 88–98; McDonald, 1978, pp. 166–71.
19 Whether this was in fact so was a matter of some controversy among the north China Communist Party members, see Zhongguo geming bowuguan, 1981, p. 224; see also Wou, 1978, p. 213.
20 Zhongguo geming gowuguan, 1981, pp. 117–234; Deng, 1953, pp. 79–84.
21 Zhongguo shehui kexue yuan, 1981, pp. 48–50; see also McDonald, 1978, p. 212; Tang Hai, 1926, p. 425; Shaffer, 1982, pp. 98–103.
22 Wang Qingbin, 1928, 2:203; KYZB 152 (28 July 1931): 883–4.
23 NSGB 12:1 (August 1925): *jinwen* 19.
24 Wang Qingbin, 1928, 2:101.
25 Ibid., 2:202.
26 McDonald, 1978, pp. 212–13; Tang Hai, 1926, pp. 425–30.
27 Tang Hai, 1926, pp. 430–1.
28 McDonald, 1978, p. 269; Shaffer, 1982, pp. 106–7.
29 *Jingbao*, 8 February 1926, see Hatano, February 1926, pp. 108–9.
30 McCormack, 1977, pp. 202–3.
31 Nishimura, 1972, p. 50.
32 Hou Defeng, 1929, pp. 249–50; Chesneaux, 1968, p. 268.
33 KYZB 32 (28 January 1929): 523; KYZB 42 (14 April 1929): 676; KYZB 52 (28 June 1929): 59; China, shiyebu, laodong nianjian bianzuan weiyuanhui, 1933, 2:45 and 1934, 2:32, 33, 35.
34 KYZB 129 (7 February 1932): 526; China, shiyebu, laodong nianjian bianzuan weiyuanhui, 1933, 2:45.
35 Liu and Shi, 1932, pp. 77–8.
36 KYZB 173 (7 January 1932): 68.
37 KYZB 200 (28 July 1932): 500.
38 For 'yellow unions', see Gourlay, 1953, pp. 103–35.
39 KYZB 254 (14 September 1933): 210.
40 KYZB 330 (14 April 1935): 282.
41 KYZB 371 (21 February 1936): 936.
42 KYZB 367 (21 January 1936): 874.
43 China, shiyebu, laodong nianjian bianzuan weiyuanhui, 1934, 2:31–2.
44 Ibid., 2:34.
45 KYZB 228 (28 February 1933): 980.
46 China, shiyebu, laodong nianjian bianzuan weiyuanhui, 1934, 2:34.
47 KYZB 137 (7 April 1931): 647; KYZB 140 (28 April 1931): 693; KYZB 143 (21 May 1931): 747; KYZB 273 (7 February 1934): 514.
48 China, shiyebu, laodong nianjian bianzuan weiyuanhui, 1934, 2:32–7.
49 KYZB 45 (7 May 1929): 726–32; Beijing shifan daxue, 1958, p. 36. China, shiyebu, laodong nianjian bianzuan weiyuanhui, 1934, 2:134.
50 Zhongguo kexue yuan, 1960, p. 315.
51 KYZB 73 (7 December 1929): 390; KYZB 102 (14 July 1930): 82–3.
52 KYZB 210 (14 October 1932): 659; KYZB 223 (21 January 1933): 873–4; KYZB 228 (28 February 1933): 980.
53 KYZB 290 (14 June 1934): 786; KYZB 367 (21 January 1936): 869.
54 See Wright, 1981a, pp. 673–5.

55 Ma Chaojun, 1959, p. 232; China, shiyebu, laodong nianjian bianzuan weiyuanhui, 1934, 2:134; *Yishibao*, 19 May 1931, in Hatano, May 1931, pp. 279–84.
56 KYZB 273 (7 February 1934): 514; KYZB 275 (21 February 1934): 545–52; KYZB 309 (7 November 1934): 1090; KYZB 315 (21 December 1934): 33–4.
57 Ma Chaojun, 1959, p. 812; CEB, 21 July 1928; KYZB 163 (21 October 1931): 1035.
58 Deng, 1953, p. 83.
59 Ma Chaojun, 1959, pp. 1104–5.
60 KYZB 56 (28 July 1929): 125.
61 KYZB 65 (7 October 1929): 263–4.
62 Ma Chaojun, 1959, p. 940: Wang Qingbin, 1928, 2:201.
63 Ma Chaojun, 1959, p. 982.
64 Ibid., p. 1215.
65 KYZB 201 (7 August 1932): 516.
66 KYZB 240 (31 May 1933): 1161.
67 NP, Nathan to Turner, 20 February 1932, 2 March 1932, 8 May 1932.
68 NP, Pryor to Turner, 20 June 1935.
69 NP, Nathan to Turner, 13 December 1931.
70 KYZB 147 (21 June 1931): 801–2.
71 KYZB 287 (21 May 1934): 737.

Chapter 11
1 Wang Kung-ping, 1977, pp. 49–50.
2 Kraus, 1980, p. 152.
3 Ibid., p. 153.
4 Coble, 1980, p. 152.
5 See Meisner, 1977, pp. 1–9.
6 Coble, 1980, p. 20.
7 Ibid., p. 263.

BIBLIOGRAPHY

This bibliography includes works cited in the notes and also a few others of major importance in the development of this project.

Archival sources
Nathan Papers. Desposited in the Bodleian Library, Oxford. These consist mostly of letters between E. J. Nathan, Chief Manager of the Kailuan Mining Administration in Tianjin, and the Chairman of the Board of the Chinese Engineering and Mining Company in London.

Newspapers and periodicals

Chinese language

Dagongbao. Tianjin, 1937.
Dongfang zazhi. Shanghai, 1904–37.
Duli pinglun. Beijing, 1932.
Gongshang banyuekan. Shanghai, 1928–37.
Guoji maoyi daobao. Shanghai, 1929–36.
Henan Zhongyuan meikuang gongsi huikan. Jiaozuo, 1931.
Jianshe weiyuanhui gongbao. Nanjing, 1930–37.
Jingji banyuekan. Beijing, 1927–8. Later *Gongshang banyuekan.*
Kuangye lianhehui jikan. Beijing, 1923–6.
Kuangye zhoubao. Nanjing, 1928–37.
Nongkuang gongbao. Nanjing, 1928–30.
Nongshang gongbao. Beijing, 1914–25.
Shandong nongkuang gongbao. Jinan, 1928–31.
Shangwu guanbao. Beijing, 1907–11.
Shiye tongji. Nanjing, 1933–6.
Tiedao gongbao. Nanjing, 1928–37.
Tongji yuebao. Nanjing, 1931–4.
Xiangdao zhoubao. Guangzhou, 1924.
Xin gingnian. Beijing, 1921.
Yinhang yuekan. Beijing, 1921–8.
Yinhang zhoubao. Shanghai, 1917–37.
Zhongwai jingji zhoukan. Beijing, 1923–7. Later *Jingji banyuekan.*

Japanese language

Mantetsu chōsa geppō. Dalian, 1919–44 (under various titles).
Naigai chōsa shiryō. Tokyo, 1932.
Shina kōgyō jihō. Dalian, 1909–42.
Tōa. Tokyo, 1928–45.
Tōyō keizai shimpō. Tokyo, 1937.
Tsūshō kōhō. Tokyo, 1917.

Western languages

Chinese Economic Bulletin. Beijing and Shanghai, 1919–35.
Chinese Economic Journal. Beijing, 1927–37.
Chinese Economic Monthly. Beijing, 1923–6. Later *Chinese Economic Journal.*
Chinese Repository. Guangzhou, 1833–51.
Contemporary Manchuria. Dalian, 1937–41.
International Labour Review. Geneva, 1935.
London and China Express. London, 1915.
Nankai Weekly Statistical Service. Tianjin, 1928–33.
North China Daily News. Shanghai, 1934.
North China Herald and Supreme Court and Consular Gazette. Shanghai, 1850–1937.
People's Tribune. Beijing, 1926.
The Times. London, 1929–37.

Books, articles, government reports, etc.

Chinese language

Bai Jiaju. *Diqici Zhongguo kuangye jiyao.* Chongqing, 1945.
Beijing shifan daxue, lishixi sannianji, yanjiuban. *Mentougou meikuang shigao.* Beijing, 1958.
Chen Zhen. *Zhongguo jindai gongye shi ziliao, diyiji, minzu ziben chuangban he jingying de gongye.* Beijing, 1957.
Zhongguo jindai gongye shi ziliao, dierji, diguozhuyi dui Zhongguo gongkuang shiye de qinlue he longduan. Beijing, 1958.
Zhongguo jindai gongye shi ziliao, disiji, Zhongguo gongye de tedian, ziben jiegou he gongye ge hangye de gaikuang. Beijing, 1961.
Zhongguo jindai gongye shi ziliao, disanji, Qing zhengfu, Beiyang zhengfu he Guomindang guanliao ziben chuangban he longduan de gongye. Beijing, 1962.
China (People's Republic of), guojia tongji ju, gongye tongji si. *Wo guo gangtie, dianli, meitan, jixie, fangzhi, zaozhi gongye de jinxi.* Beijing, 1958.
China (Republic of), caizhengbu, caizheng nianjian bianzuan chu. *Caizheng nianjian.* Shanghai, 1935.
Jiaotong tiedao bu, jiaotong shi bianzuan weiyuanhui. *Jiaotong shi, luzheng bian.* Nanjing, 1935.
Lifa yuan, bianyi chu. *Zhonghua minguo fagui huibian.* Shanghai, 1934.

Quanguo jingji weiyuanhui. *Shanxi kaocha baogao shu.* Shanghai, 1936.

Shiyebu, guoji maoyi ju. *Zhongguo shiye zhi: Jiangsu sheng.* Shanghai, 1933.

Zhongguo shiye zhi: Shandong sheng. Shanghai, 1934.

Zhongguo shiye zhi: Hunan sheng. Shanghai, 1935.

Zhongguo shiye zhi: Shanxi sheng. Shanghai, 1937.

Laodong nianjian bianzuan weiyuanhui. *Ershiyinian Zhongguo laodong nianjian.* Nanjing, 1933.

Laodong nianjian bianzuan weiyuanhui. *Ershiernian Zhongguo laodong nianjian.* Nanjing, 1934.

Zhongguo jingji nianjian bianzuan weiyuanhui. *Zhongguo jingji nianjian.* Shanghai, 1934.

Zhongguo jingji nianjian bianzuan weiyuanhui. *Minguo ershisinian Zhongguo jingji nianjian xubian.* Shanghai, 1935.

Zhongguo jingji nianjian bianzuan weiyuanhui. *Zhongguo jingji nianjian disanbian.* Shanghai, 1936.

Tiedaobu, tiedao nianjian bianzuan weiyuanhui. *Tiedao nianjian.* Shanghai, 1933.

Zhuji chu, tongji ju. *Zhonghua minguo tongji tiyao.* Chongqing, 1940.

Deng Zhongxia. *Zhongguo zhigong yundong jianshi (1919–26).* Beijing, 1953.

Ding Richu and Du Xuncheng. 'Yu Xiaqing jian lun'. *Lishi yanjiu.* 1981.3 (May–June 1981): 145–66.

Ding Wenjiang. *Zhongguo Kuangye jiyao.* Beijing, 1921.

'Wushi nian lai Zhongguo zhi kuangye'. In *Zuijin zhi wushi nian,* ed. Shenbao guan. Shanghai, 1923.

Dongbei wenhua she, nianjian bianyin chu. *Dongbei nianjian.* Shenyang, 1931.

Fei Jingzhong (Woqui zhongzi). *Dangdai mingren zhuan.* Shanghai, 1926.

Gan Houci. *Beiyang gongdu leizuan xubian.* Tianjin, 1910.

Gong Jun. *Zhongguo xin gongye fazhan shi dagang.* Shanghai, 1933.

Gu Lang. *Zhongguo shi da kuangchang diaocha ji.* Shanghai, 1916.

Guo Shihao. 'Zaoqi Kaiping meitian de kaifa'. *Nankai xuebao* 1980.6 (November 1980): 45–9.

Guomindang zhongyang dangbu. *Shi nian lai zhi Zhongguo jingji jianshe.* Nanjing, 1937.

Hebei sheng, kuangwu zhengli weiyuanhui. *Hebei kuangwu huikan.* Baoding, 1930.

Hou Defeng. *Disanci Zhongguo kuangye jiyao.* Beijing, 1929.

Disici Zhongguo kuangye jiyao. Beijing, 1932.

Hou Defeng and Cao Guoquan. 'Sanshi nian lai Zhongguo zhi meikuang shiye'. In *Sanshi nian lai zhi Zhongguo gongcheng,* ed. Zhongguo gongcheng shixue hui. Nanjing, 1948.

Hu Jixian. *Kuangye tekan.* Guangzhou, 1931.

Hu Rongquan. *Zhongguo meikuang.* Shanghai, 1935.

Huang Jiamo. *Jiawu zhan qian zhi Taiwan meiwu.* Taibei, 1961.

Huang Yanpei and Pang Song. *Zhongguo sishi nian haiguan shangwu tongji tubiao (1876–1915).* Xianggang, 1966.

Huang Yifeng. 'Chen Qiyuan jiazu he Liu Hongsheng ziben jituan'. *Gongshang shiliao* 1 (November 1980): 55–62.

Ji Di. 'Beiyang junfa zhengke zichan jiwen'. *Jindaishi ziliao* 1978.1 (1978): 163–75.

Ji Hua. 'Ni Sichong he ta zai Tianjin de touzi'. *Jindaishi ziliao* 1978.1 (1978): 156–62.

Jia Shiyi. *Minguo caizheng shi.* Shanghai, 1917.

Jiangxi sheng, qinggongye ting, taoci yanjiu suo. *Jingdezhen taoci shigao.* Beijing, 1959.

Jiao-Ji tielu guanliju. *Jiao-Ji tielu jingji diaocha huibian.* Qingdao, 1934.

Li Enhan. *Wan-Qing de shouhui kuangquan yundong.* Taibei, 1963.

Li Hongzhang. *Li Wenzhong gong quanji.* 100 vols. Nanjing, 1905–8.

Lin Dunkui and Mei Zhen. 'Zhongguo zaoqi meikuang zibenjia dui gongren de canku boxue'. *Xin jianshe* 1965.6 (June 1965): 66–9.

Liu Ao. *Xun-Tai tuisi lu.* Taibei, 1958.

Liu Dajun. *Zhongguo gongye diaocha baogao.* 3 vols. Nanjing, 1937.

Liu Jie et al. *Shanxi zaochan nianjian.* Taiyuan, 1936.

Liu Xinquan and Shi Yushou. 'Shandong Zhongxing meikuang gongren diaocha'. *Shehui kexue zazhi* 3.1 (March 1932): 35–93.

Lü Shiqiang. *Zhongguo zaoqi de lunchuan jingying.* Taibei, 1962.

Luo Zhiru. *Tongjibiao zhong zhi Shanghai.* Nanjing, 1932.

Ma Bohuang. 'Lun jiu Zhongguo Liu Hongsheng qiye fazhan zhong de jige wenti'. *Lishi yanjiu* 1980.3 (May–June 1980): 49–66.

Ma Chaojun. *Zhongguo laogong yundong shi.* Taibei, 1959.

Manzhouguo, caizhengbu. *Manzhouguo waiguo maoyi tongji nianbao, Kangde yuannian.* Dalian, 1935.

Jingjibu. *Manzhouguo waiguo maoyi tongji nianbao, Kangde sannian.* Dalian, 1937.

Mi Rucheng. *Diguozhuyi yu Zhongguo tielu.* Shanghai, 1980.

Nankai daxue, jingji yanjiu suo. *1913 nian–1952 nian Nankai zhishu ziliao huibian.* Beijing, 1958.

Peng Zeyi. *Zhongguo jindai shougongye shi ziliao.* Beijing, 1957.

Ping-Han tielu guanli weiyuanhui. *Ping-Han tielu nianjian.* Hankou, 1932.

Quan Hansheng (a) *Hanyeping gongsi shilue.* Xianggang, 1972.

(b) 'Qingji xifa shuru Zhongguo qian de meikuang shuihuan wenti'. In *Zhongguo jingjishi luncong*, by Quan Hansheng. 2 vols. vol. 2, pp. 673–9. Xianggang, 1972.

(c). 'Shanxi meikuang ziyuan yu jindai Zhongguo gongyehua de guanxi'. In *Zhongguo jingjishi luncong*, by Quan Hansheng. 2 vols. vol. 2, pp. 745–66. Xianggang, 1972.

Shanghai shangye chuxu yinhang, diaochabu. *Mei yu meiye.* Shanghai, 1935.

Shangwu yinshu guan. *Da-Qing Guangxu xin faling.* Shanghai, 1909.

Zhonghua minguo xianxing fagui daquan. Shanghai, 1933.

Bianyi suo. *Zhonghua minguo faling daquan.* 9th edn. Shanghai, 1919.

Shen Baozhen. *Shen Wensu gong zhengshu.* n.p. 1880.

Sun Jingzhi. *Huabei jingji dili.* Beijing, 1957.

Sun Yutang. *Zhong-Ri jiawu zhanzheng qian waiguo ziben zai Zhongguo jingying de jindai gongye.* Shanghai, 1955.

Zhongguo jindai gongye shi ziliao, diyiji, 1840–1895 nian. Beijing, 1957.

Tan Xichou. 'Shandong Zichuan Boshan meitian dizhi'. *Dizhi huibao* 4 (1922): 11–42.

Tang Hai. *Zhongguo laodong wenti.* Shanghai, 1926.

Tang Mingsui, Li Longqian and Zhang Weixiong. 'Dui Deng Tuo tongzhi "Cong Wanli dao Qianlong" yiwen de shangque he buchong'. *Lishi yanjiu* 1958.1 (January 1958): 41–65.

Tong Zhehui. 'Zhanshi Huabei kuangye'. *Shehui kexue zazhi* 10.1 (June 1948): 1–47.

Wang Jingyu. *Zhongguo jindai gongye shi ziliao, dierji, 1895–1914 nian.* Beijing, 1957.

Wang Mingxin, Zhong Yuling et al., eds. *Dayi xian zhi.* Preface. Dayi xian, 1930.

Wang Qingbin. *Diyici Zhongguo laodong nianjian.* Beijing, 1928.

Wang Xi. *Zhong-Ying Kaiping kuangquan jiaoshe.* Taibei, 1962.

Wang Xi and Li Enhan, eds. *Kuangwu dang.* 8 vols. Taibei, 1960.

Wang Zhenlu et al., eds. *Yi xian zhi.* 1905.

Wang Zhongluo. 'Gudai Zhongguo renmin shiyong mei de lishi'. *Wen shi zhe* 1956.12 (December 1956): 24–30.

Wei Qingyuan and Lu Su. *You guan Qingdai qianqi kuangye zhengce de yichang da lunzhan.* Beijing, 1980.

Wei Zichu. *Diguozhuyi yu Kailuan meikuang.* Shanghai, 1954.

Wu Bannong. 'Rimei qingxiao zhong zhi guomei wenti'. *Shehui kexue zazhi* 3.4 (December 1932): 479–532.

Wu Chengming. *Diguozhuyi zai jiu Zhongguo de touzi.* Beijing, 1955.

Xie Jiarong. *Dierci Zhongguo kuangye jiyao.* Beijing, 1926.

Xing Bixin et al., eds., *Dierci Zhongguo laodong nianjian.* Beijing, 1932.

Xu Gengsheng. *Zhong-wai heban meitie kuangye shihua.* Shanghai, 1947.

Xue Muqiao, chief ed. *Zhongguo jingji nianjian (1982).* Xianggang, 1982.

Yan Guanghua. 'Jiu Kailuan meikuang baogong zhi zhong diguozhuyi he fengjian baogongtou de goujie yu maodun'. *Nankai jingji yanjiu suo jikan* 1981.3 (August 1981): 34–40.

Yan Zhongping. *Zhongguo jindai jingjishi tongji ziliao xuanji.* Beijing, 1955.

Zhongguo mianfangzhi shigao, 1289–1937. Beijing, 1963.

Yang Bingyan (a) '1897–1904 nian Yingguo Fu gongsi qinzhan Henan kuangshan de yinmou huodong'. In *Zhongguo jin sanbai nian shehui jingji shi lunji,* ed. Zhou Kangxie. 5 vols. vol. 4, pp. 391–5. Xianggang, 1974.

(b) '1909 nian Henan renmin fandui Yingguo Fu gongsi jiudi shou mei de douzheng'. In *Zhongguo jin sanbai nian shehui jingji shi lunji,* ed. Zhou Kangxie. 5 vols. vol. 4, pp. 396–9. Xianggang, 1974.

Yang Dajin. *Jindai Zhongguo shiye tongzhi.* Nanjing, 1933.

Yang Duanliu and Hou Houpei. *Liushiwu nian lai Zhongguo guoji maoyi tongji.* Nanjing, 1931.

Yang Kuan. *Zhongguo gudai yetie jishu de faming he fazhan.* Shanghai, 1956.

Yu Heyin (a) *Benxihu meitie gongsi baogao.* Beijing, 1926.

(b) *Fengtian Jinxi xian Dayaogou meikuang baogao.* Beijing, 1926.

(c) *Fushun meikuang baogao.* Beijing, 1926.

(d) *Shanxi Pingding xian Yangquan fujin Baojin gongsi meikuang tiechang baogao.* Beijing, 1926.

(e) *Zhili Linyu xian Liujiang meikuang gongsi baogao.* Beijing, 1926.

Zhang Huiruo. *Diwuci Shandong kuangye baogao.* Jinan, 1936.

Zhang Shiwen. *Ding xian nongcun gongye diaocha.* Ding xian, 1936.

Zhang Shouyong et al. eds. *Huangchao zhanggu huibian.* Shanghai, 1902.

Zhang Xiaomei. *Sichuan jingji cankao ziliao.* Shanghai, 1939.

Zheng Wanyen. *Minguo shijiunian Shandong kuangye baogao.* Jinan, 1931.

Zhongguo geming bowuguan. *Beifang diqu gongren yundong ziliao xuanbian, 1921–1923.* Beijing, 1981.

Zhong [guo] gong [chandang], Datong meikuang weiyuanhui, kuangshi bianxie zu.

'1918–1936 nian de Datong meikuang'. *Lishi jiaoxue* 1962.2 (February 1962): 26–35.

Pingxiang meikuang weiyuanhui, xuanchuan bu. *Hongse de Anyuan*. Nanchang, 1959.

Zhongguo kexue yuan, Jilin sheng fenyuan, lishi yanjiu suo with Jilin shifan daxue, lishi xi. *Jindai dongbei renmin geming yundong shi, 1840–1919*. Changchun, 1960.

Shanghai jingji yanjiu suo, with Shanghai shehui kexue yuan, jingji yanjiu suo. *Shanghai jiefang qianhou wujia ziliao huibian*. Shanghai, 1958.

Zhongguo shehui kexue yuan, jindai shi yanjiu suo, with Anyuan gongren yundong jinian guan. *Liu Shaoqi yu Anyuan gongren yundong*. Beijing, 1981.

Zhongguo shixue hui. *Yangwu yundong*. 8 vols. Shanghai, 1961.

Zhongguo yinhang, jingji yanjiu shi. *Zhonghua minguo ershiliunian quanguo yinhang nianjian*. Shanghai, 1937.

Zhou Xianwen. 'Ri ju shidai Taiwan zhi kuangye jingji'. *Taiwan yinhang jikan* 9.2 (September 1957): 14–46.

Zhou Xiuluan. *Diyici shijie dazhan shiqi Zhongguo minzu gongye de fazhan*. Shanghai, 1958.

Zhu Cai. *Qingfen ge ji*. 1908.

Japanese language

Hatakeyama Hideki. 'Mitsui Miike tankō ni okeru keiei rōmu seisaku no kakuritsu katei'. *Ōsaka daigaku keizaigaku* 25.4 (March 1976): 86–132.

Hatano Ken'ichi. *Gendai Shina no kiroku*. Beijing, 1924–32, monthly.

Horiuchi Takejirō. 'Satsuraidakuji tankō higyō temmatsu'. In *Mantetsu*, edited by Ito Takeo et al. 3 vols. vol. 3, 738–45. Tokyo, 1967.

Inoue Gentai. *Chintō mondai no ketsuron to sekitan seisaku*. Qingdao, 1921.

Japan, gaimushō. *Nihon gaikō bunsho*. vol. 40 (1907). 3 parts. Tokyo, 1961.

Ajiakyoku. *Saikin Shina kankei sho mondai tekiyō, 1928*. 3 vols. Tokyo, 1929.

Ajiakyoku. *Saikin Shina kankei sho mondai tekiyō, 1929*. 5 vols. Tokyo, 1930.

Jōhōbu. *Gendai Shina jimmeikan*. Tokyo, 1928.

Jōhōbu. *Gendai Chūkaminkoku Manshūkoku jimmeikan*. Tokyo, 1932.

Jōhōbu. *Gendai Chūkaminkoku Manshū teikoku jimmeikan*. Tokyo, 1937.

Jōyakukyoku. *Joyaku isan*. 2 vols. Tokyo, 1936.

Kanda Masao. *Shisen shō sōran*. Tokyo, 1936.

Kikuta Tarō. 'Sansei no dohō seitetsu'. *Tōa keizai ronsō* 3.2 (May 1943): 84–100.

Kōzan konwakai. *Nihon kōgyō hattatsu shi*. 3 vols. Tokyo, 1932.

Kuboyama Yūzō. *Shina sekitan chōsa hōkokusho*. Tokyo, 1940.

Shina sekitan jijō. Tokyo, 1944.

Manshikai. *Manshū kaihatsu yonjū nen shi*. 3 vols. Tokyo, 1964–5.

Matsumoto Tadao. *Matsumoto bunko Chūgoku kankei shimbun kirinukishū*. Yūshōdo microfilm. Tokyo, 1967.

Minami Manshū tetsudō kabushiki kaisha (MMT). *Minami Manshū tetsudō kabushiki kaisha jū nen shi*. Dalian, 1919.

MMT, *Minami Manshū tetsudō kabushiki kaisha dianiji jū nen shi*. Dalian, 1928.

Minami Manshū tetsudō kabushiki kaisha daisanji jū nen shi. Dalian, 1938.

Chōsabu (a) *Ekiken tanden chōsa shiryō*. Dalian, 1937.

(b) *Pekin seizan tanden chōsa shiryō*. Dalian, 1937.
(c) *Sansei shō tanden chōsa shiryō*. Dalian, 1937.
(d) *Seikei tanden kaihatsu hōsaku oyobi chōsa shiryō*. Dalian, 1937.
(e) *Shisen Hakusan Shōkyū tanden chōsa shiryō*. Dalian, 1937.
Hoku-Shi keizai chōsajo. *Santō shō Kō-Sai ensen sekitan kōgyō no genkyō to sekitan zōsan keikaku no gaiyō*. Beijing or Harbin, 1941.
Keizai chōsakai (a) *Manshū rōdō jijō sōran*. Dalian, 1936.
(b) *Shina sekitan shijō ni taisuru kongo no hōsaku*. Xinjing, 1936.
Kōgyōbu kōmuka. *Santō shō kōgyō shiryō*. Dalian, 1914.
Rōmuka. *Minami Manshu kōzan rōdō jijō*. Dalian, 1931.
Sangyōbu. *Kita Shina keizai sōkan*. Tokyo, 1938.
Shomubu chōsaka. *Kairan tankō chōsa shiryō*. Dalian, 1929.
Moto Santō tetsudō san dai kikan no genjō: tetsudō, tankō kōwan. Dalian, 1928.
Sōsaishitsu, kōhōka. *Minami Manshū tetsudō kabushiki kaisha sanjū nen ryakushi*. Dalian, 1937.
Tenshin jimusho chōsaka. *Kita Shina kōgyō kiyō*. Tianjin, 1936.
Mishina Yoritada. *Hoku-Shi minzoku kōgyō no hattatsu*. Tokyo, 1942.
Nakamura Takatoshi. *Hatō seido no kenkyū*. Tokyo, 1944.
Nakamura Yoshihito. *Kita Manshū no shigen to sangyō gaikan*. Harbin, 1929.
Negishi Tadashi. *Chūkaminkoku jitsugyō meikan*. Tokyo, 1934.
Nichi-Man shōji kabushiki kaisha. *Hoku-Shi sekitankai no genkyō*. Xinjing, 1937.
Nishimura Shigeo. 'Dai kakumei-ki ni okeru Tōsanshō, rōdō mondai o chūshin ni'. *Ajia kenkyū* 19.3 (October 1972): 29–63.
Oka Itarō, ed. *Santō keizai jijō*. Jinan, 1919.
Okabe Toshiyoshi. 'Shina joshi bōseki rōdōsha sōshutsu katei no tokushitsu: Sōshutsu katei o chūshin to suru Shina no kindaiteki joshi rōdōsha no mondai', parts I and II. *Tōa keizai ronsō* 2.2 (May 1942): 139–64, 2.3 (September 1942): 163–93.
Ōyama Shikitarō. *Kōgyō rōdō to oyakata seido*. Tokyo, 1964.
Saitō Ryōe. *Tai-Shi keizai seisaku no aru kihon mondai*. Tokyo, 1938.
Sugiyama Shinya. 'Bakumatsu Meiji shoki no sekitan yushutsu to Shanhai sekitan jijō'. In *Kindai ikōki no Nihon keizai*, ed. Shinbo Hiroshi and Yasuba Yasukichi, pp. 199–218. Tokyo, 1979.
Sumiya Mikio. *Nihon sekitan sangyō no bunseki*. Tokyo, 1968.
Takimoto Seiichi and Mukai Shikamatsu. *Nihon sangyō shiryō taikei*. 12 vols. Tokyo, 1926–7.
Tanaka Tadao. *Shina keizai kenkyū*. Tokyo, 1920.
Tezuka Masao. *Jihen zen ni okeru Shina sekitan no seisan to ryūdō*. Tokyo, 1940.
'Shina tankō no dohō keitai'. *Tōa kenkyūjo hō* 20 (February 1943): 117–76.
Shina jūkōgyō hattatsu shi. Kyoto, 1944.
Tōa dōbunkai. *Shina shōbetsu zenshi*. 18 vols. Tokyo, 1917–20.
Tōa kenkyūjo. *Shogaikoku no tai-Shi tōshi*. 3 vols. Tokyo, 1942–3.
Tokunaga Kiyoyuki. 'Shanhai Dairen bukka shisū'. *Tōa keizai kenkyū* 14.1 (January 1930): 102–21.

Western Languages

Adshead, S. A. M. 'An Energy Crisis in Early Modern China'. *Ch'ing-shih Wen-t'i* 3.2 (December 1974): 20–8.

Allen, G. C. *A Short Economic History of Japan*. 2nd edn. London, 1962.

Arnold, Julean H. *China: A Commercial and Industrial Handbook*. Washington, 1926.

Ashton, Thomas S., and Sykes, Joseph. *The Coal Industry of the Eighteenth Century*. 2nd edn. Manchester, 1964.

Baran, Paul A. *The Political Economy of Growth*. London, 1973.

Barrow, Sir John. *Travels in China*. 2nd edn. London, 1806.

Bergère, Marie-Claire. *Capitalisme National et Impérialisme: La Crise des Filatures Chinoises en 1923*. Paris, 1980.

Biggerstaff, Knight. 'The Secret Correspondence of 1867–1868: Views of Leading Chinese Statesmen Regarding the Further Opening of China to Western Influence'. *Journal of Modern History* 22.2 (June 1950): 122–36.

Boorman, Howard L., and Howard, Richard C., eds. *Biographical Dictionary of Republican China*. 4 vols. New York, 1967–71.

Brown, Shannon R. 'The Ewo Filature: A Study in the Transfer of Technology to China in the 19th Century'. *Technology and Culture* 20.3 (July 1979): 550–68.

'Cakes and Oil: Technology Transfer and Chinese Soybean Processing, 1860–1895'. *Comparative Studies in Society and History* 23.3 (July 1981): 449–63.

Brown, Shannon R., and Wright, Tim. 'Technology, Economics and Politics in the Modernization of China's Coal Mining Industry: The First Phase, 1850–1895'. *Explorations in Economic History* 18.1 (January 1981): 60–83.

Buchanan, Daniel H. *The Development of Capitalist Enterprise in India*. New York, 1934.

Buck, David D. *Urban Change in China: Politics and Development in Tsinan, Shantung, 1890–1949*. Madison, 1978.

Buck, John Lossing. *Chinese Farm Economy*. Chicago, 1930.

Land Utilization in China. 3 vols. Nanjing, 1937.

Buxton, Neil K. *The Economic Development of the British Coal Industry: From Industrial Revolution to the Present Day*. London, 1978.

Caldwell, G. S. 'Experiences on a Chinese Coalfield'. *Transactions of the Institution of Mining Engineers* 43 (1911–12): 361–9.

Carlson, Ellsworth C. *The Kaiping Mines (1877–1912)*. 2nd edn. Cambridge, Mass., 1971.

Chan, Wellington K. K. *Merchants, Mandarins and Modern Enterprise in Late Ch'ing China*. Cambridge, Mass., 1977.

Chang, John Key. *Industrial Development in Pre-Communist China*. Chicago, 1969.

Chang, Kia-ngau. *China's Struggle for Railroad Development*. New York, 1943.

Chao, Kang. 'The Growth of a Modern Cotton Textile Industry and the Competition with Handicrafts'. In *China's Modern Economy in Historical Perspective*, ed. Dwight H. Perkins, pp. 167–202. Stanford, 1975.

The Development of Cotton Textile Production in China. Cambridge, Mass., 1977.

Chesneaux, Jean. *The Chinese Labor Movement*. Translated by Hope M. Wright, Stanford, 1968.

Chi, Madeleine. 'Bureaucratic Capitalists in Operation: Ts'ao Ju-lin and his New Communications Clique'. *Journal of Asian Studies* 34.3 (May 1975): 675–88.

China, Inspectorate-General of Customs (IMC). *Decennial Reports on the Trade, Navigation, Industry, etc. of the Ports Open to Foreign Commerce in China and Corea, and on the Conditions and Development of the Treaty Port Provinces, 1922–1931*. Shanghai, 1932.

Reports on Trade of China. Shanghai, 1865–81, annually.

Returns of Trade and Trade Reports. Shanghai, 1882–1919, annually.

China (Republic of), Ministry of Industry, Bureau of Mines. 'Organization of Production, Processing and Distribution of Coal and Coal Products and Liquid and Gaseous Fuels in China', in *Transactions of the Third World Power Conference*, vol. 3, pp. 337–60. Washington, 1938.

Chu, Samuel C. *Reformer in Modern China: Chang Chien, 1853–1926.* New York, 1965.

Clark, Robert S., and Sowerby, Arthur de Carle. *Through Shen-Kan: The Account of the Clark Expedition in North China, 1908–09.* London, 1912.

Coble, Parks M., Jr. *The Shanghai Capitalists and the Nationalist Government, 1927–1937.* Cambridge, Mass., 1980.

Cochran, Sherman. *Big Business in China: Sino-foreign Rivalry in the Cigarette Industry, 1890–1930.* Cambridge, Mass., 1980.

Collins, William F. *Mineral Enterprise in China.* London, 1918.

Des Forges, Roger V. *Hsi-liang and the Chinese National Revolution.* New Haven, 1973.

Drake, Noah F. 'The Coalfields around Tse Chou, Shansi, China'. Abstracted in *Transactions of the Institution of Mining Engineers* 25 (1902–3): 821.

Eastman, Lloyd E. *The Abortive Revolution: China Under Nationalist Rule, 1927–1937.* Cambridge, Mass., 1974.

Eckstein, Alexander, Chao, Kang, and Chang, John Key. 'The Economic Development of Manchuria: The Rise of a Frontier Economy'. *Journal of Economic History* 34.1 (March 1974): 239–64.

Elvin, Mark. *The Pattern of the Chinese Past.* Stanford, 1972.

'Comment'. *Modern China* 4.3 (July 1978): 329–30.

Endacott, George B. *An Eastern Entrepot: A Collection of Documents Illustrating the History of Hong Kong.* London, 1964.

Esherick, Joseph W. *Reform and Revolution in China: The 1911 Revolution in Hunan and Hubei.* Berkeley, 1976.

Fairbank, John K, et al., eds. *The I. G. in Peking: Collected Letters of Robert Hart.* 2 vols. Cambridge, Mass., 1975.

Feuerwerker, Albert. *China's Early Industrialization: Sheng Hsuan-huai and Mandarin Enterprise.* Cambridge, Mass., 1958.

'Industrial Enterprise in Twentieth-Century China: The Chee Hsin Cement Co.' In *Approaches to Modern Chinese History*, ed. Albert Feuerwerker et al., pp. 304–41. Berkeley, 1967.

Economic Trends in the Republic of China. Ann Arbor, 1977.

Fleming, George. *Travels on Horseback in Mantchu Tartary: Being a Summer's Ride Beyond the Great Wall of China.* London, 1863.

Fogel, Robert W., and Engerman, Stanley L., eds. *The Reinterpretation of American Economic History.* New York, 1971.

Gamble, Sidney D. *How Chinese Families Live in Peiping.* New York, 1933.

Ting Hsien, A North China Rural Community. New York, 1954.

Gibson, Finlay A. *The Coal Mining Industry of the United Kingdom, The Various Coalfields Thereof and the Principal Foreign Countries of the World.* Cardiff, 1922.

Gillin, Donald B. *Warlord: Yen Hsi-shan in Shansi Province, 1911–1949.* Princeton, 1967.

Gourlay, Walter E. '"Yellow" Unionism in Shanghai: A Study of Kuomintang Technique in Labor Control, 1927–1937'. *Papers on China* 7 (February 1953): 103–35.

Great Britain, Department of Overseas Trade. *Report on the Commercial, Industrial and Economic Situation in China*. London, 1919–1935, annually or biennially.

Griffin, Alan R. *Coalmining*. London, 1971.

Mining in the East Midlands, 1550–1947. London, 1975.

The British Coalmining Industry: Retrospect and Prospect. Buxton, 1977.

Grosier, Jean Baptiste Gabriel Alexandre. *De la Chine, ou Description Génerale de cet Empire*. 3rd edn. 7 vols. Paris, 1818–20.

Hardy, Randall W. *China's Oil Future: A Case of Modest Expectations*. Boulder, 1978.

Hartwell, Robert M. 'A Revolution in the Chinese Iron and Coal Industries during the Northern Sung, 960–1126 A.D.'. *Journal of Asian Studies*. 21.2 (February 1962): 153–62.

'A Cycle of Economic Change in Imperial China: Coal and Iron in North-east China, 750–1350'. *Journal of the Economic and Social History of the Orient*. 10.1 (July 1967): 102–60.

Ho, Ping-ti. *Studies on the Population of China, 1368–1953*. Cambridge, Mass., 1959.

Hommel, Rudolf P. *China at Work: An Illustrated Record of the Primitive Industries of China's Masses, and Thus an Account of Chinese Civilization*. New York, 1937.

Hou, Chi-ming. *Foreign Investment and Economic Development in China, 1840–1937*. Cambridge, Mass., 1965.

Howe, Christopher. *Wage Patterns and Wage Policy in Modern China, 1919–1972*. Cambridge, 1973.

China's Economy: A Basic Guide. London, 1978.

Hsia, Ronald. *Steel in China: Its Output Behaviour, Productivity and Growth Pattern*. Wiesbaden, 1971.

Hsiao, Liang-lin. *China's Foreign Trade Statistics, 1864–1949*. Cambridge, Mass., 1974.

Ikonnikov, Alexander B. *The Coal Industry of China*. Canberra, 1977.

International Labour Office (ILO) (a) *Industrial Labour in India*. Geneva, 1938.

(b) *The World Coalmining Industry*. 2 vols. Geneva, 1938.

International Labour Organization, Coal Mines Committee. *Productivity in Coal Mines*. Geneva, 1951.

Irish University Press (IUP). *Irish University Press Reprints of British Parliamentary Papers, Area Studies: China*. 42 vols. Shannon, 1971.

Jevons, H. Stanley. *The British Coal Trade*. London, 1915.

Kailan Mining Administration, The. *Kaiping Coal*. Tianjin, c. 1920.

Karnik, V. B. *Strikes in India*. Bombay, 1967.

Kennedy, Thomas L. *The Arms of Kiangnan: Modernization in the Chinese Ordnance Industry, 1860–1895*. Boulder, 1978.

Kerr, Clark, and Siegel, Abraham. 'The Inter-Industry Propensity to Strike – an International Comparison'. In *Industrial Conflict in Britain*, ed. Eric W. Evans and S. W. Creigh, pp. 233–54, 283–8. London, 1977.

Kidron, Michael. *Foreign Investments in India*. London, 1965.

Kinder, Claude W. 'Railways and Collieries of North China'. *Minutes of the*

Proceedings of the Institute of Civil Engineers 103 (1890–1): 278–304.

Kingsmill, Thomas W. 'Inland Communications in China'. *Journal of the North China Branch of the Royal Asiatic Society* new series 28 (1898): 1–213.

Klein, Frederick R. 'When Steam Darkened the Sail: Geographic and Public Policy Factors Affecting the Timing of Conversion from Sail to Steam Marine Power'. Unpublished PhD dissertation, Columbia University, 1968.

Kraus, Richard A. *Cotton and Cotton Goods in China, 1918–1936.* New York, 1980.

Kula, Witold. *An Economic Theory of the Feudal System.* Translated by Lawrence Garner. London, 1976.

Kurgan-van Hentenryk, G. *Jean Jadot: Artisan de l'Expansion Belge en Chine.* Brussels, 1965.

Landes, David S. *The Unbound Prometheus: Technological Change and Industrial Development in Western Europe from 1750 to the Present.* Cambridge, 1972.

Langton, John. *Geographical Change and Industrial Revolution: Coalmining in South West Lancashire, 1590–1799.* Cambridge, 1979.

Lefevour, Edward. *Western Enterprise in Late Ch'ing China: A Selective Survey of Jardine, Matheson and Company's Operations, 1842–1895.* Cambridge, Mass., 1968.

Levy, Howard S. *Chinese Footbinding: The History of a Curious Erotic Custom.* New York, 1966.

Lewis, Charlton M, III. 'Some Notes on the Ko-lao Hui in late Ch'ing China'. In *Popular Movements and Secret Societies in China, 1840–1950,* ed. Jean Chesneaux, pp. 97–112. Stanford, 1972.

Lieu, D. K. (Liu Dajun). *The Silk Industry of China.* Shanghai, 1941.

Lippit, Victor. 'The Development of Underdevelopment in China'. *Modern China* 4.3 (July 1978): 251–328.

Liu, Kwang-ching. *Anglo-American Steamship Rivalry in China, 1862–1874.* Cambridge, Mass., 1962.

Liu, Ta-chung and Yeh, Kung-chia. *The Economy of the Chinese Mainland: National Income and Economic Development, 1933–1959.* Princeton, 1965.

Longfield, Claude M. *The Past, Present and Future of Australian Power Supplies.* Melbourne, 1947.

McCloskey, Donald N. 'International Differences in Productivity? Coal and Steel in America and Britain before World War I'. In *Essays on a Mature Economy: Britain after 1840,* ed. Donald N. McCloskey, pp. 285–309. Princeton, 1971.

McCormack, Gavan. *Chang Tso-lin in Northeast China, 1911–1928.* Stanford, 1977.

McDonald, Angus W., Jr. *The Urban Origins of Rural Revolution: Elites and Masses in Hunan Province, China, 1911–1927.* Berkeley and Los Angeles, 1978.

McKay, John P. *Pioneers for Profit: Foreign Entrepreneurship and Russian Industrialization, 1885–1913.* Chicago, 1970.

MacMurray, John V. A. *Treaties and Agreements with and Concerning China, 1894–1919.* 2 vols. New York, 1921.

Mandel, Ernest. *Marxist Economic Theory.* Translated by Brian Pearce. London, 1968.

Mauldon, Frank R. E. *The Economics of Australian Coal.* Melbourne, 1929.

Meisner, Maurice. *Mao's China: A History of the People's Republic.* New York, 1977.

Meng, T'ien-p'ei, and Gamble, Sidney D. *Prices, Wages and the Standard of Living in Peking, 1900–1924.* Supplement to the *Chinese Social and Political Science Review*, July 1926.

Milward, Alan S., and Saul, S. B. *The Development of the Economies of Continental Europe, 1850–1914.* London, 1977.

The Economic Development of Continental Europe, 1780–1870. 2nd edn., London, 1979.

Mitchell, Brian R. *European Historical Statistics, 1750–1970.* London, 1975.

Moller, W. A. 'Mining in Manchuria'. *Transactions of the Institution of Mining Engineers.* 25 (1902–3): 139–45.

Morris, J. H., and Williams, L. J. *The South Wales Coal Industry 1841–1875.* Cardiff, 1958.

Moulder, Frances V. *Japan, China and the Modern World Economy: Toward a Reinterpretation of East Asian Development, ca. 1600 to ca. 1918.* Cambridge, 1977.

Murphey, Rhoads. *Shanghai: Key to Modern China.* Cambridge, Mass., 1953.

Myers, Ramon H. *The Chinese Peasant Economy: Agricultural Development in Hopei and Shantung, 1890–1949.* Cambridge, Mass., 1970.

Nef, John U. *The Rise of the British Coal Industry.* 2 vols. London, 1932.

Ohkawa Kazushi et al., eds. *Estimates of Long-term Economic Statistics of Japan Since 1868.* vol. 8: *Prices.* Tokyo, 1967. vol. 10: *Mining and Manufacturing.* Tokyo, 1972.

Orchard, John E. 'Shanghai'. *Geographical Review.* 26.1 (January 1936): 1–31.

Perkins, Dwight H. *Agricultural Development in China (1368–1968).* Chicago, 1969.

'Growth and Changing Structure of China's Twentieth Century Economy'. In *China's Modern Economy in Historical Perspective*, ed. Dwight H. Perkins, pp. 115–65. Stanford, 1975.

Polo, Marco. *The Travels.* Translated by Ronald Latham. London, 1958.

Rawski, Thomas G. *China's Transition to Industrialism: Producer Goods and Economic Development in the Twentieth Century.* Ann Arbor, 1980.

Read, Thomas T. 'The Earliest Industrial Use of Coal'. *Transactions of the Newcomen Society* 20 (1939–40): 119–33.

'Economic-Geographic Aspects of China's Iron Industry'. *Geographical Review* 33.1 (January 1943): 42–55.

Reid, Alexander. 'Chinese Mines and Miners'. *Transactions of the Institution of Mining Engineers.* 23 (1901–2): 26–37.

Richthofen, Ferdinand von. *Baron Richthofen's Letters, 1870–1872.* Shanghai, 1872.

China: Ergebnisse Eigener Reisen und darauf gegründeter Studien. 5 vols. vol. 2. Berlin, 1882.

Tagebücher aus China. 2 vols. Berlin, 1907.

Riskin, Carl. 'Surplus and Stagnation in Modern China'. In *China's Modern Economy in Historical Perspective*, ed. Dwight H. Perkins, pp. 49–84. Stanford, 1975.

'The Symposium Papers: Discussion and Comments'. *Modern China* 4.3 (July 1978): 359–76.

Royal Commission on Labour in India. *Report of the Royal Commission on Labour in India.* London, 1931.

Sakatani, Yoshiro. *Manchuria: A Survey of its Economic Development.* New York, 1980.

Schrecker, John E. *Imperialism and Chinese Nationalism: Germany in Shantung.* Cambridge, Mass., 1971.

Schurr, Sam H., and Netschert, Bruce C. *Energy in the American Economy, 1850–1975.* Baltimore, 1960.

Seth, Bal Raj. *Labour in the Indian Coal Industry.* Bombay, 1940.

Shaffer, Lynda. *Mao and the Workers: The Hunan Labor Movement, 1920–1923.* New York, 1982. (See also Womack, Lynda S.)

Sheba, Togo, ed. *Japan–Manchoukuo Year Book, 1936.* Tokyo, 1935.

Japan–Manchoukuo Year Book, 1937. Tokyo, 1936.

Japan–Manchoukuo Year Book, 1938. Tokyo, 1937.

Japan–Manchoukuo Year Book, 1939. Tokyo, 1938.

Shurick, A. T. *The Coal Industry.* London, 1924.

South Manchurian Railway Company (SMR). *Fifth Report on Progress in Manchuria to 1936.* Dalian, 1936.

Sixth Report on Progress in Manchuria to 1939. Dalian, 1939.

Srivastava, V. L. *A Socio-Economic Survey of the Workers in the Coalmines of India (with particular reference to Bihar).* Calcutta, 1970.

Sturmey, S. G. *British Shipping and World Competition.* London, 1962.

Sun, E-tu Zen. 'Mining Labour in the Ch'ing Period'. In *Approaches to Modern Chinese History*, ed. Albert Feuerwerker et al., pp. 45–67. Berkeley, 1967.

Sun, Kungtu C, and Huenemann, Ralph W. *The Economic Development of Manchuria in the First Half of the Twentieth Century.* Cambridge, Mass., 1969.

Sung, Ying-hsing (Song Yingxing). *T'ien-kung K'ai-wu: Chinese Technology in the Seventeenth Century.* Translated by E-tu Zen Sun and Shiou-chuan Sun. University Park, Pennsylvania State University, 1966.

Sutcliffe, Robert B. *Industry and Underdevelopment.* London, 1971.

Ting, Leonard G. 'Recent Developments in China's Cotton Industry'. *Nankai Social and Economic Quarterly* 9.2 (July 1936): 398–445.

'The Coal Industry in China', parts I and II. *Nankai Social and Economic Quarterly* 10.1 (January 1937): 32–74, 10.2 (July 1937): 192–277.

United States, Bureau of Mines. *Mineral Facts and Problems*, 1975 ed. Washington, 1976.

United States, Central Intelligence Agency. *China: The Coal Industry.* Washington, 1976.

Walters, R. H. *The Economic and Business History of the South Wales Steam Coal Industry, 1840–1914.* New York, 1977.

Wang, Kung-ping. *Controlling Factors in the Future Development of the Chinese Coal Industry.* New York, 1947.

Mineral Resources and Basic Industries in the People's Republic of China. Boulder, 1977.

Williamson, Alexander. *Journeys in North China, Manchuria and Eastern Mongolia, with some account of Corea.* 2 vols. London, 1870.

Womack, Lynda S. 'Anyuan: The Cradle of the Chinese Workers' Revolutionary Movement, 1921–1922'. In *Columbia Essays in International Affairs.* vol. 5, pp. 166–201. New York, 1969. (See also Shaffer, Lynda).

Woodhead, H. G. W., ed. *China Year Book.* London and Tianjin, 1912–39, annually or biennially.

Wou, Odoric Y. K. *Militarism in Modern China: The Career of Wu P'ei-fu, 1916–1939.* Canberra, 1978.

Wright, Tim. 'Shandong Mines in the Modern Chinese Coal Industry up to 1937'. PhD dissertation, Cambridge University, 1976.

1980 (a) 'Entrepreneurs, Politicians and the Chinese Coal Industry, 1895–1937'. *Modern Asian Studies* 14.4 (October 1980): 579–602.

1980 (b) 'Sino-Japanese Business in China: The Luda Company, 1921–1937'. *Journal of Asian Studies* 39.4 (August 1980): 711–27.

1981 (a) '"A Method of Evading Management" – Contract Labor in Chinese Coal Mines before 1937'. *Comparative Studies in Society and History* 23.4 (October 1981): 656–78.

1981 (b) 'Growth of the Modern Chinese Coal Industry: An Analysis of Supply and Demand, 1896–1936'. *Modern China* 7.3 (July 1981): 317–50.

'Nationalist Policies and the Regulation of Chinese Industry: Competition and Control in Coal Mining'. To be included in *Ideal and Reality: Social and Political Change in Modern China, 1860–1949*, ed. David Pong and Edmund Fung. Forthcoming.

'A New Series for Electric Power Production in pre-1937 China'. Unpublished paper.

Wu, Yuan-li. *Economic Development and the Use of Energy Resources in Communist China.* New York, 1963.

Yasuba, Yasukichi. 'Freight Rates and Productivity in Ocean Transportation for Japan, 1875–1943'. *Explorations in Economic History* 15.1 (January 1978): 11–39.

Young, Arthur N. *China's Nation-Building Effort, 1927–1937: The Financial and Economic Record.* Stanford, 1971.

INDEX

agricultural economy, bankruptcy of, 3, 110, 111, 195
alcoholic drinks, distillation of, 8, 60, 65
Anglo-Chinese Finance and Trade Corporation, 152
Anhui, 65, 111, 141, 149, 158, 164
Anshan Ironworks, 58
anthracite coal, 7, 17, 80, 86, 88
antimony, 66
Anyuan, 187
Anyuan Rail and Mine Workers' Club, 185, 187; see also Pingxiang mine
arsenals, 56, 139-41; see also Jiangnan, Nanjing and Tianjin arsenals

Badaohao, mines at, 126, 146
Bank of China, 110
banks, Chinese, 22, 23, 145, 149, 150-1, 158
Baochang Company, 133
Baoding, 106
Baojin Company, 200; capital, 19, 88; competition with small mines, 32, 33; ironworks, 58; management, 143, 146, 180; operations, 26, 39, 143, 206n38; prices, 112; profits, 94-5, 101, 143; taxes, 157; transport, 88-9, 143; workers, 26, 172, 173, 174
Baran, Paul, 20
Beijing, 67, 69, 160, 184; coal market, 11, 45, 46, 47, 83, 107; coal mines near, 8, 11, 51, 156; use of coal in, 8, 69
Bei–Ning railway, 44, 86, 106, 107
Beipiao Company, 109, 126, 146, 200, 206n38
Belgian interests in China, 123, 124, 132, 148
Belgium, coal mining in, 12, 173, 194
Bengbu, 157
Benxihu Company, 200; capital, 22, 122; ironworks, 58, 60; management, 127, 129, 130, 146; mining accidents, 172, 173, 174, 176; operations, 38, 41, 206n37; recruitment of labour, 164, 166;

strikes, 187; tax, 131-2; workers, 24, 25, 179
Bishan, mines at, 42
bituminous coal, 7, 17, 80, 86
Bodong Company, 39, 137, 200, 206n38
Boshan xian: ceramics industry, 8, 64-5; glass industry, 65, 66; iron-making, 64; mining, 6, 11, 19, 32, 33, 42, 205n18; sales of coal, 35, 46, 47; transport, 83, 84, 133-4; wages, 28, 34, 204n62; workers, 34, 164, 192
Boxer Uprising, 103, 120, 123, 125
brick-making, 60, 65, 102
British-American Tobacco, 65, 97
British interests in China, 118, 119, 122-3, 127, 196; see also Kailuan Mining Administration; Mentougou Company; Peking Syndicate
Buck, David D., 97
Buck, John Lossing, 66, 67, 68
bureaucrats: investment in coal mines, 139-60 passim, 197
Buxton, Neil K., 57

Cao Rulin, 148, 150
capital, Chinese, 3, 22-3, 120, 130, 135-6, 138, 139-60, 196-7
capital, foreign, 2, 3, 4, 21-2, 90, 117-38, 141-2, 196-7; see also under individual countries
capital, supply of, 3, 18-23, 58, 81, 87, 90, 135-6, 147, 155, 195
cartels and sales agreements, 70, 71, 154-5, 197, 220n82
cement industry, 57
ceramics industry, 8, 64, 65
Chahar, 164
Changcheng Company, 126, 146, 188, 192, 200
Changchun, 44, 69
Chang, John Key, 1, 11, 12, 57, 102, 110, 194
Changsha, 84, 152